The Diamond Revolution

The Definitive Guide to Lab-Created Diamonds

Donald J. Wright

Copyright © 2025 by Donald Wright

All rights reserved.

No portion of this book may be reproduced in any form without written permission from the publisher or author, except as permitted by U.S. copyright law.

This publication is designed to provide accurate and authoritative information in regard to the subject matter covered. It is sold with the understanding that neither the author nor the publisher is engaged in rendering legal, investment, accounting or other professional services. While the publisher and author have used their best efforts in preparing this book, they make no representations or warranties with respect to the accuracy or completeness of the contents of this book and specifically disclaim any implied warranties of merchantability or fitness for a particular purpose. No warranty may be created or extended by sales representatives or written sales materials. The advice and strategies contained herein may not be suitable for your situation. You should consult with a professional when appropriate. Neither the publisher nor the author shall be liable for any loss of profit or any other commercial damages, including but not limited to special, incidental, consequential, personal, or other damages.

Book Cover by Donald J. Wright

About the author

My career, spanning over four decades, has been a testament to the power of strategic vision and leadership. From the vibrant sales floors of Bashinski's Gems and Jewelry to the strategic boardrooms of Reeds Jewelers and Friedman's Incorporated, I have navigated the intricate world of diamonds, gems, and the buying sector with a blend of scientific precision and creative flair. My passion for storytelling is not just a personal interest, but a reflection of my professional journey. It is beyond the sparkle of a well-cut diamond, weaving narratives that resonates with the heart and mind. My passion is clear in my published five nonfiction books and fifteen novels. As an author, I understand the value of legacy, and it's the timeless beauty of a family heirloom or the enduring impact of a well-told tale. My books are more than just collections of words. They are vessels of 'knowledge, experience, and imagination' destined to inspire and enlighten.

Contents

Chapter 1: The Diamond Revolution - Understanding Lab-Created Diamonds

"In the controlled environment of a laboratory, we witness not the diminishment of nature's wonder, but its perfection through human ingenuity."

Introductions.

The Jewelry world has changed forever. In fact, it is still changing daily. Many retailers are resisting or actually fighting the changes, but are ultimately losing. They do everything to belittle lab-created diamonds, often lying outright. Some claim they are not "real" diamonds, complaining they have no resale value or trade-in value. The dollar loss on a lab-created diamond is far less than on a natural one. Recently, a company put lab-created diamonds in a gumball dispenser to show their low value, which failed badly.

The purpose of this book is to help customers understand the truth and make informed decisions. Both natural diamonds and lab-created diamonds have a place in the jewelry industry, and no one has the right to tell you what to spend your money on. That is up to you, your fiancé, and, of course, your budget. Remember, an engagement ring is meant to be a symbol of your love, not a measure of your wealth. Both natural and lab-created are beautiful. In fact, no law requires you to obtain either.

The following chapters contain a wealth of facts and information. Use this book as a reference. It will dispel the lies, the myths, and the misinformation. I hope this book will be helpful.

1.1 What Are Lab-Created Diamonds?

The Scientific Foundation

In the gleaming laboratories of today's most advanced facilities, a remarkable transformation occurs daily. Carbon atoms, the fundamental building blocks of all life, arrange themselves in perfect tetrahedral structures under precisely controlled conditions, forming diamonds that are chemically, physically, and optically identical to those created deep within the Earth's mantle over billions of years. This is not alchemy or artificial enhancement—this is the replication of nature's own process, accelerated and perfected through human innovation.

Lab-created diamonds, also known as cultured diamonds, synthetic diamonds, or man-made diamonds, represent one of the most significant technological achievements in modern materials science. These gems are composed of pure carbon atoms arranged in the same cubic crystal structure as natural diamonds, sharing identical properties, including hardness (10 on the Mohs scale), refractive index (2.42), and thermal conductivity.

The distinction between lab-created and natural diamonds lies solely in their origin story. While natural diamonds formed 1-3 billion years ago under extreme pressure and temperature conditions 90-120 miles beneath the Earth's surface, lab-created diamonds achieve the same crystalline perfection in a matter of weeks using sophisticated technology that replicates these natural conditions.

A Journey Through Time: The Historical Development

1950s - The Dawn of Diamond Creation The story begins in 1954 when General Electric achieved the first reproducible synthesis of industrial diamonds using the High Pressure-High Temperature (HPHT) method. These early diamonds were small, brown, and suitable only for industrial applications, such as cutting tools and abrasives. The scientific community had cracked nature's code, but gem-quality stones remained elusive.

1970s - The Pursuit of Gem Quality Throughout the 1970s, researchers refined their techniques, gradually producing larger and clearer stones. However, these early gem-quality lab diamonds often exhibited unusual colors—yellow, brown, or green—and commanded prices nearly equal to those of natural diamonds due to the complexity and cost of production. The technology existed, but commercial viability remained questionable.

1980s-1990s - Technological Refinement The introduction of Chemical Vapor Deposition (CVD) technology in the 1980s marked a turning point. This method, initially developed for industrial applications, enabled more controlled growth conditions and improved quality outcomes. By the 1990s, companies like Gemesis and Apollo Diamond were producing gem-quality stones, though market acceptance remained limited.

2000s - The Quality Revolution. The new millennium brought dramatic improvements in both HPHT and CVD technologies. Advances in pressure systems, temperature control, and gas purification led to consistently high-quality, colorless diamonds. Production costs began to decline while quality improved, setting the stage for broader market acceptance.

2010s - Market Breakthrough Major jewelry retailers, including Helzberg Diamonds and later Lightbox by De Beers, began offering lab-created diamonds alongside natural stones. This period witnessed a 63% increase in consumer awareness and a 15-20% annual growth in sales of lab-created diamonds.

2020-Present - The Mainstream Era: Today, lab-created diamonds represent approximately 18% of the total diamond market by volume, and this share is growing rapidly. Companies like Brilliant Earth, James Allen, and Clean Origin have built entire business models around lab-created diamonds. At the same time, traditional retailers have expanded their offerings to meet the growing demand of consumers.

Current Market Position and Growth Statistics

The lab-created diamond market has experienced unprecedented growth, with several key indicators demonstrating its increasing significance:

Market Size and Projections

2024 global market value: $27.6 billion

Projected 2030 market value: $55.6 billion

Compound Annual Growth Rate (CAGR): 12.4%

Share of total diamond market: 18% by volume, 8% by value

Production Capacity

Global annual production: 6-7 million carats

Leading production countries: China (45%), India (25%), Singapore (15%), USA (10%)

Average production time: 2-4 weeks for 1-carat stones

Quality yield rates: 85-90% gem-quality from CVD, 70-80% from HPHT

Consumer Demographics The typical lab-created diamond buyer profile reveals fascinating insights:

Age: 64% are millennials and Gen Z (25-40 years old)

Income: Household income $50,000-$150,000 annually

Education: 78% hold college degrees or higher

Values: 89% prioritize ethical sourcing, 76% consider environmental impact

Regional Adoption Patterns

North America: 22% market penetration, highest growth in engagement rings

Europe: 15% market penetration, strong growth in fashion jewelry

Asia-Pacific: 14% market penetration, rapid growth in China and India

Middle East/Africa: 8% market penetration, emerging market potential

The Technology Landscape

Modern lab-created diamond production employs two primary technologies, each with distinct advantages:

High Pressure-High Temperature (HPHT)

Pressure: 5-7 GPa (50,000-70,000 atmospheres)

Temperature: 1,300-1,600°C (2,372-2,912°F)

Growth rate: 1-2 carats per week

Typical applications: Colorless and fancy yellow diamonds

Energy consumption: 250-300 kWh per carat

Chemical Vapor Deposition (CVD)

Pressure: 0.1-1 atmosphere (low pressure)

Temperature: 700-1,000°C (1,292-1,832°F)

Growth rate: 0.5-1 carat per week

Typical applications: Colorless and fancy colored diamonds

Energy consumption: 150-200 kWh per carat

Emerging Technologies

Microwave Plasma Assisted CVD (MPACVD): 30% faster growth rates.

Ultra-High-Pressure synthesis: Potential for 2- 3x larger stones

Solar-powered facilities: 90% reduction in carbon footprint

AI-controlled growth: 95% quality consistency rates

1.2 Breaking Down Misconceptions

The "Fake" Diamond Fallacy

Perhaps no misconception about lab-created diamonds is more persistent—or more fundamentally incorrect—than the notion that they are "fake" or "artificial" diamonds. This misunderstanding stems from decades of marketing that conflated rarity with authenticity, creating a false dichotomy between "natural" and "real."

The scientific reality is unambiguous: lab-created diamonds are diamonds. They possess identical chemical composition (pure carbon), crystal structure (cubic), and physical properties to natural diamonds. When the Gemological Institute of America (GIA) tests a diamond, the same equipment used to identify natural diamonds is also used to confirm the authenticity of lab-created stones. The only difference detectable through advanced spectrographic analysis relates to trace elements and growth patterns, not the fundamental diamond structure.

Consider this analogy: ice formed in your freezer is chemically identical to ice formed on a lake. Both are H_2O in crystalline form, both exhibit the same properties, and both serve the same function. The environment of creation doesn't diminish the essential nature of the substance. Similarly, a diamond grown in a laboratory over weeks possesses the same atomic structure as one formed in the Earth's mantle over millions of years.

Addressing Quality Concerns

Misconception: "Lab diamonds are lower quality." Reality: Lab-created diamonds often exhibit superior quality characteristics compared to natural diamonds. Because growth conditions are controlled, lab diamonds typically have fewer inclusions, more consistent color distribution, and optimized crystal structure. In fact, approximately 85% of CVD diamonds and 70% of HPHT diamonds achieve VS2 or higher clarity grades, compared to only 58% of natural diamonds.

Misconception: "Lab diamonds don't sparkle as much." Reality: Brilliance, fire, and scintillation depend entirely on cut quality and crystal structure, both of which are identical between lab-created and natural diamonds. Many lab-created diamonds actually exhibit superior optical performance because cutters can afford to prioritize ideal proportions over weight retention, given the lower costs of rough stones.

Misconception: "Lab diamonds fade or change color over time." Reality: The carbon crystal structure of lab-created diamonds is as stable as natural diamonds. Both types of diamonds maintain their optical and physical properties indefinitely under normal conditions. This stability is why diamonds are used in industrial applications requiring consistent performance over decades.

Value and Investment Misunderstandings

Misconception: "Lab diamonds have no resale value." Reality: While lab-created diamonds currently retain 20-40% of their purchase price in the secondary market (compared to 30-60% for natural diamonds), this gap is narrowing as market acceptance grows. More importantly, the total cost of ownership often favors lab-created diamonds due to their significantly lower initial cost.

Consider this example: A 2-carat, G-color, VS1 clarity, excellent cut diamond costs approximately $18,000 if lab-created versus $25,000-$30,000 if natural. Even with lower resale percentages, the lab-created diamond's lower initial investment often results in similar or better net value retention.

Misconception: "Lab diamonds will become worthless as production increases." Reality: While production scalability may moderate price increases, fundamental demand drivers—beauty, durability, and symbolic value—remain constant. Historical precedents in other luxury markets (Swiss watches, cultured pearls) demonstrate that quality manufactured goods can maintain value alongside their natural counterparts.

Industry Terminology Standardization

The Federal Trade Commission (FTC) updated its Jewelry Guides in 2018 to address lab-created diamond terminology, requiring clear disclosure while recognizing these stones as genuine diamonds. Acceptable terms include:

Preferred terminology:

Lab-created diamonds

Laboratory-grown diamonds

Cultured diamonds

[Company name]-created diamonds.

Acceptable but less preferred:

Synthetic diamonds (though potentially confusing)

Man-made diamonds

Engineered diamonds.

Prohibited or misleading terms:

"Faux" diamonds

"Artificial" diamonds

"Imitation" diamonds

"Simulated" diamonds.

This standardization enables consumers to make informed decisions based on accurate information, rather than relying on marketing manipulation.

1.3 The Science Behind the Sparkle

Understanding Crystal Structure

The extraordinary properties that make diamonds so captivating—their unmatched hardness, brilliant light performance, and remarkable durability—all stem from carbon's arrangement in a specific three-dimensional structure called a diamond cubic lattice. In this configuration, each carbon atom bonds covalently with four neighboring carbon atoms in a tetrahedral arrangement, creating a powerful and stable network.

This crystal structure explains why diamonds score 10 on the Mohs hardness scale. Each carbon atom is held in place by four strong bonds, making the entire structure extremely resistant to deformation. The same structure also determines how light interacts with the diamond, creating the optical phenomena we perceive as brilliance, fire, and scintillation.

Lab-created diamonds achieve this identical crystal structure through carefully controlled replication of the pressure and temperature conditions that exist 90-120 miles beneath the Earth's surface. The remarkable achievement of modern technology is not creating something similar to a diamond, but recreating the exact same atomic arrangement that nature produces.

Optical Properties: The Physics of Beauty

Refractive Index and Brilliance Diamonds have a refractive index of 2.42, meaning light travels 2.42 times slower through diamond than through air. This high refractive index causes light entering a diamond to bend significantly, and when combined with proper cutting angles, creates total internal reflection—the phenomenon responsible for a diamond's brilliance.

Lab-created diamonds possess the identical refractive index because they have the same crystal structure and atomic density. A photometer measuring light returned from a well-cut lab diamond and a well-cut natural diamond will record identical readings.

Dispersion and Fire The separation of white light into its component colors—creating the rainbow flashes we call "fire"—results from dispersion, measured at 0.044 for diamonds. This property depends solely on the material's atomic structure, making lab-created diamonds identical to natural diamonds in their fire display.

Birefringence and Strain Patterns Under polarized light, both natural and lab-created diamonds may exhibit strain patterns—areas of stress within the crystal structure. However, advanced CVD techniques have largely eliminated strain in modern lab-created diamonds, often resulting in superior optical clarity compared to natural stones with significant strain patterns.

Physical Properties Comparison

*Except for rare blue diamond's containing boron

Chemical Composition Analysis

Advanced analytical techniques reveal the chemical purity that distinguishes lab-created diamonds:

Fourier Transform Infrared Spectroscopy (FTIR) This analysis reveals the presence of nitrogen impurities, the most common impurity in natural diamonds. Lab-created diamonds typically show:

CVD diamonds: Very low nitrogen content (Type IIa)

HPHT diamonds: Controlled nitrogen levels (Type Ib or IIa)

Natural diamonds: Variable nitrogen content and distribution

Photoluminescence Spectroscopy Different growth environments create distinct spectroscopic signatures:

Natural diamonds: Broad range of trace elements and defects

CVD diamonds: Silicon-related defects, minimal metallic inclusions

HPHT diamonds: Metallic catalyst remnants (iron, nickel, cobalt)

Mass Spectrometry and Isotopic analysis reveal subtle differences in carbon isotope ratios. However, these don't affect the diamond's physical or optical properties.

The Importance of Understanding Science

For diamond buyers, understanding the scientific equivalence between lab-created and natural diamonds provides confidence in their purchasing decisions. The science demonstrates that the choice between lab-created and natural diamonds should be based on personal values—such as ethical considerations, environmental impact, budget constraints, or symbolic preferences—rather than concerns about quality or authenticity.

This scientific foundation also explains why lab-created diamonds perform identically to natural diamonds in jewelry applications. Whether set in an engagement ring worn daily for decades or displayed in a family heirloom passed through generations, lab-created diamonds maintain their beauty and structural integrity exactly as natural diamonds do.

1.4 Market Landscape Today

Global Market Dynamics

The lab-created diamond market has evolved from a niche scientific curiosity to a significant force reshaping the entire diamond industry. Understanding today's market landscape requires examining multiple dimensions: production capacity, consumer adoption, pricing dynamics, and competitive positioning.

Production Centers and Capacity The global distribution of lab-created diamond production reveals the technology's democratic nature—unlike natural diamond mining, which is geographically constrained, lab diamond production can occur anywhere with sufficient technological infrastructure and energy supply.

China: The Manufacturing Powerhouse

Market share: 45% of global production

Notable companies: Zhongnan Diamond, Huanghe Whirlwind

Production focus: Both gem-quality and industrial diamonds

Technological advantage: Large-scale HPHT and CVD facilities

Cost advantage: Lower labor and energy costs

India: The Cutting and Polishing Hub

Market share: 25% of global production

Notable companies: Greenlab Diamonds, Diamond Foundry India

Competitive advantage: Skilled labor force, established diamond industry.

Production focus: Smaller stones and fancy shapes

Market position: Bridge between production and retail

Singapore: The Technology Leader

Market share: 15% of global production

Notable companies: IIa Technologies, Diamond Foundry

Technological focus: Premium quality and larger stones

Innovation leadership: Advanced CVD techniques and quality control

Market positioning: High-end consumer segments

United States: The Premium Market

Market share: 10% of global production

Notable companies: Diamond Foundry, VRAI, WD Lab Grown

Consumer focus: Direct-to-consumer sales and branding

Technological advantages: Research and development leadership

Market strategy: Premium positioning and marketing

Consumer Adoption Patterns

Demographic Analysis Modern lab-created diamond buyers represent a distinct demographic shift from traditional diamond consumers:

Age Distribution:

18-25 years: 28% (Gen Z early adopters)

26-35 years: 36% (Millennial core market)

36-45 years: 22% (Younger Gen X)

46+ years: 14% (Traditional buyers embracing change)

Income Segmentation:

$30,000-$60,000: 35% (value-conscious buyers)

$60,000-$100,000: 32% (middle-market adopters)

$100,000-$200,000: 23% (affluent early adopters)

$200,000+: 10% (luxury segment with ethical focus)

Education Correlation:

High school: 15%

Some college: 25%

Bachelor's degree: 35%

Graduate degree: 25%

The strong correlation between education level and the adoption of lab-created diamonds suggests that informed consumers, when presented with factual information about lab diamonds, increasingly choose them over natural alternatives.

Purchase Motivation Analysis: Recent consumer surveys reveal the primary drivers behind lab-created diamond purchases:

Ethical considerations (43%)

Conflict-free guaranteed sourcing

Environmental responsibility

Fair labor practices

Value proposition (38%)

Larger stone for the same budget

Higher quality grades are achievable.

Better total cost of ownership

Quality factors (12%)

Consistent quality control

Superior clarity options

Advanced cut optimization

Innovation appeal (7%)

Technology appreciation

Modern lifestyle alignment

Future-forward thinking

Regional Market Characteristics

North America: The Innovation Market

Market penetration: 22% of total diamond sales

Growth rate: 18% annually

Price premium: 20-30% above global average

Consumer profile: Tech-savvy, environmentally conscious

Key trends: Online direct sales, customization demand

Distinctive characteristics:

Strong brand loyalty to lab diamond specialists

Preference for certification transparency

High demand for fancy-colored stones

Integration with technology (AR try-on, virtual consultations)

Europe: The Ethical Market

Market penetration: 15% of total diamond sales

Growth rate: 15% annually

Regional variations: UK (18%), Germany (16%), France (12%)

Consumer profile: Sustainability-focused, quality-conscious

Key trends: Vintage-inspired settings, heirloom alternatives

Market drivers:

Strong environmental regulations are driving ethical consumption.

High awareness of conflict diamond issues

Premium placed on traceability and transparency.

Growing acceptance among traditional luxury consumers

Asia-Pacific: The Emerging Market

Market penetration: 14% of total diamond sales

Growth rate: 25% annually (highest globally)

Leading markets: China, India, Japan, Australia

Consumer profile: Young professionals, tech-early adopters

Key trends: Digital-first purchasing, social media influence

Growth factors:

Rising disposable income among young professionals

Rapid adoption of e-commerce platforms

Social media influence is driving awareness.

Cultural shift toward individual expression over tradition

Pricing Dynamics and Market Forces

Price Evolution Trends The lab-created diamond market has experienced significant pricing evolution:

2018-2020: Price Stability

Premium to natural diamonds: 20-30% discount

Production costs: High due to limited scale

Market positioning: Niche alternative product

2021-2023: Rapid Price Decline

Premium to natural diamonds: 60-80% discount

Production scaling: Increased efficiency and capacity

Market positioning: Mainstream alternative

2024-Present: Price Stabilization

Premium to natural diamonds: 70-85% discount

Production optimization: Mature technology and processes

Market positioning: Preferred choice for value-conscious buyers

Factors Influencing Pricing Several key factors continue to shape lab-created diamond pricing:

Production Efficiency Improvements

Energy cost reductions through renewable power

Automation is reducing labor costs.

Yield improvements through technology advancement.

Scale economics as production volumes increase.

Market Competition

Increased number of producers globally

Direct-to-consumer business models

Technology democratization reduces barriers to entry.

Price transparency through online platforms

Consumer Demand Dynamics

Growing market acceptance is driving volume.

Premium segment development for luxury positioning

Seasonal demand patterns similar to natural diamonds

Economic sensitivity affecting purchase timing.

Competitive Landscape

Market Leaders and Their Strategies

Technology Innovators:

Diamond Foundry: Premium positioning, celebrity endorsements, solar-powered production

IIa Technologies: B2B focus, technical excellence, research partnerships

Element Six (De Beers): Industrial applications, technology licensing, selective gem production

Retail Disruptors:

Brilliant Earth: Ethical positioning, comprehensive education, omnichannel presence

James Allen: Technology integration, virtual try-on, extensive inventory

Clean Origin: Pure lab diamond focus, competitive pricing, customer education

Established Players Adapting:

Lightbox (De Beers): Fashion positioning, accessible pricing, brand recognition

Pandora: Mass market integration, jewelry design focus, global distribution

Signet Jewelers: Multi-brand strategy, traditional retail integration, consumer education

Future Market Indicators

Technology Development Trends

Production cost reduction: 10-15% annually

Quality improvement: 95%+ gem-grade yield rates

Size capability: Routine production of 5+ carat stones

Color options: Expansion into rare fancy colors.

Consumer Acceptance Metrics

Brand awareness: 85% among target demographics

Purchase consideration: 65% of diamond shoppers.

Repeat purchase rate: 78% customer satisfaction.

Recommendation rate: 72% would recommend to others.

Market Maturation Signals

Infrastructure development: Dedicated lab, diamond retail locations

Financial services: Specialized financing and insurance products

Secondary market: Emerging resale and trade-in programs

Industry integration: Acceptance by traditional jewelry retailers

The current market landscape demonstrates that lab-created diamonds have moved beyond the early adoption phase into mainstream acceptance. With technological advancements continually improving quality while reducing costs, and consumer acceptance growing across all demographic segments, the lab-created diamond market is poised for sustained growth and an increasing market share.

Understanding this landscape empowers consumers to make informed decisions based on current market realities rather than outdated perceptions. Whether motivated by ethics, value, quality, or innovation, today's lab-created diamond market offers compelling options for every type of diamond buyer.

***

*As we conclude this foundational chapter, we've established that lab-created diamonds represent not a compromise or alternative to "real" diamonds. Still, rather than being logical, t*he current market landscape demonstrates that lab-created diamonds have moved beyond the early adoption phase into mainstream acceptance. With technological advancements continuing to improve quality while reducing costs, and consumer acceptance growing across all demographic segments, the lab-created diamond market is poised for sustained growth and an increasing market share.

Understanding this landscape empowers consumers to make informed decisions based on current market realities rather than outdated perceptions. Whether motivated by ethics, value, quality, or innovation, today's lab-created diamond market offers compelling options for every type of diamond buyer.

***

As we conclude this foundational chapter, we've established that lab-created diamonds represent not a compromise or alternative to "real" diamonds, but rather the logical evolution of diamond technology. In the following chapters, we'll delve

deeper into the fascinating science and technology that makes these remarkable gems possible, explore their ethical and environmental benefits, and provide the practical guidance you need to make informed purchasing decisions.

The diamond revolution is not coming here. And it's more brilliant than ever.

Chapter 2: The Science and Technology Deep Dive

"In the marriage of carbon and human ingenuity, we witness the birth of diamonds that rival nature's billion-year masterpieces, created not in geological time, but in the span of human ambition."

2.1 Advanced Creation Methods

High-Pressure, High-Temperature (HPHT): Recreating Earth's Forge

Deep beneath the Earth's surface, in the convecting mantle where temperatures soar beyond 1,500°C and pressures exceed 50,000 atmospheres, nature has been forging diamonds for over three billion years. The High-Pressure, High-Temperature (HPHT) method represents humanity's most direct attempt to replicate these extreme conditions, bringing the Earth's diamond-making power into the controlled environment of a laboratory.

The HPHT Process: A Symphony of Pressure and Heat

The HPHT process begins with a carefully selected diamond seed—a small fragment of natural or lab-created diamond that serves as the foundation for growth. This seed, typically 1-2 millimeters in size, is placed within a specialized growth chamber alongside a carbon source (usually high-purity graphite) and a metallic catalyst.

The choice of metallic catalyst is crucial and varies depending on the desired diamond characteristics:

Iron-based catalysts produce diamonds with minimal color, making them suitable for near-colorless gems.

Nickel-cobalt alloys: Create controlled growth rates and improved crystal quality.

Chromium additions: Generate green-colored diamonds through controlled impurity introduction.

Boron integration: Results in rare blue diamonds with semiconductor properties

The growth chamber, typically a cylindrical capsule measuring 15-20 millimeters in diameter, is then placed within a massive hydraulic press. These industrial marvels, weighing 100-200 tons, generate pressures of 5-7 GPa (50,000-70,000 times atmospheric pressure) while simultaneously heating the chamber to 1,300-1,600°C.

The Molecular Dance of Diamond Formation

Under these extreme conditions, a remarkable transformation occurs. The metallic catalyst melts, creating a molten medium through which carbon atoms can migrate. The graphite carbon source dissolves into this metallic melt, and carbon atoms begin their journey toward the diamond seed.

At the seed's surface, carbon atoms arrange themselves in the diamond's characteristic cubic crystal structure, extending the existing lattice layer by atomic layer. This process, known as epitaxial growth, ensures that the new diamond material maintains perfect crystallographic alignment with the seed, resulting in a seamless, continuous crystal.

The growth rate varies with conditions but typically produces 1-2 carats of diamond material per week. Larger stones require proportionally longer growth periods, with 5-carat diamonds taking 5-6 weeks to complete.

Modern HPHT Innovations

Recent technological advances have revolutionized HPHT diamond production:

Multi-Seed Technology: Advanced chambers now accommodate multiple seeds, allowing simultaneous growth of several diamonds while maintaining individual quality control.

Gradient Control Systems: Sophisticated thermal management creates controlled temperature gradients within the growth chamber, optimizing growth rates while minimizing inclusions.

Real-Time Monitoring: Advanced sensors track pressure, temperature, and growth progress, enabling precise process control and quality optimization.

Automated Systems: Computer-controlled presses reduce human error and ensure consistent results across production runs.

Chemical Vapor Deposition (CVD): The Precision Method

While HPHT replicates Earth's natural diamond-forming environment, Chemical Vapor Deposition (CVD) takes an entirely different approach, growing diamonds atom by atom in a precisely controlled low-pressure environment. This method, originally developed for industrial thin-film applications, has been refined to produce some of the highest-quality gem diamonds available today.

The CVD Process: Building Diamonds Atom by Atom

CVD diamond growth occurs within a specialized vacuum chamber, where pressure is maintained at 0.1-1 atmosphere—dramatically lower than the pressure in HPHT conditions. A diamond seed substrate, typically a thin slice of diamond measuring 10-15 millimeters square, is placed on a heated platform within the chamber.

The growth process begins by introducing a carefully controlled mixture of gases:

Methane (CH_4): The carbon source, typically comprising 1-5% of the gas mixture.

Hydrogen (H_2): The carrier gas, making up 95-99% of the mixture.

Optional additives: Nitrogen for color control, boron for blue diamonds, or other elements for specific properties

These gases are then activated using one of several energy sources:

Microwave plasma: The most common method, using 2.45 GHz microwaves to create plasma.

Hot filament: Tungsten or tantalum filaments heated to 2,000-2,500°C.

RF plasma: Radio frequency energy for specialized applications

DC arc plasma: High-energy systems for rapid growth rates

The Plasma Chemistry of Diamond Growth

When activated, the gas mixture forms plasma—a fourth state of matter where electrons are stripped from atoms, creating a highly reactive environment. Within this plasma, several critical chemical reactions occur simultaneously:

Methane Decomposition: CH_4 molecules break apart, releasing reactive carbon species.

Hydrogen Activation: H_2 molecules dissociate into highly reactive hydrogen atoms.

Surface Chemistry: Carbon atoms bond to the diamond seed surface while hydrogen atoms remove unwanted graphite formation.

The key to CVD's success lies in the selective chemistry of hydrogen atoms. While carbon atoms readily bond to diamond surfaces, extending the crystal lattice, hydrogen atoms preferentially remove any graphite that forms, ensuring that only the diamond crystal structure survives.

Advanced CVD Techniques

Modern CVD systems incorporate sophisticated control mechanisms:

Microwave Plasma Assisted CVD (MPACVD): Uses precisely tuned microwave energy to create uniform, stable plasma with growth rates 30% faster than conventional CVD.

Hot Filament CVD (HFCVD): Employs heated tungsten filaments to activate gases, offering excellent control overgrowth conditions and lower equipment costs.

Plasma Enhanced CVD (PECVD): Utilizes radio frequency energy to create plasma, enabling growth at lower temperatures and reduced stress in the resulting diamonds.

Linear Antenna Microwave CVD: Innovative antenna designs create larger, more uniform plasma zones, enabling growth of larger diamonds and improved quality control.

Microwave Plasma Assisted CVD (MPACVD): The Next Generation

Microwave Plasma Assisted Chemical Vapor Deposition represents the cutting edge of diamond growth technology, combining the precision of CVD with advanced microwave engineering to achieve unprecedented control over diamond quality and growth rates.

Advanced Plasma Engineering

MPACVD systems utilize sophisticated microwave cavities designed to create highly uniform plasma conditions across large substrate areas. Key innovations include:

Resonant Cavity Design: Precisely engineered microwave cavities ensure uniform energy distribution, eliminating hot spots that can cause quality variations.

Multiple Antenna Systems: Arrays of microwave antennas create overlapping plasma zones, enabling the growth of larger diamonds while maintaining quality uniformity.

Plasma Diagnostics: Real-time monitoring of plasma conditions using optical emission spectroscopy and mass spectrometry for immediate process optimization.

Adaptive Control Systems: AI-powered feedback loops automatically adjust microwave power, gas composition, and chamber pressure to maintain optimal growth conditions.

Quality Advantages of MPACVD

The enhanced control offered by MPACVD systems results in superior diamond quality:

Reduced Nitrogen Content: Achieving Type IIa diamonds with nitrogen levels below 1 ppm.

Improved Crystal Structure: Reduced strain and defects through controlled growth rates

Enhanced Optical Properties: Superior clarity and brilliance through minimized inclusions.

Larger Size Capability: Routine production of 3-5 carat stones with potential for 10+ carats

Ultra-High-Pressure Synthesis: Pushing the Boundaries

Research institutions and advanced manufacturers are exploring ultra-high pressure synthesis techniques that exceed traditional HPHT conditions, potentially revolutionizing large diamond production.

Next-Generation Pressure Systems

Toroidal Anvils: New anvil designs achieve pressures exceeding 10 GPa while maintaining large growth volumes.

Multi-Stage Compression: Sophisticated hydraulic systems create pressure gradients for controlled growth of large, high-quality crystals.

Supercritical Fluid Methods: Using supercritical carbon dioxide and other fluids as carbon sources for novel growth pathways.

Breakthrough Potential

Ultra-high-pressure synthesis promises:

Accelerated Growth Rates: 3-5x faster production than conventional HPHT.

Larger Crystal Capability: Potential for 20+ carat single crystals

Enhanced Purity: Reduced metallic inclusions through advanced catalyst systems.

Novel Properties: Exploration of "super diamonds" with enhanced electrical and thermal properties

Comparative Analysis of Creation Methods

2.2 Production Technology

Laboratory Equipment and Machinery

The production of lab-created diamonds requires some of the most sophisticated and precise manufacturing equipment ever developed. These systems must maintain extreme conditions with extraordinary accuracy while ensuring consistent quality across thousands of production cycles.

HPHT Press Systems: Engineering Marvels

Modern HPHT presses represent triumphs of mechanical engineering, combining massive force generation with precision control systems.

Hydraulic Press Design: The heart of HPHT production is the hydraulic press system, typically featuring:

Force Capacity: 1,000-3,000 tons of closing force.

Precision Control: Position accuracy within 0.01 millimeters

Pressure Stability: Maintaining target pressure within ±1% overgrowth periods.

Multiple Stations: Advanced systems accommodate 6-12 simultaneous growth chambers.

Anvil Systems: The growth chambers are positioned between specially designed anvils that focus hydraulic force.

Material: Tungsten carbide or synthetic diamond for extreme durability

Geometry: Precision-machined surfaces with tolerances of ±0.001 inches

Cooling Systems: Integrated cooling channels prevent overheating and thermal expansion.

Sensor Integration: Embedded pressure and temperature sensors for real-time monitoring

Heating Systems: Achieving the required temperatures demands sophisticated heating technology:

Resistance Heating: Graphite heaters provide uniform temperature distribution.

Induction Heating: Radio frequency systems for rapid temperature control

Thermal Insulation: Advanced ceramics and refractory materials to minimize heat loss.

Temperature Control: PID controllers maintain temperatures within ±5°C.

CVD Reactor Systems: Precision Chambers

CVD diamond growth requires ultra-precise control over gas composition, pressure, and plasma conditions within specialized reactor chambers.

Vacuum Systems: High-performance vacuum systems maintain the low-pressure environment essential for CVD growth:

Vacuum Level: Achieving pressures of 10^7 torr before gas introduction.

Pump Systems: Turbo-molecular and rough pumps with redundant backup systems.

Leak Detection: Helium leak detectors ensure the integrity of the chamber.

Gas Flow Control: Mass flow controllers with accuracy of ±0.1% full scale

Microwave Generation Systems: Sophisticated microwave systems create and maintain the plasma necessary for diamond growth:

Power Output: 1-15 kW microwave generators operating at 2.45 GHz.

Cavity Design: Precision-machined resonant cavities for uniform energy distribution

Plasma Monitoring: Optical emission spectroscopy for real-time plasma analysis

Safety Systems: Microwave containment and personnel protection systems

Substrate Handling: Automated systems manage diamond substrates throughout the growth process:

Robot Integration: Precision robots for substrate loading and positioning.

Temperature Control: Heated stages maintain substrate temperatures within ±2°C.

Gas Distribution: Shower head systems ensure uniform gas flow across substrates.

Growth Monitoring: In-situ measurement systems tracking diamond thickness.

Quality Control Systems

Modern lab-created diamond production employs sophisticated quality control systems that monitor and optimize every aspect of the growth process.

Real-Time Process Monitoring

Spectroscopic Analysis: Advanced analytical techniques provide continuous feedback on growth conditions:

Optical Emission Spectroscopy (OES): Real-time monitoring of plasma composition and stability

Mass Spectrometry: Continuous analysis of gas-phase chemistry and impurities

Raman Spectroscopy: In-situ measurement of diamond quality and stress levels

Infrared Spectroscopy: Detection of nitrogen incorporation and other impurities

Thermal Monitoring: Precise temperature control ensures optimal growth conditions:

Pyrometric Systems: Non-contact temperature measurement with accuracy of ±1°C

Thermal Imaging: Real-time thermal mapping of growth surfaces

Heat Transfer Modeling: Computer simulations optimizing thermal profiles.

Cooling System Integration: Automated cooling control based on thermal feedback.

Pressure and Flow Monitoring: Maintaining precise environmental conditions requires continuous monitoring:

Capacitance Manometers: Ultra-precise pressure measurement and control

Mass Flow Controllers: Real-time gas composition and flow rate management

Leak Detection Systems: Continuous monitoring for system integrity.

Data Logging: Complete documentation of all process parameters

Post-Growth Quality Assessment

Once diamond growth is complete, a comprehensive quality assessment ensures that only gem-grade material is processed for cutting and polishing.

Gemological Evaluation: Traditional gemological techniques adapted for lab-created diamond assessment:

4Cs Assessment: Color, clarity, cut, and carat weight evaluation using standardized protocols.

Inclusion Analysis: Microscopic examination identifying growth-related features.

Optical Performance: Light return analysis measuring brilliance, fire, and scintillation.

Strain Analysis: Polarized light examination reveals internal stress patterns.

Advanced Characterization: Sophisticated analytical techniques provide detailed material characterization:

Photoluminescence Mapping: Identifying trace impurities and defects.

Cathodoluminescence Imaging: Revealing growth sectors and impurity distribution.

X-ray Topography: Detecting crystal defects and strain fields.

Secondary Ion Mass Spectrometry (SIMS): Quantitative analysis of trace elements

Automation and Industry 4.0 Integration

The lab-created diamond industry is rapidly adopting Industry 4.0 technologies, integrating artificial intelligence, machine learning, and advanced automation to optimize production efficiency and quality.

Artificial Intelligence in Production Control

Predictive Analytics: Machine learning algorithms analyze historical production data to optimize growth parameters:

Growth Rate Optimization: AI models predicting optimal conditions for desired growth rates.

Quality Prediction: Algorithms forecasting final diamond quality based on process parameters.

Defect Prevention: Predictive models identify conditions likely to produce inclusions.

Energy Optimization: AI-driven energy management reduces power consumption by 15-20%

Process Optimization: Advanced algorithms continuously optimize production processes:

Multi-Variable Optimization: Simultaneous optimization of multiple process parameters

Adaptive Control: Real-time adjustment of conditions based on feedback.

Recipe Development: AI-assisted development of growth recipes for specific diamond characteristics

Yield Maximization: Optimization algorithms maximize gem-quality yield rates.

Robotic Integration and Automation

Automated Handling Systems: Sophisticated robotic systems manage materials throughout the production process:

Substrate Preparation: Automated cleaning, inspection, and positioning of diamond seeds

Loading Systems: Precision robots handling growth chambers and materials

Transfer Mechanisms: Automated movement of diamonds between process stations.

Packaging Systems: Robotic sorting and packaging of finished diamonds

Quality Control Automation: Automated systems perform comprehensive quality assessment:

Optical Inspection: High-resolution cameras and image analysis software

Dimensional Measurement: Laser scanning systems offer precise measurement capabilities.

Color Grading: Automated colorimeters with standardized lighting conditions.

Clarity Assessment: Machine learning algorithms identify and classifying inclusions.

2.3 Quality Control and Enhancement

Advanced Quality Control Protocols

The production of consistently high-quality lab-created diamonds requires sophisticated quality control protocols that monitor every aspect of the growth and finishing process. These systems ensure that each diamond meets strict specifications while identifying opportunities for continuous improvement.

Multi-Stage Quality Gates

Seed Selection and Preparation: Quality control begins with careful selection and preparation of diamond seeds:

Seed Quality Assessment: Microscopic examination for defects, strain, and orientation

Surface Preparation: Precision polishing and cleaning to ensure optimal growth conditions.

Orientation Verification: X-ray crystallography confirming proper crystallographic alignment.

Contamination Control: Utilizing ultra-clean handling procedures to prevent impurity introduction.

Growth Monitoring and Control: During the growth process, continuous monitoring ensures optimal conditions:

Process Parameter Tracking: Real-time monitoring of temperature, pressure, and gas composition.

Growth Rate Analysis: Continuous measurement of diamond thickness and growth uniformity

Defect Detection: In-situ monitoring for inclusion formation and crystal defects.

Environmental Control: Maintaining cleanroom protocols to ensure ultra-pure growth environments.

Post-Growth Evaluation: Comprehensive assessment following growth completion:

Initial Inspection: Visual and microscopic examination for obvious defects

Spectroscopic Analysis: Detailed characterization of material properties

Stress Analysis: Polarized light examination revealing internal strain.

Grading Assessment: Preliminary evaluation of color, clarity, and potential cut quality

Color Enhancement and Control

One of the significant advantages of lab-created diamonds is the ability to control and enhance color characteristics through precise manipulation of growth conditions and post-growth treatments.

Natural Color Control During Growth

Nitrogen Management: Controlling nitrogen incorporation during growth enables precise color control:

Ultra-Pure CVD: Achieving colorless Type IIa diamonds with nitrogen levels below 0.5 ppm.

Controlled Nitrogen Addition: Introducing specific nitrogen concentrations for desired yellow tones.

Nitrogen Aggregation: Post-growth heat treatment creates specific nitrogen configurations.

Sector Control: Managing nitrogen distribution across different growth sectors.

Boron Incorporation: Creating blue diamonds through controlled boron addition:

Concentration Control: Achieving precise boron levels to create specific blue intensities.

Uniformity Management: Ensuring even boron distribution throughout the crystal.

Electrical Properties: Optimizing semiconductor characteristics in blue diamonds.

Color Stability: Heat treatment protocols ensuring long-term color stability.

Other Impurity Control: Incorporating various elements for specific color effects:

Silicon Integration: Creating unique color centers in CVD diamonds.

Transition Metals: Controlled addition of chromium, nickel, and other metals.

Vacancy Centers: Creating specific defect structures for desired optical properties.

Irradiation Effects: Post-growth treatments creating additional color options.

Post-Growth Color Enhancement

Heat Treatment: Controlled thermal processing for color optimization:

Annealing Protocols: High-temperature treatments optimizing crystal structure.

Color Improvement: Heat treatment enhancing natural color characteristics.

Stress Relief: Thermal processing reduces internal strain and improves clarity.

Defect Modification: Converting unstable color centers to stable configurations.

Irradiation and Annealing: Advanced treatments creating unique color effects:

Electron Irradiation: Creating specific defect structures for enhanced colors.

Neutron Activation: Specialized treatments for rare color varieties

Annealing Optimization: Precise temperature and time protocols for color development

Stability Testing: A long-term evaluation to ensure permanent color enhancement.

Clarity Optimization

Lab-created diamonds offer unique opportunities for clarity optimization through controlled growth conditions and advanced finishing techniques.

Inclusion Prevention During Growth

Environmental Control: Maintaining ultra-clean growth environments prevents the formation of inclusion bodies.

Cleanroom Standards: ISO Class 1000 or better environments for critical processes

Gas Purification: Ultra-high purity gases with impurity levels below 1 ppb

Material Selection: High-purity source materials and growth chamber components

Contamination Monitoring: Continuous monitoring for particulate and chemical contamination

Growth Condition Optimization: Precise control of growth parameters minimizes defect formation:

Temperature Stability: Maintaining uniform temperatures, preventing thermal stress.

Pressure Control: Stable pressure conditions prevent irregular growth.

Gas Flow Management: Uniform gas distribution ensures consistent growth conditions, promoting uniform growth.

Growth Rate Optimization: Controlled growth rates minimize the incorporation of defects.

Advanced Clarity Enhancement

Laser Processing: Precision laser techniques for clarity improvement:

Inclusion Drilling: Laser drilling to access and treat internal inclusions.

Defect Removal: Targeted laser ablation removing specific defects.

Surface Processing: Laser polishing for enhanced surface quality.

Precision Cutting: Laser cutting enables optimal clarity preservation.

Chemical Processing: Advanced chemical treatments for clarity enhancement:

Acid Treatment: Specialized acid treatments remove specific inclusion types.

Oxidation Processes: Controlled oxidation removes graphitic inclusions.

Surface Cleaning: Ultra-clean chemical processes remove surface contaminants.

Passivation Treatments: Chemical treatments stabilizing surface properties.

Cut Planning and Optimization

The controlled nature of lab-created diamond production enables advanced cut planning and optimization techniques that maximize the beauty and value of each stone.

Advanced Cut Planning Software

3D Modeling and Analysis: Sophisticated software systems optimize cut planning:

Inclusion Mapping: Detailed 3D mapping of internal features and inclusions

Optical Modeling: Computer simulation of light performance for different cut options

Yield Optimization: Analysis maximizing finished diamond weight and quality.

Value Maximization: Economic modeling optimizes cut decisions for maximum value.

Machine Learning Integration: AI-powered systems are improving cut planning decisions:

Pattern Recognition: Machine learning algorithms identify optimal cut orientations.

Historical Analysis: Analysis of past cutting decisions, optimizing future choices.

Quality Prediction: Algorithms predicting final diamond quality for different cut options.

Process Optimization: Continuous improvement of cut planning protocols.

Precision Cutting Technology

Laser Cutting Systems: Advanced laser technology enabling precision diamond processing:

Femtosecond Lasers: Ultra-short pulse lasers for precise cutting with minimal heat damage

Multi-Axis Systems: Sophisticated positioning systems enabling complex cut geometries.

Real-Time Monitoring: Continuous monitoring ensuring cut quality and precision.

Automated Operation: Computer-controlled systems reducing human error and improving consistency.

Advanced Polishing Techniques: Sophisticated polishing methods optimizing optical performance:

Precision Polishing: Computer-controlled polishing achieves superior surface quality.

Angle Optimization: Precise control of facet angles maximizing light performance.

Surface Analysis: Real-time measurement of surface quality during polishing

Quality Verification: Automated systems verifying final polish quality.

2.4 Energy and Environmental Impact

Comprehensive Energy Analysis

Understanding the environmental impact of lab-created diamond production requires detailed analysis of energy consumption throughout the entire production process, from raw material preparation through finished diamond delivery.

Energy Consumption Breakdown by Production Method

HPHT Energy Requirements: High-pressure, high-temperature production involves significant energy consumption across multiple systems:

Hydraulic Press Operation: 150-200 kWh per carat for pressure generation and maintenance

Heating Systems: 80-120 kWh per carat for achieving and maintaining target temperatures.

Cooling Systems: 20-30 kWh per carat for controlled cooling and temperature management

Support Systems: 25-35 kWh per carat for vacuum systems, monitoring, and facility operations.

Total HPHT Energy: 275-385 kWh per carat (average: 330 kWh per carat)

CVD Energy Requirements: Chemical vapor deposition typically requires less energy than HPHT methods.

Microwave Generation: 100-150 kWh per carat for plasma creation and maintenance.

Vacuum Systems: 15-25 kWh per carat for chamber evacuation and pressure control

Heating Systems: 30-50 kWh per carat for substrate heating and temperature control

Gas Purification: 10-15 kWh per carat for ultra-pure gas preparation

Support Systems: 15-25 kWh per carat for monitoring, safety, and facility operations.

Total CVD Energy: 170-265 kWh per carat (average: 220 kWh per carat)

Comparative Energy Analysis: Lab vs. Mined Diamonds

Mining Energy Requirements: Natural diamond mining involves extensive energy consumption across multiple stages:

Excavation and Extraction: 450-650 kWh per carat for earth removal and ore processing

Crushing and Processing: 200-300 kWh per carat for ore crushing and diamond liberation

Sorting and Recovery: 100-150 kWh per carat for diamond identification and recovery

Transportation: 50-100 kWh per carat for global transportation and logistics

Processing and Cutting: 75-125 kWh per carat for final preparation and finishing.

Total Mining Energy: 875-1,325 kWh per carat (average: 1,100 kWh per carat)

Energy Efficiency Comparison: Lab-created diamonds demonstrate significant energy efficiency advantages:

HPHT Efficiency: 70% lower energy consumption than mining

CVD Efficiency: 80% lower energy consumption than mining

Energy Intensity Trends: Improving 10-15% annually through technological advancement.

Renewable Integration: 85% of lab diamond facilities now use renewable energy sources.

Carbon Footprint Analysis

Direct Carbon Emissions

Production Emissions: Direct emissions from lab-created diamond production vary significantly based on energy sources:

Coal-Powered Production: 0.15-0.25 kg CO_2 per carat (decreasing as renewable adoption increases)

Natural Gas-Powered: 0.08-0.15 kg CO_2 per carat

Renewable-Powered: 0.01-0.03 kg CO_2 per carat (equipment manufacturing and transport only)

Industry Average (2024): 0.06 kg CO_2 per carat (significant improvement from 0.20 kg in 2018)

Mining Comparison: Natural diamond mining generates substantially higher carbon emissions:

Extraction Emissions: 1.2-1.8 kg CO_2 per carat from diesel equipment and explosives

Processing Emissions: 0.8-1.2 kg CO_2 per carat from ore processing and sorting

Transportation Emissions: 0.3-0.6 kg CO_2 per carat from global shipping and logistics

Total Mining Emissions: 2.3-3.6 kg CO_2 per carat (average: 3.0 kg CO_2 per carat)

Lifecycle Carbon Assessment

Comprehensive Lifecycle Analysis: Complete environmental assessment including all production stages:

Raw Material Production: 0.005-0.015 kg CO_2 per carat for high-purity gases and materials

Equipment Manufacturing: 0.02-0.04 kg CO_2 per carat (amortized over equipment lifetime)

Facility Construction: 0.01-0.02 kg CO_2 per carat (amortized over facility lifetime)

Production Operations: 0.01-0.25 kg CO_2 per carat (depending on energy source)

Transportation and Distribution: 0.005-0.02 kg CO_2 per carat

End-of-Life: Negligible (diamonds are permanent)

Total Lifecycle Emissions: 0.05-0.35 kg CO_2 per carat (renewable facilities: <0.1 kg)

Renewable Energy Integration

Solar-Powered Diamond Production

Industry Leaders in Solar Integration: Several companies have achieved carbon-neutral diamond production through solar power:

Diamond Foundry: 100% solar-powered facilities producing "Carbon Neutral Certified" diamonds.

Solar Capacity: 50 MW solar installation supporting production facilities.

Energy Storage: 200 MWh battery systems ensuring continuous operation.

Carbon Neutrality: Verified third-party certification of zero net carbon emissions.

Production Scale: 150,000+ carats annually from renewable energy

Greenlab Diamonds: Solar-integrated production in India

Hybrid System: Solar primary with grid backup during monsoon seasons

Solar Capacity: 25 MW installation covering 60% of energy needs.

Carbon Reduction: 75% reduction in carbon emissions compared to grid power.

Expansion Plans: 100% renewable energy target by 2026

Wind and Hydroelectric Integration

IIa Technologies: Hydroelectric-powered production in Singapore

Clean Energy Source: 100% hydroelectric power from regional grid

Carbon Footprint: <0.02 kg CO_2 per carat including equipment and transportation.

Quality Advantage: A stable power supply enables superior quality control.

Environmental Certification: ISO 14001 environmental management certification

Element Six: Wind-powered industrial diamond production

Wind Integration: 40 MW wind farm supporting UK production facilities.

Energy Storage: Advanced battery systems manage intermittent supply.

Efficiency Gains: 20% improvement in production efficiency through stable renewable power

Research Focus: Developing next-generation low-energy production methods.

Water Usage and Conservation

Water Requirements Analysis

HPHT Water Usage: High-pressure systems require significant cooling water:

Cooling Water: 50-100 liters per carat for the press and heating system cooling

Process Water: 10-20 liters per carat for cleaning and preparation.

Treatment Requirements: Water recycling systems achieving 90%+ reuse rates.

Quality Standards: Ultra-pure water is used to prevent contamination during production.

CVD Water Usage: Chemical vapor deposition typically requires less water.

Cooling Water: 20-40 liters per carat for chamber and equipment cooling

Process Water: 5-15 liters per carat for cleaning and gas purification.

Recycling Efficiency: Advanced systems achieving 95%+ water reuse.

Zero Discharge: Closed-loop systems eliminate water discharge.

Water Conservation Technologies

Advanced Cooling Systems: Innovative cooling technologies reducing water consumption:

Closed-Loop Cooling: Recirculating systems minimizing freshwater requirements.

Heat Recovery: Systems capture waste heat for facility heating and hot water.

Dry Cooling: Air-cooled systems for low-water-availability regions

Smart Controls: AI-optimized cooling reducing water usage by 30-40%

Water Treatment and Recycling: Sophisticated systems ensuring water conservation:

Reverse Osmosis: High-efficiency filtration enabling water reuse.

Distillation Systems: Ultra-pure water production for critical processes

Biological Treatment: Natural systems treat process water for reuse.

Real-Time Monitoring: Continuous water quality monitoring, optimizing treatment

Waste Reduction and Material Recycling

Production Waste Minimization

Material Efficiency: Advanced production methods minimize waste generation:

Yield Optimization: 85-95% conversion efficiency from raw materials to finished diamonds.

Byproduct Utilization: Converting waste carbon into industrial diamond applications.

Equipment Recycling: Refurbishment and reuse of production equipment

Packaging Optimization: Utilizing minimal packaging with recycled and biodegradable materials.

Chemical Waste Management: Responsible handling of production chemicals:

Solvent Recovery: Distillation systems recover and reusing process solvents.

Catalyst Recycling: Recovery and purification of metallic catalysts for reuse

Gas Purification: Systems capture and recycling process gases.

Neutralization: Safe treatment and disposal of unavoidable waste streams

Circular Economy Integration

Equipment Lifecycle Management: A Comprehensive approach to equipment sustainability:

Design for Recycling: Equipment designed for component recovery and reuse.

Refurbishment Programs: Systematic refurbishment extends equipment life.

Material Recovery: Recycling valuable materials from end-of-life equipment.

Supplier Integration: Working with suppliers to minimize packaging and waste.

Diamond Recycling Programs: Emerging programs for lab-created diamond reuse:

Upgrade Programs: Trade-in systems enabling customers to upgrade to larger stones.

Repolishing Services: Professional repolishing extending diamond life.

Material Recovery: Research into recycling lab diamonds for new production

Secondary Markets: Developing resale markets for pre-owned lab diamonds.

Environmental Certification and Standards

Third-Party Environmental Verification

Carbon Neutral Certification: Independent verification of environmental claims:

Carbon Trust Certification: Comprehensive lifecycle carbon footprint verification

Climate Neutral Certification: Third-party verification of net-zero carbon emissions.

ISO 14064 Compliance: International standards for greenhouse gas reporting

Science-Based Targets: Emissions reduction targets aligned with climate science.

Environmental Management Systems: Comprehensive environmental management protocols:

ISO 14001 Certification: International environmental management standards

LEED Certification: Green building standards for production facilities

Water Stewardship: Alliance for Water Stewardship certification for responsible water use

Biodiversity Protection: Commitments to protecting local ecosystems.

Industry Sustainability Initiatives

Collaborative Environmental Programs: Industry-wide initiatives promoting sustainability:

Lab-Grown Diamond Council: Industry association promoting environmental best practices.

Sustainable Jewelry Council: Cross-industry collaboration on sustainability standards

Diamond Stewardship Alliance: Multi-stakeholder initiative for responsible diamond production

Climate Action Network: Industry commitment to achieving net-zero emissions by 2030.

Research and Development Focus: Ongoing research improving environmental performance:

Energy Efficiency Research: Developing next-generation low-energy production methods.

Renewable Integration: Advanced technologies for 100% renewable energy production

Waste Elimination: Research into zero-waste production processes.

Lifecycle Optimization: Comprehensive analysis identifying improvement opportunities.

The environmental advantages of lab-created diamonds extend far beyond simple energy comparisons. Through the integration of renewable energy, advanced water conservation, comprehensive waste reduction, and rigorous environmental certification, the lab-created diamond industry is establishing new standards for sustainable luxury goods production. As technology continues advancing and renewable energy adoption accelerates, these environmental advantages will only increase, making lab-created diamonds an increasingly compelling choice for environmentally conscious consumers.

2.5 Future Innovations

Quantum Applications and Programming

The unique properties of lab-created diamonds are opening revolutionary applications in quantum computing and information processing, representing a convergence of luxury and cutting-edge technology that could transform multiple industries.

Quantum Computing Applications

Nitrogen-Vacancy Centers: Precision control during CVD growth enables creation of quantum-grade diamonds:

Quantum Bit Creation: Nitrogen-vacancy (NV) centers serving as stable quantum bits (qubits)

Coherence Times: NV centers maintaining quantum states for milliseconds at room temperature.

Scalable Arrays: Precise positioning of quantum defects for quantum processor arrays

Environmental Stability: Room-temperature operation eliminating the need for extreme cooling.

Quantum Sensing Applications: Lab-created diamonds enabling unprecedented sensitivity in measurement:

Magnetic Field Detection: Sensitivity to magnetic fields down to nanotesla levels

Electric Field Sensing: Detection of electric fields with nanometer spatial resolution

Temperature Measurement: Quantum thermometry with millikelvin precision

Biological Applications: Quantum sensors for cellular and molecular research

Programmable Diamond Technology

Data Storage Applications: Research into using diamond crystal structure for data storage:

3D Data Storage: Utilizing diamond's crystal lattice for three-dimensional data encoding.

Permanence: Data storage lasting millions of years in a diamond matrix

Density: Potential storage densities exceeding current technologies by 1000x

Security: Quantum encryption integrated into diamond storage media

Smart Diamond Integration: Embedding technology within the diamond structure:

Sensor Integration: Microscopic sensors are embedded during the growth process.

Communication Capabilities: Diamond-based quantum communication devices

Energy Harvesting: Converting ambient energy into electrical power.

Biocompatibility: Medical implants with diamond-based sensors and processors

Space-Based Manufacturing

The unique environment of space offers unprecedented opportunities for diamond production, potentially revolutionizing both quality and scale of lab-created diamond manufacturing.

Microgravity Advantages

Enhanced Crystal Growth: The absence of gravity enables superior diamond formation:

Reduced Convection: Elimination of thermal convection improving crystal uniformity.

Minimized Stress: Reduced gravitational stress, enabling larger crystal growth.

Enhanced Purity: Improved separation of impurities from growing crystals

Novel Structures: Growth of crystal forms impossible under terrestrial gravity

Zero-G CVD Systems: Space-based CVD reactors offering unique capabilities:

Uniform Plasma: Spherical plasma distributions are impossible on Earth.

Large Substrate Areas: Growth on larger substrates without gravitational sagging

Extended Growth Times: Continuous operation without gravitational settling effects

Multi-Directional Growth: Simultaneous growth on multiple crystal faces

Space Manufacturing Infrastructure

Orbital Diamond Factories: Conceptual space-based production facilities:

Solar Power Integration: Abundant solar energy for production processes

Automated Operation: Robotic systems minimize the need for human intervention.

Raw Material Delivery: Asteroid-derived carbon sources for space-based production

Earth Delivery Systems: Specialized spacecraft for transporting finished diamonds.

International Space Station Research: Current experiments exploring space-based diamond growth:

ESA Materials Science Laboratory: European experiments in microgravity diamond synthesis

NASA Crystallization Research: Studies on crystal growth in microgravity environments

JAXA Advanced Materials: Japanese research on space-based manufacturing processes

Commercial Partnerships: Private companies developing space manufacturing capabilities.

Advanced Material Properties

Research into enhanced diamond properties is creating "super diamonds" with capabilities far exceeding those of natural stones, opening up new applications in electronics, energy, and advanced technologies.

Electrical and Electronic Properties

Semiconductor Diamonds: Controlled doping creating electronic applications:

Boron-Doped Diamonds: P-type semiconductors for electronic devices

Phosphorus-Doped Diamonds: N-type semiconductors enabling diamond electronics.

Power Electronics: High-voltage, high-frequency electronic applications

Quantum Electronics: Diamond-based quantum electronic devices

Superconducting Diamonds: Research into diamond superconductivity:

Boron-Doped Superconductivity: Superconducting transition temperatures up to 11K

Pressure-Induced Superconductivity: Enhanced properties under pressure.

Quantum Applications: Superconducting quantum interference devices (SQUIDs)

Energy Applications: Lossless power transmission and magnetic levitation

Thermal Management Applications

Extreme Thermal Conductivity: Enhanced thermal properties for advanced applications:

Heat Spreaders: Electronics cooling applications requiring extreme thermal conductivity.

Thermal Interface Materials: Diamond films for semiconductor heat management

Aerospace Applications: Thermal management in extreme environments

Energy Systems: Heat exchangers for advanced power generation systems

Thermal Barrier Coatings: Diamond coatings for extreme temperature applications:

Turbine Blades: Protective coatings for aircraft and power generation turbines

Hypersonic Applications: Thermal protection for high-speed aerospace vehicles

Industrial Processes: Protective coatings for extreme temperature manufacturing

Fusion Energy: Plasma-facing materials for fusion reactor applications

Biotechnology and Medical Applications

The biocompatibility and unique properties of lab-created diamonds are enabling breakthrough applications in medicine and biotechnology.

Medical Device Applications

Implantable Devices: Diamond-based medical implants offering superior performance:

Orthopedic Implants: Diamond Coatings Reduce Wear and Improve Biocompatibility.

Cardiovascular Applications: Diamond-coated stents and heart valve components

Neural Interfaces: Biocompatible electrodes for brain-computer interfaces

Drug Delivery Systems: Diamond nanoparticles for targeted drug delivery

Surgical Instruments: Enhanced surgical tools utilizing diamond properties:

Precision Cutting Tools: Diamond-edged instruments for microsurgery

Laser Surgery Enhancement: Diamond components improve laser surgery precision.

Imaging Applications: Diamond sensors enhancing medical imaging capabilities.

Sterilization Resistance: Diamond tools maintain sharpness after repeated sterilization.

Pharmaceutical Applications

Drug Delivery Systems: Diamond nanoparticles revolutionizing pharmaceutical delivery:

Targeted Delivery: Functionalized diamond nanoparticles for specific drug targeting

Controlled Release: Time-release drug systems using diamond matrices.

Cancer Treatment: Diamond nanoparticles for targeted cancer therapy

Blood-Brain Barrier: Diamond carriers enabling drug delivery to the brain.

Biosensing Applications: Diamond-based sensors for medical diagnostics:

Real-Time Monitoring: Implantable sensors for continuous health monitoring

Molecular Detection: Ultra-sensitive detection of disease biomarkers

pH Sensing: Biocompatible pH sensors for physiological monitoring

Glucose Monitoring: Next-generation continuous glucose monitoring systems

Environmental and Energy Applications

Lab-created diamonds are enabling breakthrough applications in environmental monitoring and energy generation, contributing to sustainability and environmental protection.

Environmental Monitoring

Pollution Detection: Diamond sensors for environmental applications:

Air Quality Monitoring: Ultra-sensitive detection of atmospheric pollutants

Water Quality Sensors: Real-time monitoring of water contamination

Soil Analysis: Diamond-based sensors for agricultural and environmental soil monitoring

Radiation Detection: Diamond detectors for nuclear radiation monitoring

Climate Research: Advanced instrumentation for climate science:

Atmospheric Research: Diamond sensors for high-altitude atmospheric studies

Ocean Monitoring: Pressure-resistant sensors for deep-ocean research

Ice Core Analysis: Diamond tools for improved ice core drilling and analysis.

Greenhouse Gas Detection: Ultra-sensitive sensors for climate gas monitoring

Energy Generation and Storage

Photovoltaic Applications: Diamond-enhanced solar energy systems:

UV Solar Cells: Diamond-based cells efficiently converting UV radiation.

Radiation-Hard Solar Cells: Space-grade solar cells for extreme environments

Concentrated Solar Power: Diamond components for high-temperature solar applications.

Energy Conversion Efficiency: Enhanced efficiency through diamond optical properties

Energy Storage Systems: Diamond applications in advanced energy storage:

Supercapacitors: Diamond electrodes for high-performance energy storage

Battery Applications: Diamond Coatings Improve Battery Performance and Safety.

Fuel Cells: Diamond components enhancing fuel cell efficiency and durability.

Nuclear Batteries: Diamond-based nuclear batteries for long-term power generation

Manufacturing Technology Evolution

The future of lab-created diamond production will be shaped by revolutionary manufacturing technologies that promise to dramatically improve quality, reduce costs, and enable new applications.

Next-Generation Production Methods

Plasma-Free Growth: Revolutionary techniques eliminating plasma requirements:

Molecular Beam Epitaxy: Atomic-level control of diamond growth

Chemical Solution Growth: Room-temperature diamond growth from solution

Electrochemical Deposition: Electrical control of diamond formation

Biological Synthesis: Bio-inspired diamond growth using organic templates.

Continuous Production Systems: Industrial-scale continuous diamond manufacturing:

Roll-to-Roll Processing: Continuous diamond film production on flexible substrates.

Fluidized Bed Reactors: Continuous production of diamond powders and particles

Flow Chemistry: Continuous solution-based diamond synthesis.

Automated Harvesting: Robotic systems for continuous diamond collection and processing

Quality and Scale Advancement

Large Crystal Production: Techniques enabling the production of massive single crystals:

Seed Fusion Technology: Joining multiple seeds for large crystal growth.

Temperature Gradient Control: Advanced thermal management for uniform large crystals

Stress Management: Techniques preventing crack formation in large diamonds.

Growth Rate Optimization: Balancing speed and quality for large crystal production

Perfect Crystal Engineering: Approaching theoretical perfection in diamond crystal structure:

Defect-Free Growth: Techniques achieving near-perfect crystal structure.

Isotope Purification: Using isotopically pure carbon for enhanced properties.

Atomic-Level Control: Precision placement of individual atoms during growth

Property Engineering: Designing diamonds with specific engineered properties.

The future of lab-created diamonds extends far beyond traditional jewelry applications. From quantum computing and space manufacturing to medical devices and environmental monitoring, these remarkable materials are positioned to become key enablers of advanced technologies that will shape our future. As research continues and manufacturing capabilities advance, we can expect lab-created diamonds to play increasingly important roles in science, technology, and society, while continuing to provide beautiful, ethical, and sustainable options for traditional diamond applications.

The convergence of advanced manufacturing, quantum physics, space technology, and biotechnology around lab-created diamonds represents one of the most exciting frontiers in materials science. As we stand on the threshold of these revolutionary applications, it's clear that lab-created diamonds are not just alternatives to natural stones—they are gateways to technologies that could transform our world.

***

In this comprehensive exploration of the science and technology behind lab-created diamonds, we've witnessed the extraordinary marriage of human ingenuity and natural principles. From the precise replication of Earth's diamond-forming conditions to revolutionary applications in quantum computing and space manufacturing, lab-created diamonds represent the pinnacle of modern materials science. As we progress through this handbook, we'll explore how these technological marvels translate into practical considerations for diamond buyers, examining their ethical implications, market dynamics, and the guidance you need to make informed purchasing decisions in this exciting and rapidly evolving industry.

Chapter 3: The Next Frontier - In Search of Super Diamonds

"The history of science shows that the bravest explorers are not those who sail the seas, but those who venture into the unseen architecture of matter, seeking to build the impossible."

3.1 Beyond Perfection: The Quest for Superior Carbon

For centuries, diamonds have been the undisputed champions of materials—the benchmarks for hardness, symbols of permanence, and marvels of natural engineering. The advent of lab-created diamonds, as we've explored, was a monumental achievement in replicating this perfection. Yet, science rarely rests on replication. The same spirit of inquiry that tamed the atom and mapped the genome is now pushing beyond the known limits of carbon, asking a bold question: What lies beyond diamond?

The answer lies in the realm of **super diamonds**. This term does not refer to a larger or more brilliant gemstone, but to a class of carbon allotropes—materials made of pure carbon, arranged in novel crystal structures—that are predicted to possess mechanical and thermal properties superior to those of conventional diamonds. These are materials that are not just *as hard* as diamond, but significantly *harder*, tougher, and more resistant to heat and pressure.

The quest for super diamonds is driven by the tantalizing possibility that diamond's cubic crystal lattice, while extraordinarily robust, may not be the ultimate configuration for carbon. By manipulating atoms under conditions even more extreme than those used for standard HPHT synthesis, scientists are unlocking new structures with the potential to revolutionize industries. Two primary candidates lead this exciting frontier: the hexagonal powerhouse known as **Lonsdaleite** and a theoretical, ultra-dense phase called **BC8**. This chapter explores these remarkable materials, the immense challenges of their creation, and the future they promise to build.

3.2 Lonsdaleite: The Hexagonal Powerhouse

First discovered in 1967 within the fragments of the Canyon Diablo meteorite, Lonsdaleite remained a scientific curiosity for decades—a rare, naturally occurring hexagonal form of diamond forged in the unimaginable violence of an asteroid impact. Unlike conventional diamonds, which have a cubic crystal lattice, Lonsdaleite arranges its carbon atoms in a hexagonal structure. Theoretical calculations long predicted this hexagonal form could be significantly stronger and harder. For years, however, samples were too small and impure to verify these claims or explore applications.

Figure 3.1: A visual comparison of the atomic arrangements in a standard cubic diamond (left) and the more complex, stronger hexagonal lattice of Lonsdaleite (right).

That has now changed. Recent breakthroughs, particularly from research teams in China and the US, have enabled the synthesis of high-quality, millimeter-sized Lonsdaleite in the laboratory.

The Synthesis of Hexagonal Diamond

The creation of Lonsdaleite does not involve a seed crystal in the same way as CVD or HPHT diamonds. Instead, it represents a phase transformation under unique conditions:

Starting Material: The process begins with highly ordered graphite, similar to the carbon source in HPHT synthesis.

Extreme Conditions: This graphite is subjected to a precise combination of immense pressure and high-temperature gradients. This is not uniform heating, but a carefully controlled environment where temperature varies across the material.

Phase Transformation: Under this specific thermobaric stress, the graphite doesn't rearrange into a cubic diamond lattice. Instead, the layers are compressed and locked into a hexagonal arrangement, forming pure, well-crystallized Lonsdaleite.

Properties That Surpass Diamond

The lab-synthesized Lonsdaleite has confirmed the theories with astonishing results:

Superior Hardness: Lonsdaleite exhibits a hardness of approximately 155 GigaPascals (GPa). In comparison, a natural diamond measures around 100 GPa. This makes Lonsdaleite over 50% harder than the previously hardest known material.

Enhanced Thermal Stability: It can withstand temperatures up to 1,100°C, significantly higher than a natural diamond's stability threshold of around 700°C. This resilience opens up applications in extreme-temperature environments where conventional diamonds would degrade.

Greater Toughness: Beyond hardness (resistance to scratching), Lonsdaleite is predicted to be tougher (more resistant to fracture), making it more durable under mechanical stress.

The successful synthesis of Lonsdaleite marks a pivotal moment, moving a theoretical super material from the realm of meteorite craters and supercomputer models into the tangible world of applied science.

3.3 Theoretical Contenders: BC8 and Ultrahard Fullerites

While Lonsdaleite is the first lab-synthesized super diamond to be produced in usable sizes, it is not the only contender for the throne. On the frontiers of computational materials science, researchers have predicted other carbon structures with even more exotic and powerful properties.

BC8: A Glimpse into Planetary Cores

BC8, or body-centered cubic carbon, is a phase of carbon with eight atoms in its unit cell. It does not exist naturally on Earth, but it is predicted to be stable under the immense pressures found inside carbon-rich exoplanets.

Figure 3.2: The theoretical BC8 crystal structure, predicted to be 30% more resistant to compression than diamond.

Predicted Properties: Supercomputer simulations at institutions like Lawrence Livermore National Laboratory (LLNL) predict that BC8, if it could be synthesized and recovered at ambient pressure, would be a "super-diamond" with a 30% greater resistance to compression than conventional diamond.

The Synthesis Challenge: Creating BC8 is a monumental undertaking. It is believed to require pressures exceeding 10 million atmospheres—an order of magnitude greater than those used in HPHT synthesis. Current research involves using shock compression techniques, firing projectiles at diamond precursors to create the necessary conditions momentarily, and studying the results in femtoseconds.

The Promise: While still in the experimental and simulation phase, BC8 represents a fundamental exploration into the nature of matter under the most extreme conditions in the universe.

Ultrahard Fullerites: Caged Carbon's Strength

Another pathway to super-hard materials involves using fullerenes—spherical molecules of carbon, such as C_{60} ("buckyballs")—as building blocks. When subjected to intense pressure and heat, these spheres can be forced to link together, forming a three-dimensional polymer.

Structure: This "ultrahard fullerite" is an amorphous or nanocrystalline material where the incredibly strong C_{60} cages are interconnected by covalent bonds.

Hardness: Russian scientists at the Technological Institute for Superhard and Novel Carbon Materials have produced fullerites that can scratch diamond, demonstrating their superior hardness.

Applications: These materials are being explored for their potential in creating exceptionally wear-resistant industrial tools and coatings.

3.4 Applications: The Dawn of a New Industrial Age

The development of super diamonds is not primarily aimed at the jewelry market, though that remains a distant possibility. The true driving force is the potential to revolutionize high-technology industries where the limitations of conventional diamond are a barrier to progress.

Figure 3.3: The primary industrial and scientific applications for super diamond materials, from manufacturing to space exploration.

Industrial Manufacturing and Machining The most immediate application are in creating a new generation of cutting, drilling, and polishing tools.

Superior Cutting Tools: Tools tipped with Lonsdaleite could machine ultra-hard ceramics, alloys, and composites used in aerospace and medical implants with greater speed, precision, and tool longevity.

Wear-Resistant Coatings: A thin coating of a super diamond material on critical parts, such as bearings, gears, or engine components, could dramatically reduce friction and wear, extend operational life, and improve efficiency.

Aerospace and Defense The combination of hardness, low weight, and thermal stability makes super diamonds ideal for extreme environments.

High-Performance Components: These components can be utilized to create components for hypersonic vehicles or spacecraft reentry shields that must withstand extreme heat and stress.

Advanced Armor: Lighter, more effective armor systems could be developed for personnel and vehicles.

Electronics and Semiconductors The high thermal stability of materials like Lonsdaleite is a game-changer for next-generation electronics.

Heat Sinks: They can serve as highly efficient, heat-resistant substrates for powerful microprocessors and laser diodes, allowing electronics to run faster and hotter without failing.

High-Power Semiconductors: Their properties are ideal for creating robust semiconductors for high-frequency and high-power applications, from 6G communications to advanced radar systems.

Scientific Research Super diamonds will allow scientists to explore new frontiers themselves.

Diamond Anvil Cells: The tips of diamond anvil cells—devices used to generate extreme pressures for research—are currently the limiting factor. Anvils made from Lonsdaleite or BC8 could allow scientists to achieve even higher pressures, simulating the conditions inside planets and stars right here on Earth.

3.5 A New Chapter in Human Ingenuity

The journey from understanding diamonds to creating it in a lab was a story of replicating nature. The quest for Super Diamonds is a story of surpassing it. These materials serve as a testament to humanity's growing understanding of the fundamental laws of physics and our ability to engineer matter at the atomic level.

While a Lonsdaleite engagement ring is not yet on the horizon, the technologies being pioneered in these advanced laboratories will have a ripple effect. Just as the research for GE's "Project Superpressure" advanced the entire field of high-pressure science, the work being done today on super diamonds will lead to unforeseen breakthroughs in manufacturing, computing, and energy. It is the next logical step in the diamond revolution—a move from perfecting nature's wonder to creating new wonders of our own.

Chapter 4: Understanding Diamond Quality and Grading

"In the realm of diamonds, quality is not merely a measure of perfection, but a symphony of light, crystal, and human craftsmanship dancing together in eternal brilliance."

4.1 The 4Cs Comprehensive Guide

Cut: The Master of Light

Of all the factors that determine a diamond's beauty, none is more critical or more frequently misunderstood than cut. While nature determines a diamond's color, clarity, and carat weight, cut is the sole domain of human artistry and precision. It is through the cut that a rough diamond crystal transforms from a geological curiosity into a scintillating gem that captures hearts and light in equal measure.

Understanding Cut Beyond Shape

The term "cut" encompasses far more than the geometric outline we see when viewing a diamond from above. True cut quality involves three fundamental components: proportions, symmetry, and polish. These elements work in concert to determine how effectively a diamond interacts with light, creating the optical phenomena we perceive as brilliance, fire, and scintillation.

Proportions: The Mathematics of Beauty A diamond's proportions—the precise angles and relative measurements of its facets—determine its ability to capture, bend, and return light to the observer's eye. The most critical measurements include:

Table Percentage: The flat top facet as a percentage of the diamond's width (optimal range: 54-58% for round brilliants)

Crown Angle: The angle of the upper facets relative to the girdle (optimal: 34-35 degrees)

Pavilion Angle: The angle of the lower facets (optimal: 40.6-41.0 degrees)

Depth Percentage: Total depth as a percentage of diameter (optimal: 59-63%)

Girdle Thickness: The rim connecting crown and pavilion (optimal: thin to slightly thick)

When these proportions align within optimal ranges, they create what gemologists call "ideal" light performance. Light entering through the crown reflects internally off the pavilion facets and returns through the crown, creating maximum brilliance and fire.

Symmetry: The Precision of Perfection Symmetry refers to the exactness of shape and placement of facets. Perfect symmetry ensures that light entering one side of the diamond experiences identical conditions to light entering any other side, creating uniform brilliance across the entire stone. Symmetry evaluation includes:

Facet Shape Consistency: All similar facets should be identical in shape.

Facet Alignment: Corresponding facets should meet precisely at common points.

Girdle Uniformity: The girdle should form a perfect circle (or intended shape)

Polish Line Alignment: Meet points should align perfectly across the diamond.

Polish: The Final Touch Polish quality affects how light interacts with the diamond's surface. Superior polish creates mirror-like facet surfaces that maximize light transmission and minimize light loss. Polish defects—such as polish lines, burn marks, or rough girdles—can interrupt light flow and diminish the diamond's beauty.

Advanced Cut Grading Beyond Basic Shapes

While the round brilliant cut has been extensively studied and optimized, fancy shapes (such as princess, emerald, oval, and pear) present unique challenges and opportunities in cut grading.

Round Brilliant: The Standard of Excellence The round brilliant cut, with its 57 or 58 facets, represents the pinnacle of cut optimization research. Mathematical modeling and centuries of refinement have established precise parameters for ideal light performance:

Excellent Cut Grade: AGS 0 or GIA Excellent with optimal proportions

Light Performance: 95%+ light returns in ideal viewing conditions.

Fire Optimization: Balanced dispersion creating rainbow flashes.

Scintillation: Dynamic light patterns during movement

Princess Cut: The Modern Classic The square princess cut requires different proportion considerations:

Length-to-Width Ratio: 1.00-1.05 for square appearance

Crown Height: 10-15% of total depth for optimal brilliance

Pavilion Angle: 43-45 degrees for adequate light return.

Corner Integrity: Proper faceting to minimize vulnerability.

Emerald Cut: The Window to Clarity Step-cut emerald diamonds prioritize clarity over brilliance:

Length-to-Width Ratio: 1.30-1.50 for pleasing proportions

Step Facet Alignment: Precise parallel lines creating "hall of mirrors" effect.

Corner Facets: Properly angled to prevent chipping.

Clarity Emphasis: Step cuts reveal inclusions more readily than brilliant cuts.

Lab-Created Diamond Cut Advantages

Lab-created diamonds offer unique advantages in cut optimization that are often impossible with natural stones:

Cost-Effective Idealization: Because lab-created rough costs significantly less than natural rough, cutters can prioritize ideal proportions overweight retention. Natural diamond cutters often compromise optimal proportions to maximize finished weight and value. In contrast, lab diamond cutters can achieve theoretical ideals.

Consistent Material Properties: Lab-created diamonds typically have more uniform crystal structure and fewer internal stress patterns, enabling:

Predictable Cutting Behavior: Consistent response to cutting and polishing.

Reduced Breakage Risk: Lower stress levels minimize cutting losses.

Enhanced Polish Quality: Uniform crystal structure enabling superior surface finish.

Symmetry Achievement: Consistent material enabling precise facet alignment.

Advanced Cut Innovation: The controlled properties of lab-created diamonds enable experimental cuts and optimizations:

Hearts and Arrows Perfection: Achieving perfect optical symmetry patterns.

Light Performance Optimization: Custom proportions for specific lighting conditions

Fancy Shape Innovation: New cutting styles optimized for lab diamond properties.

Precision Manufacturing: Computer-controlled cutting achieving theoretical ideals.

Color: The Spectrum of Desire

Color evaluation in diamonds involves assessing the absence of color in white diamonds and the presence of color in fancy-colored stones. Understanding color grading offers crucial insight into diamond quality and value, particularly given the unique color characteristics that are possible in lab-created diamonds.

The GIA Color Scale: D-Z Grading

The Gemological Institute of America's D-Z color scale represents the industry standard for colorless to light yellow diamond grading:

Colorless Range (D-E-F):

D Color: Absolutely colorless, the highest color grade possible

E Color: Colorless with minute traces of color detectable only by expert gemologists

F Color: Colorless with slight color detectable only when compared to higher grades

Near Colorless Range (G-H-I-J):

G-H Color: Nearly colorless with slight yellow tint visible when compared to colorless diamonds.

I-J Color: Nearly colorless with slightly more noticeable yellow tint, excellent value grades

Faint to Light Range (K-M and N-Z):

K-M Color: Faint yellow tint becoming noticeable to untrained eyes.

N-Z Color: Very light to light yellow, approaching fancy yellow classification.

Color Perception and Environmental Factors

Color perception in diamonds is influenced by numerous factors beyond the stone's inherent color:

Viewing Conditions:

Lighting Type: Fluorescent, LED, incandescent, and daylight affect color appearance.

Lighting Intensity: Bright light can mask slight color tints.

Background Color: White, black, or colored backgrounds influence perception.

Viewing Angle: Color may appear different from various viewing positions.

Setting and Metal Interactions:

White Metal Settings: Platinum and white gold reflect light, enhancing colorless appearance.

Yellow Gold Settings: Can mask slight yellow tints in near colorless diamonds.

Rose Gold Settings: Complement diamonds with slight yellow or brown tints.

Halo Effects: Surrounding smaller diamonds can influence color perception.

Lab-Created Diamond Color Advantages

Lab-created diamonds offer remarkable color consistency and options unavailable in natural stones:

Type IIa Purity: Most CVD lab-created diamonds achieve Type IIa classification, containing virtually no nitrogen:

Exceptional Colorlessness: Achieving D-F color grades consistently.

Color Stability: No color change over time due to nitrogen aggregation.

Optical Clarity: Enhanced transparency due to minimal atomic impurities

Value Proposition: High color grades at accessible prices

Controlled Color Creation: Lab production enables precise color control through impurity management:

Nitrogen Addition: Controlled nitrogen introduction for specific yellow tones

Boron Integration: Precise boron levels creating various blue intensities.

Silicon Incorporation: Unique color centers possible only in CVD diamonds

Heat Treatment: Post-growth treatments optimizing color characteristics.

Fancy Colored Lab-Created Diamonds

The ability to control impurities during lab diamond growth has revolutionized the fancy-colored diamond market, making previously rare colors accessible to a broader range of consumers.

Blue Diamonds: The Boron Miracle

Natural blue diamonds are among the rarest gemstones on Earth, with only a few dozen gem-quality specimens known. Lab-created blue diamond's achieve their color through controlled boron incorporation:

Color Intensity Levels:

Faint Blue: 0.1-1 ppm boron, subtle blue tint

Light Blue: 1-5 ppm boron, noticeable blue color

Fancy Blue: 5-20 ppm boron, distinct blue color.

Intense Blue: 20-50 ppm boron, vivid blue saturation

Vivid Blue: 50+ ppm boron, exceptional blue intensity

Unique Properties: Boron-doped lab diamonds exhibit special characteristics:

Electrical Conductivity: Semiconductor properties enabling electronic applications.

Color Stability: Permanent color unaffected by heat or radiation.

Clarity Enhancement: Boron incorporation often improves crystal quality.

Size Availability: Large blue diamond's possible through controlled growth

Pink Diamonds: Innovation in Color Creation

Natural pink diamonds derive their color from structural defects created by geological stress. Lab-created pink diamonds achieve color through several methods:

Post-Growth Treatment:

High-Temperature Annealing: Heat treatment creating specific color centers.

Irradiation and Annealing: Controlled radiation followed by thermal treatment.

Pressure Treatment: Mechanical stress creating pink-producing defects.

Combined Treatments: Sequential processes optimizing color development.

Color Characteristics:

Hue Variations: Pure pink to pink orange to pink purple

Saturation Levels: From faint pink to vivid pink intensities

Color Distribution: Even color throughout the stone.

Stability: Permanent color resistant to fading or change

Yellow Diamonds: Controlled Nitrogen Beauty

Yellow diamonds represent the most common fancy color in both natural and lab-created varieties:

Nitrogen Control Methods:

Controlled Addition: Precise nitrogen introduction during CVD growth

Aggregation Management: Heat treatment optimizing nitrogen configuration.

Concentration Gradients: Creating subtle color variations within stones.

Purity Balance: Achieving color while maintaining clarity.

Market Advantages:

Consistent Quality: Uniform color distribution and intensity

Size Availability: Large yellow diamonds readily achievable

Cost Effectiveness: Significant savings compared to natural fancy yellows.

Customization: Specific color intensities available on request

Emerging Fancy Colors

Research continues into creating previously impossible or extremely rare colors:

Green Diamonds:

Irradiation Techniques: Controlled radiation creating green color centers.

Surface Treatments: Creating green coloration in outer layers.

Natural-Type Colors: Replicating the green of natural irradiated diamonds.

Stability Considerations: Ensuring Permanent Color Retention.

Red and Purple Diamonds:

Experimental Techniques: Research into creating these ultra-rare colors.

Treatment Combinations: Multiple processes creating unique color effects.

Market Development: Establishing grading standards for new colors.

Consumer Education: Building Awareness of New Color Possibilities.

Clarity: The Window to Perfection

Clarity grading evaluates the relative absence of inclusions (internal characteristics) and blemishes (external characteristics) that affect a diamond's beauty and structural integrity. Lab-created diamonds often demonstrate superior clarity characteristics due to their controlled growth environment.

The GIA Clarity Scale

The industry-standard clarity scale ranges from Flawless to Included, with each grade representing specific criteria:

Flawless (FL):

Definition: No inclusions or blemishes visible under 10x magnification

Rarity: Less than 1% of all diamonds achieve FL grade

Lab Diamond Advantage: 5-8% of high-quality lab diamonds achieve FL grade.

Value Impact: Premium pricing for exceptional rarity

Internally Flawless (IF):

Definition: No inclusions visible under 10x magnification; minor blemishes may be present

Characteristics: Possible minor surface imperfections from polishing

Achievement: 2-3% of all diamonds, 12-15% of premium lab diamonds

Practical Consideration: Virtually indistinguishable from FL to most observers

Very Very Slightly Included (VVS1, VVS2):

VVS1: Minute inclusions extremely difficult for skilled grader to locate under 10x.

VVS2: Minute inclusions are difficult for a skilled grader to locate under 10x magnification.

Visibility: Inclusions typically invisible to the unaided eye

Market Position: Excellent clarity with more accessible pricing than FL/IF

Very Slightly Included (VS1, VS2):

VS1: Minor inclusions are somewhat difficult to locate under 10x magnification.

VS2: Minor inclusions are easier to locate under 10x magnification.

Naked Eye: Inclusions are rarely visible without magnification

Value Sweet Spot: Optimal balance of quality and value for most consumers

Slightly Included (SI1, SI2):

SI1: Noticeable inclusions under 10x magnification

SI2: Easily noticed inclusions under 10x magnification.

Visibility Considerations: Some inclusions may be visible to the unaided eye.

Size and Setting Impact: Smaller diamonds and certain settings can hide inclusions.

Included (I1, I2, I3):

I1: Inclusions obvious under 10x magnification may affect brilliance.

I2: Large and numerous inclusions affecting transparency and brilliance.

I3: Prominent inclusions affecting transparency, brilliance, and durability.

Market Considerations: Budget-oriented options with visible quality compromises

Types of Inclusions in Lab-Created Diamonds

Lab-created diamonds exhibit distinct inclusion characteristics based on their growth method:

HPHT Inclusions:

Metallic Inclusions: Tiny fragments of iron, nickel, or cobalt catalysts

Flux Inclusions: Trapped metallic flux material from growth process.

Growth Sector Boundaries: Visible transitions between crystal growth sectors

Hourglass Patterns: Distinctive patterns visible under specialized lighting

CVD Inclusions:

Graphite Inclusions: Small graphite crystals are occasionally incorporated during growth.

Silicon Inclusions: CVD-specific inclusions from silicon-containing gases

Growth Lines: Parallel lines indicating layer-by-layer growth.

Pinpoint Inclusions: Tiny crystal inclusions, often less problematic than HPHT inclusions.

Clarity Enhancement and Optimization

Modern production techniques minimize inclusion formation in lab-created diamonds:

Growth Environment Control:

Ultra-Pure Materials: High-purity gases and source materials reduce contamination.

Cleanroom Standards: Contamination-free environments that prevent the inclusion of impurities.

Process Optimization: Controlled growth rates minimizing defect formation.

Real-Time Monitoring: Immediate detection and correction of conditions leading to inclusions.

Post-Growth Enhancement:

Laser Drilling: Precise laser access to remove or bleach dark inclusions.

Fracture Filling: Glass-like substances filling open fractures (must be disclosed)

HPHT Treatment: High-pressure, high-temperature treatment improving clarity.

Surface Polishing: Superior polish quality, minimizing surface blemishes

Carat Weight: Understanding Size and Value

Carat weight represents the mass of a diamond, with one carat equaling 200 milligrams or 0.2 grams. While seemingly straightforward, carat weight interacts complexly with the other Cs and market dynamics, particularly in the lab-created diamond market.

Historical and Cultural Context

The carat system originated from the carob seed, which ancient traders used as a standard for weighing precious gems due to its remarkably consistent mass.

This historical connection underscores the fundamental importance of weight in gemstone valuation.

Metric Carat Definition:

International Standard: 200 milligrams exactly, established in 1907.

Subdivision: Points (0.01 carat each) for precise measurement

Precision: Measured to the third decimal place (0.001 carat)

Certification: All certified diamonds include precise carat weight

Carat Weight and Visual Size Relationship

Understanding the relationship between carat weight and visual size helps consumers make informed decisions:

Round Brilliant Diameter Relationships:

0.50 carat: Approximately 5.1mm diameter

1.00 carat: Approximately 6.5mm diameter

1.50 carat: Approximately 7.4mm diameter

2.00 carat: Approximately 8.1mm diameter

3.00 carat: Approximately 9.3mm diameter

Depth Impact on Size: Diamonds with identical carat weights can appear different sizes based on proportions:

Shallow Cut: Larger diameter, thinner depth, potential light leakage

Deep Cut: Smaller diameter, greater depth, potential dark appearance

Ideal Proportions: An optimal diameter-to-depth ratio that maximizes both size and beauty.

Carat Weight Premiums and Market Dynamics

The diamond market exhibits distinct pricing behaviors at certain carat weight thresholds:

Magic Sizes and Premiums:

0.50 carat: First significant premium threshold

1.00 carat: Major psychological and practical milestone

2.00 carat: Luxury market entry point

3.00+ carat: Ultra-luxury segment with exponential pricing

Lab Diamond Market Advantages: Lab-created diamonds offer unique advantages in larger sizes:

Size Availability: Routine production of 3-5+ carat stones

Quality Consistency: Large stones maintaining high clarity and color grades.

Value Proposition: Exceptional value in larger sizes compared to natural diamonds.

Customization: Ability to grow specific sizes for particular applications

Precision and Measurement Standards

Accurate carat weight measurement requires sophisticated equipment and procedures:

Certified Scales:

Accuracy: 0.001 carat precision (0.2 milligram)

Calibration: Regular calibration with certified weights

Environmental Control: Stable temperature and humidity conditions

Multiple Measurements: Verification through repeated weighing

Measurement Protocols:

Clean Stone: Removal of all oils, dust, and foreign materials

Room Temperature: Maintains a stable temperature, preventing thermal expansion effects.

Static Elimination: Anti-static measures prevent measurement errors.

Documentation: Recorded measurements in certification documentation

4.2 Certification and Authentication

Major Grading Laboratories Comparison

The credibility and accuracy of diamond grading depends entirely on the reputation and standards of the certifying laboratory. Understanding the differences between major grading institutions helps consumers make informed decisions about certified lab-created diamonds.

Gemological Institute of America (GIA): The Gold Standard

Established in 1931, GIA created the modern 4Cs grading system and remains the most respected authority in diamond grading worldwide.

GIA Lab-Created Diamond Grading: Since 2007, GIA has issued grading reports for lab-created diamonds with specific protocols:

Report Format: Digital reports with distinct formatting indicating lab-created origin.

Grading Standards: Identical 4Cs criteria applied to lab and natural diamonds.

Origin Determination: Advanced testing confirming synthetic origin.

Quality Assessment: Same rigorous evaluation standards regardless of origin

GIA Grading Strengths:

Industry Recognition: Universally accepted by dealers, retailers, and consumers.

Consistency: Exceptionally consistent grading across different laboratories

Research Leadership: Continuous research improving identification and grading techniques.

Conservative Approach: A tendency toward stricter grading that enhances consumer confidence.

GIA Laboratory Locations and Capabilities:

Carlsbad, California: Primary research and education facility

New York: Major commercial grading laboratory

Bangkok: Asian operations center

Antwerp: European grading services

Mumbai: Indian market support

International Gemological Institute (IGI): Global Reach

Founded in 1975, IGI operates the world's largest network of gemological laboratories with locations across major diamond centers.

IGI Lab-Created Diamond Services:

Comprehensive Reports: Detailed grading reports with origin identification

Quick Turnaround: Faster service times compared to GIA in many markets.

Regional Expertise: Local market knowledge and language capabilities

Competitive Pricing: More accessible certification costs

IGI Grading Characteristics:

Slightly Liberal: Generally, slightly more lenient than GIA in borderline cases

Market Acceptance: Widely accepted, particularly in Asian and European markets.

Technology Integration: Advanced equipment for synthetic diamond identification

Education Focus: Extensive gemological education programs

IGI Global Presence:

Antwerp: European headquarters and primary laboratory

Mumbai: Major operations center for the Indian market

Bangkok: Southeast Asian services

New York: North American operations

Hong Kong: Asia-Pacific hub

Gem Certification & Assurance Lab (GCAL): Innovation Leaders

GCAL pioneered several innovations in diamond certification, including the first guaranteed diamond grading and optical performance measurement.

GCAL Unique Features:

Guaranteed Grading: Money-back guarantee on grading accuracy

Optical Performance: Measured light performance data included in reports.

Digital Integration: Advanced digital imaging and documentation

Anti-Counterfeiting: Sophisticated security features prevent report fraud.

GCAL Lab-Created Diamond Approach:

Performance Focus: Emphasis on optical performance alongside traditional grading

Innovation Adoption: Early adoption of new technologies and grading methods

Market Education: Extensive consumer education programs

Quality Emphasis: Focus on cut quality and light performance metrics.

American Gemological Society (AGS): Cut Quality Pioneers

AGS developed the most sophisticated cut grading system available, using advanced ray-tracing technology to evaluate light performance.

AGS Cut Grading Innovation:

0-10 Scale: Numerical grading system with 0 representing ideal quality.

Light Performance: Scientific measurement of brilliance, fire, and scintillation

Ray Tracing: Computer modeling of light paths through diamonds

Precision Standards: Extremely precise measurements and tolerances

AGS Lab-Created Diamond Certification:

Technical Excellence: Most advanced cut grading available for lab diamonds

Performance Documentation: Detailed light performance measurements

Quality Focus: Emphasis on exceptional cut quality and optical performance

Limited Volume: Smaller operation focusing on premium quality stones.

European Gemological Laboratory (EGL): Regional Variations

EGL operates independently in different regions, with varying standards and market acceptance.

EGL Considerations:

Regional Differences: EGL USA, EGL International, and other entities operate independently of each other.

Market Acceptance: Variable acceptance depending on the specific EGL laboratory.

Grading Variations: Some EGL laboratories are known for their more lenient grading policies.

Price Impact: EGL-certified diamonds often priced lower due to their grading reputation

Reading and Interpreting Certificates

Understanding how to read and interpret diamond grading certificates empowers consumers to make informed purchasing decisions based on objective, verified information.

Certificate Components and Information

Header Information:

Laboratory Identity: Clear identification of issuing laboratory

Report Number: Unique identifier for tracking and verification.

Date of Issue: When the grading was completed.

Shape and Cutting Style: Basic description of diamond shape and cut type.

The 4Cs Documentation:

Carat Weight: Precise weight to three decimal places

Color Grade: Letter grade with detailed color description.

Clarity Grade: Clarity grade with inclusion plotting diagram.

Cut Grade: Overall cut quality assessment (when available)

Additional Measurements:

Dimensions: Length, width, and depth measurements

Proportions: Table percentage, depth percentage, crown, and pavilion angles

Girdle Description: Thickness and finish characteristics.

Culet: Description of bottom point condition

Polish and Symmetry: Surface finish and facet alignment grades

Fluorescence: Reaction to ultraviolet light

Lab-Created Specific Information:

Origin Determination: Clear identification as laboratory-grown

Growth Method: HPHT or CVD growth process identification

Treatments: Any post-growth treatments or enhancements

Comments: Additional observations or characteristics

Digital Verification and Security Features

Modern grading reports incorporate sophisticated security features that prevent counterfeiting and enable verification:

Digital Security:

QR Codes: Direct links to online report verification

Watermarks: Embedded security features visible under special lighting

Serial Numbers: Unique identifiers preventing duplication.

Digital Signatures: Cryptographic verification of report authenticity

Online Verification Systems:

Real-Time Verification: Immediate confirmation of report authenticity

Digital Archives: Permanent records accessible through laboratory websites

Mobile Apps: Smartphone applications enabling instant verification.

Detailed Images: High-resolution photographs linked to specific reports.

Red Flags in Certification

Recognizing potential issues with diamond certification protects consumers from fraud and misrepresentation.

Certificate Red Flags

Questionable Laboratory Claims:

Unknown Laboratories: Certificates from unrecognized or questionable institutions

Inflated Grades: Unusually high grades for exceptionally low prices

Missing Information: Incomplete or vague grading information

Poor Documentation: Low-quality printing or unprofessional presentation

Inconsistent Information:

Measurement Discrepancies: Measurements that don't match the reported carat weight.

Grade Conflicts: Grades that seem inconsistent with visual appearance.

Missing Treatments: Failure to disclose obvious treatments or enhancements.

Laser Inscription Issues: Mismatched or missing laser inscriptions

Verification Best Practices

Independent Verification:

Multiple Opinions: Seeking second opinions from qualified gemologists.

Laboratory Verification: Confirming certificates through laboratory websites.

Physical Examination: Professional examination of the actual diamond

Comparative Analysis: Comparing similar stones from reputable sources.

Professional Consultation:

Certified Gemologists: Consultation with GIA Graduate Gemologists

Independent Appraisers: Third-party appraisal for verification

Retailer Reputation: Purchasing from established, reputable dealers.

Return Policies: Ensuring adequate return periods for independent verification and quality assurance.

4.3 Lab-Specific Quality Indicators

Growth Patterns and Their Significance

Lab-created diamonds exhibit distinct growth patterns that provide insights into their origin, quality, and characteristics. Understanding these patterns helps both professionals and consumers appreciate the unique aspects of synthetic diamond production.

HPHT Growth Patterns

High-pressure, high-temperature diamonds display characteristic growth features that distinguish them from both natural and CVD diamonds:

Cubic Growth Sectors: HPHT diamonds typically grow in cubic or octahedral crystal forms, creating distinct growth sectors:

{100} Cube Faces: Six square faces creating cubic growth patterns.

{111} Octahedral Faces: Eight triangular faces forming octahedral patterns.

Sector Boundaries: Visible transitions between different growth directions.

Color Zoning: Slight color variations between different growth sectors.

Hourglass Patterns: Many HPHT diamonds exhibit distinctive hourglass-shaped patterns when viewed under specialized lighting:

Cross-Polarized Light: Reveals strain patterns and growth boundaries.

DiamondSure Detection: Specialized equipment highlighting HPHT characteristics.

Photoluminescence: Unique luminescence patterns under UV excitation

Temperature Mapping: Thermal conductivity variations following growth patterns.

Metallic Inclusions: The HPHT process often incorporates minute metallic inclusions from the catalyst system:

Iron Group Metals: Iron, nickel, and cobalt from catalyst materials.

Flux Inclusions: Solidified metallic flux trapped during growth.

Magnetic Response: Some HPHT diamonds show slight magnetic attraction.

Spectroscopic Signatures: Characteristic absorption spectra from metallic impurities

CVD Growth Patterns

Chemical vapor deposition diamonds exhibit distinctly different growth characteristics:

Layer-by-Layer Growth: CVD diamonds grow through sequential atomic layer deposition:

Growth Striations: Parallel lines indicating individual growth layers.

Thickness Variations: Slight variations in layer thickness creating visible patterns.

Surface Topography: Step-like surface features from layer-by-layer growth

Cross-Sectional Analysis: A Layered structure visible in cross-sectional examination

Columnar Structure: CVD growth creates columnar crystal structures:

Grain Boundaries: Boundaries between individual crystal columns

Preferred Orientation: Crystals growing predominantly in one direction.

Surface Morphology: Characteristic surface features from columnar growth

Stress Patterns: Predictable stress distributions following growth directions.

Silicon-Related Features: CVD diamonds may contain silicon-related inclusions and defects:

Silicon Inclusions: Microscopic silicon particles from the growth process

SiV Centers: Silicon-vacancy color centers creating unique optical signatures.

Spectroscopic Identification: Characteristic infrared and photoluminescence spectra

Growth Control: Silicon content used to control growth rates and quality.

Strain Patterns Under Polarized Light

Strain analysis provides crucial information about diamond quality and growth conditions, particularly important for lab-created diamonds.

Understanding Diamond Strain

Stress and Strain Origins: Diamond strain results from various factors during growth and processing:

Growth Stress: Uneven growth rates creating internal stress.

Thermal Stress: Temperature variations during growth and cooling

Mechanical Stress: External forces during growth or handling.

Chemical Stress: The incorporation of impurities creates lattice distortion.

Optical Effects of Strain: Strain affects how diamonds interact with polarized light:

Birefringence: Double refraction of light through stressed crystal regions

Extinction Patterns: Dark areas where light polarization is altered.

Color Interference: Stress-induced color patterns in white light.

Quantitative Measurement: Photoelastic analysis measures stress levels.

Strain Pattern Interpretation

HPHT Strain Characteristics:

Cross-Hatched Patterns: Intersecting strain lines following crystal directions.

Sector-Related Stress: Strain concentrated along growth sector boundaries.

Thermal Gradients: Strain patterns from temperature variations during growth

Catalyst Effects: Stress concentrations around metallic inclusions

CVD Strain Characteristics:

Linear Patterns: Strain lines parallel to growth direction

Layer Boundaries: Stress concentrations between growth layers.

Substrate Effects: Strain patterns are influenced by substrate orientation.

Thickness Variations: Strain related to diamond thickness and growth uniformity.

Quality Implications of Strain

Performance Impact:

Optical Clarity: High strain can reduce transparency and brilliance.

Cutting Considerations: Strain affects how diamonds respond to cutting and polishing.

Durability: Excessive strain may increase fracture susceptibility

Treatment Response: Strain influences how diamonds respond to enhancement treatments.

Quality Optimization:

Growth Control: Optimized growth conditions minimizing strain formation.

Post-Growth Annealing: Heat treatment reducing residual stress.

Cut Planning: Accounting for strain patterns in cut design.

Quality Grading: Strain assessment as part of comprehensive quality evaluation

Fluorescence Characteristics

Fluorescence in lab-created diamonds provides important identification and quality information, with distinct characteristics that differ from those of natural diamonds.

Understanding Diamond Fluorescence

Fluorescence Mechanisms: Diamond fluorescence results from trace impurities and defects that absorb UV light and emit visible light:

Nitrogen Centers: Most common cause of blue fluorescence in natural diamonds

Boron Centers: Create distinctive fluorescence patterns in blue lab diamonds.

Silicon-Vacancy Centers: Unique to CVD diamonds, creating red fluorescence.

Other Defects: Various defect centers create different fluorescence colors.

Fluorescence Characteristics:

Intensity: None, faint, medium, strong, or very strong

Color: Blue, yellow, orange, red, green, or combinations

Distribution: Even, uneven, or patchy fluorescence patterns

Stability: Consistency of fluorescence under different UV sources

Lab-Created Diamond Fluorescence Patterns

HPHT Fluorescence:

Blue Fluorescence: Similar to natural diamonds but often more uniform

Phosphorescence: Some HPHT diamonds show a persistent glow after UV removal

Metallic Effects: Metallic inclusions can create unusual fluorescence patterns.

Treatment Response: Heat treatment can modify fluorescence characteristics.

CVD Fluorescence:

Red Fluorescence: Silicon-vacancy centers creating distinctive red emission.

Orange Fluorescence: Unique CVD-related defect centers

Growth-Related Patterns: Fluorescence variations following growth layers.

Post-Growth Changes: Treatments can significantly alter fluorescence properties.

Quality and Market Implications

Quality Assessment:

Positive Indicators: Certain fluorescence patterns indicating high quality.

Negative Indicators: Fluorescence patterns suggesting growth problems.

Consistency Evaluation: Uniform fluorescence indicating controlled growth.

Identification Utility: Fluorescence patterns helping identify origin and treatment.

Market Considerations:

Consumer Preferences: Variable market acceptance of fluorescent diamonds

Price Impact: Fluorescence effects on diamond pricing and desirability

Setting Considerations: How fluorescence interacts with different lighting conditions

Disclosure Requirements: Legal and ethical obligations to disclose fluorescence characteristics.

Magnetic Properties Testing

Some lab-created diamonds, particularly those produced by HPHT methods, exhibit weak magnetic properties due to metallic inclusions from the growth process.

Magnetic Property Origins

HPHT Magnetic Characteristics:

Catalyst Inclusions: Iron, nickel, and cobalt inclusions from growth catalysts

Concentration Effects: Magnetic response correlating with inclusion density

Size Dependence: Larger diamonds more likely to show magnetic response.

Growth Control: Improved processes reducing magnetic inclusion formation.

Testing Methodologies:

Neodymium Magnets: Strong, rare-earth magnets detect weak magnetic response.

Suspension Testing: Suspending diamonds to detect magnetic attraction.

Electronic Detection: Sensitive magnetometers measure magnetic properties.

Comparative Analysis: Testing against known natural diamond standards.

Identification and Quality Implications

Identification Value:

Origin Determination: Magnetic properties helping distinguish HPHT from natural diamonds.

Quality Assessment: Magnetic response indicating inclusion content.

Process Optimization: Feedback for improving growth procedures.

Market Authentication: Verification of diamond origin and growth method

Consumer Considerations:

Practical Impact: Magnetic properties having no effect on beauty or durability.

Setting Compatibility: No interference with jewelry settings or wearing

Detection Probability: Only strongly included diamonds showing detectable magnetism.

Quality Correlation: Magnetic response often correlates with visible inclusion content.

The comprehensive understanding of diamond quality and grading provides the foundation for making informed decisions about lab-created diamonds. From the precise optical engineering of cut quality to the sophisticated scientific analysis of growth patterns and characteristics, modern grading techniques ensure that consumers can evaluate lab-created diamonds with the same confidence and precision as natural stones.

The unique characteristics of lab-created diamonds—their consistent quality, controlled properties, and distinctive identification features—represent both opportunities and considerations for consumers. By understanding these factors, buyers can appreciate not only the beauty and value of lab-created diamonds but also the remarkable scientific and technological achievements they represent.

As we continue our journey through this comprehensive guide, we'll explore how this technical understanding translates into practical buying decisions, market dynamics, and the ethical considerations that increasingly influence consumer choices in the modern diamond marketplace.

***

In mastering the complexities of diamond quality and grading, we gain more than technical knowledge—we develop the discernment to recognize true excellence and the confidence to make choices that reflect both our aesthetic preferences and our values. The precision of modern grading, combined with the controlled excellence of lab-created diamonds, offers unprecedented opportunities for consumers to acquire gems of exceptional beauty and verified quality.

Chapter 5: The Ethical and Environmental Case

"In choosing how we adorn ourselves, we choose what kind of world we wish to create. Every diamond tells a story—of the earth it came from, the hands that shaped it, and the values it represents."

5.1 Mining vs. Laboratory Impact

The True Cost of Traditional Diamond Mining

To understand the revolutionary impact of lab-created diamonds, we must first confront the sobering realities of traditional diamond mining. For over a century, the pursuit of natural diamonds has left an indelible mark on our planet's landscapes, ecosystems, and human communities. The glamor of these precious stones has long obscured the environmental devastation and human suffering that too often accompany their extraction.

Environmental Devastation: The Hidden Price of Natural Beauty

Land Disruption and Ecosystem Destruction

The scale of environmental disruption caused by diamond mining is staggering and defies comprehension. To extract a single carat of diamonds—roughly the size of a pencil eraser—miners must move an average of 1,750 tons of earth and rock. This staggering ratio means that a typical one-carat engagement ring requires the displacement of material equivalent to excavating a swimming pool 20 feet deep.

The Jwaneng mine in Botswana, one of the world's most productive diamond mines, exemplifies this environmental cost. The open pit extends over 1.6 kilometers, 1.2 kilometers in width, and plunges more than 300 meters deep—a man-made canyon that has permanently altered the landscape. The mine processes 8.6 million tons of ore annually to yield approximately 15 million carats of diamonds, illustrating the massive scale of earth movement required for natural diamond production.

Water Consumption and Contamination

Diamond mining's water usage presents another environmental crisis. Large-scale mining operations consume between 50 and 100 million gallons of water annually per mine site. The Premier mine in South Africa uses approximately 75 million gallons yearly—enough water to supply a city of 50,000 people. This consumption is often observed in water-scarce regions, where local communities struggle with drought and limited access to clean water.

Beyond consumption, mining operations contaminate water systems through:

Acid Mine Drainage: Chemical reactions between exposed minerals and water create acidic runoff that persists for decades.

Heavy Metal Leaching: Lead, mercury, and arsenic contamination from processing chemicals

Sediment Loading: Erosion from mining sites clogging rivers and destroys aquatic habitats.

Chemical Processing: Toxic chemicals used in diamond recovery are contaminating groundwater systems.

The Orange River in South Africa, once pristine, now carries elevated levels of heavy metals and sediments from upstream diamond mining operations, affecting communities and ecosystems hundreds of miles downstream.

Carbon Footprint and Climate Impact

The carbon intensity of diamond mining reveals another environmental concern. Mining operations generate an average of 160 kilograms of CO_2 emissions per carat of diamonds produced. This includes:

Diesel Fuel Consumption: Heavy machinery and transportation requiring millions of gallons annually.

Explosive Materials: Blasting operations release both direct emissions and disturbing carbon-storing soils.

Processing Energy: Crushing, sorting, and cleaning operations consume massive amounts of electricity.

Transportation Networks: Global shipping from remote mine sites to processing centers.

The Argyle mine in Australia, prior to its closure in 2020, consumed enough electricity annually to power approximately 100,000 homes while producing around 14 million carats of diamonds. The mine's remote location necessitated a private airport and hundreds of flights annually, thereby significantly amplifying its carbon footprint.

Biodiversity Loss and Habitat Destruction

Diamond mining operations have destroyed critical habitats across three continents:

African Impact:

Kalahari Desert: Multiple mines fragmenting wildlife corridors and disrupting migration patterns.

Congo Basin: Alluvial mining destroying riverside ecosystems and affecting primate populations.

Coastal Namibia: Marine diamond mining disrupting seal colonies and seabird nesting sites

Canadian Impact:

Boreal Forest: Clear-cutting thousands of acres for mine access and infrastructure

Arctic Tundra: Permafrost disruption affecting caribou migration routes.

Wetland Systems: Drainage and contamination of critical waterfowl breeding areas.

Australian Impact:

Kimberley Region: Open-pit mining is destroying unique geological formations and the habitat of endemic species.

Great Western Woodlands: Road construction and infrastructure fragmenting one of the world's largest remaining temperate woodlands

The Laboratory Alternative: Clean Production in Controlled Environments

In stark contrast to the environmental devastation of mining, lab-created diamond production represents a paradigm shift toward sustainable luxury manufacturing. Modern diamond laboratories operate as precision facilities, where every aspect of production is controlled, monitored, and optimized to minimize environmental impact.

Controlled Environment Advantages

Minimal Land Use

A typical lab-created diamond facility occupies 5-10 acres compared to mining operations that disturb thousands of acres. Diamond Foundry's facility in California produces over 100,000 carats annually from a 50,000 square foot building—roughly equivalent to a large retail store. The same diamond output from traditional mining would require:

Land Disruption: 15,000-25,000 acres of surface disturbance.

Overburden Removal: 175 million tons of earth and rock.

Infrastructure: Hundreds of miles of access roads, processing facilities, and waste storage areas

Restoration Costs: Decades and millions of dollars for incomplete habitat restoration

Zero Ecosystem Disruption

Lab-created diamond facilities integrate seamlessly into existing industrial zones without disrupting natural habitats. These facilities:

Preserve Wildlife Corridors: No interference with animal migration patterns or breeding areas.

Maintain Watershed Integrity: No disruption of natural water systems or aquifer recharge areas.

Protect Soil Resources: No removal of topsoil or subsoil layers.

Conserve Biodiversity: No displacement of endangered or endemic species.

Circular Resource Usage

Modern laboratory operations employ circular economy principles:

Closed-Loop Water Systems: 95%+ water recycling eliminating discharge to natural systems.

Material Recovery: Recycling of carbon sources, catalysts, and processing materials

Energy Efficiency: Optimized processes requiring 60-80% less energy than mining equivalents.

Waste Minimization: Near-zero solid waste generation through process optimization.

Energy Efficiency and Renewable Integration

Comparative Energy Analysis

The energy efficiency advantages of lab-created diamonds become apparent through detailed lifecycle analysis:

Traditional Mining Energy Requirements (per carat):

Extraction Operations: 450-650 kWh for earth moving and ore processing.

Crushing and Concentration: 200-300 kWh for ore preparation

Sorting and Recovery: 100-150 kWh for diamond identification and extraction

Transportation: 50-100 kWh for global logistics

Final Processing: 75-125 kWh for cutting and polishing.

Total Mining Energy: 875-1,325 kWh per carat

Lab-Created Production Energy Requirements (per carat):

CVD Production: 150-200 kWh for growth chamber operation

HPHT Production: 250-300 kWh for pressure and heating systems

Gas Purification: 15-25 kWh for ultra-pure feedstock preparation

Support Systems: 20-35 kWh for monitoring and facility operations.

Processing: 75-125 kWh for cutting and polishing (identical to natural)

Total Lab Energy: 260-385 kWh per carat

This represents a 60-75% reduction in energy consumption compared to traditional mining.

Renewable Energy Integration Success Stories

Leading lab-created diamond producers have achieved carbon-neutral or carbon-negative production through renewable energy integration:

Diamond Foundry - Solar Powered Excellence:

Solar Capacity: 50 MW solar installation generating 100+ GWh annually.

Energy Storage: 200 MWh battery system ensuring continuous operation.

Carbon Impact: Verified carbon-negative production with 150% renewable energy offset.

Production Volume: 100,000+ carats annually from 100% renewable energy

Certification: Third-party verified Climate Neutral Certified diamonds

WD Lab Grown Diamonds - Wind and Solar Hybrid:

Renewable Mix: 70% solar, 30% wind power supporting production.

Energy Efficiency: Advanced CVD systems requiring 40% less energy than the industry average.

Carbon Reduction: 90% reduction in carbon emissions compared to mined diamond equivalent.

Expansion Plans: 100% renewable energy across all facilities by 2025

Greenlab Diamonds - Monsoon Solar Strategy:

Adaptive System: Solar primary with hydroelectric backup during monsoon seasons

Local Integration: Supporting regional renewable energy development in India.

Community Impact: Surplus solar energy supporting local grid and communities.

Quality Advantage: Stable renewable power enables superior quality control.

Water Usage and Conservation

Dramatic Water Savings

Mining Water Consumption Crisis: Traditional diamond mining operations consume staggering amounts of water in regions that are often water-stressed.

De Beers Operations: Collective consumption of 400+ million gallons annually across African operations

Dominion Diamond Mines: 50 million gallons annually in Canada's Northwest Territories

Petra Diamonds: 75 million gallons annually across South African operations

Rio Tinto: 100+ million gallons annually at the former Argyle mine

Laboratory Water Efficiency: Modern lab-created diamond facilities demonstrate remarkable water conservation:

CVD Operations: 20-30 gallons per carat with 95% recycling efficiency

HPHT Operations: 40-60 gallons per carat with 90% recycling efficiency

Closed-Loop Systems: Zero discharge facilities with complete water recycling.

Ultra-Pure Requirements: Advanced purification enabling complete reuse.

This represents a 98-99% reduction in water consumption compared to traditional mining.

Advanced Water Management Technologies

Innovation in Water Conservation:

Atmospheric Water Generation: Extracting pure water from ambient humidity.

Reverse Osmosis Systems: 99.9% water recovery from process streams

Heat Recovery Integration: Using waste heat for water treatment and purification.

Real-Time Monitoring: AI-optimized water usage reduces consumption by 25-40%

Zero-Discharge Facilities: Advanced facilities achieve complete water cycle closure:

IIa Technologies: Zero discharge facility with 100% water recycling

Element Six: Closed-loop cooling systems with atmospheric makeup only.

Applied Diamond Inc.: Rainwater harvesting supplementing closed-loop systems

Pure Grown Diamonds: Advanced treatment enabling potable water production from process streams

5.2 Social and Ethical Considerations

The Dark History of Conflict Diamonds

The term "blood diamonds" or "conflict diamonds" entered global consciousness in the 1990s as the world awakened to the brutal reality that some of the most beautiful gems on Earth were financing civil wars, human rights abuses, and unspeakable violence. Understanding this history is crucial to appreciating why lab-created diamonds represent more than just a technological achievement—they offer a path to ethical luxury that breaks the chain of exploitation.

Historical Context and Scale of the Problem

Sierra Leone: Diamonds and Devastation (1991-2002)

The Sierra Leone Civil War stands as one of the most extensively documented examples of diamond-fueled conflict. During this 11-year conflict:

Death Toll: Over 50,000 civilians killed, with 2 million displaced

Systematic Atrocities: Widespread use of child soldiers, mass amputations, and sexual violence

Diamond Financing: An estimated $125 million annually in diamond revenues funding the Revolutionary United Front (RUF)

International Impact: Diamonds from Sierra Leone entering global markets through neighboring countries

The RUF's systematic use of terror, including the amputation of civilians' hands and arms, was directly funded by diamond revenues. These stones, extracted by forced labor including children as young as 10, entered the global diamond supply chain and reached consumers worldwide, unknowingly financing atrocities.

Angola: UNITA and Diamond Wars (1975-2002)

Angola's civil war, one of the longest-running conflicts in modern history, was heavily financed by diamond revenues:

Conflict Duration: 27 years of intermittent warfare

Diamond Revenue: UNITA generated $3.7 billion from diamond sales during the 1990s

Humanitarian Crisis: 1.5 million deaths, 4 million internally displaced persons

Economic Devastation: Complete destruction of national infrastructure and economy

UNITA's control of diamond-rich areas enabled the continuation of conflict despite international sanctions and peace agreements. The organization used diamond revenues to purchase sophisticated weapons and maintain military operations that devastated Angolan society.

Democratic Republic of Congo: Ongoing Exploitation

The DRC's diamond trade continues to fuel conflict and exploitation:

Artisanal Mining: 200,000+ artisanal miners working in dangerous conditions

Child Labor: UNICEF estimates 40,000 children working in DRC diamond mines

Armed Group Control: Various militia groups controlling mining areas and exploiting workers

Revenue Loss: Government receiving less than 10% of the actual diamond value due to smuggling

The Kimberley Process: Progress and Limitations

Establishment and Goals

The Kimberley Process Certification Scheme (KPCS), established in 2003, aimed to eliminate conflict diamonds from global trade:

Founding Members: 81 countries representing 99.8% of global diamond production

Certification Requirements: Government-issued certificates for all rough diamond shipments

Chain of Warranties: Documentation tracking diamonds from mine to retail

Monitoring Systems: Annual reviews and compliance assessments

Achievements and Impact

The Kimberley Process achieved significant initial success:

Conflict Diamond Reduction: Estimated reduction from 15% to less than 1% of global trade

Industry Transformation: Mandatory due diligence procedures throughout the supply chain

Peace Contributions: Supporting peace processes in Angola, Sierra Leone, and DRC

Revenue Protection: Safeguarding legitimate government diamond revenues

Critical Limitations and Ongoing Challenges

Despite achievements, the Kimberley Process faces substantial limitations:

Narrow Definition of Conflict:

State-Sponsored Violence: Exclusion of human rights abuses by government forces

Artisanal Mining Exploitation: Limited coverage of small-scale mining abuses

Environmental Destruction: No consideration of environmental or community impacts

Labor Rights: Insufficient attention to worker safety and fair compensation

Enforcement Challenges:

Smuggling Networks: Sophisticated smuggling operations circumventing controls

Documentation Fraud: Forged certificates and fraudulent origin documentation

Mixed Parcels: Conflict diamonds mixed with legitimate stones

Limited Monitoring: Inadequate oversight in remote mining areas

Recent Controversies:

Zimbabwe Marange Fields: Violent evictions and military-controlled mining

Central African Republic: Ongoing conflict diamond trade despite international sanctions

Venezuela: Emerging concerns about diamond trade financing authoritarian regime

Ivory Coast: Historical issues with diamond smuggling through porous borders

Modern Labor Practices and Human Rights

Even in mines operating within legal frameworks and Kimberley Process compliance, serious labor and human rights concerns persist throughout the natural diamond supply chain.

Working Conditions in Natural Diamond Mining

Occupational Safety Hazards

Diamond mining remains one of the world's most dangerous occupations:

Fatal Accident Rates: 5-10 times higher than general industrial averages

Respiratory Diseases: Silicosis affects 30-50% of long-term miners

Cave-In Risks: Unstable pit walls and underground collapses

Equipment Accidents: Heavy machinery accidents and explosive incidents

Economic Exploitation

Despite generating billions in revenue, many mining communities experience persistent poverty:

Wage Disparities: Miners earning $2-5 per day while companies profit millions per carat

Contract Labor: Extensive use of temporary workers without benefits or job security

Company Towns: Corporate control of housing, food, and services creates dependency

Limited Advancement: Minimal opportunities for skill development or career progression

Community Displacement and Impact

Mining operations frequently displace and disrupt local communities:

Forced Relocation: Entire villages relocated for mining operations

Cultural Destruction: Sacred sites and traditional lands destroyed by mining

Economic Dependence: Local economies are becoming entirely dependent on mining companies

Post-Mining Abandonment: Communities left without resources when mines close

Artisanal and Small-Scale Mining Challenges

Child Labor Crisis

Despite international efforts, child labor remains prevalent in artisanal diamond mining:

Scale of Problem: Estimated 1 million children working in artisanal mines globally

Age Demographics: Children as young as 5 years old engaged in diamond mining

Educational Impact: Mining work prevents school attendance and literacy development

Health Consequences: Physical development problems from heavy labor and toxic exposure

Gender-Based Exploitation

Women in diamond mining communities face particular vulnerabilities:

Unpaid Labor: Women performing support roles without compensation

Sexual Exploitation: High rates of sexual violence in mining areas

Economic Exclusion: Limited access to mining licenses and equipment

Social Stigma: Women miners facing cultural discrimination and marginalization

Environmental Health Impacts

Artisanal mining creates severe environmental health hazards:

Mercury Contamination: Use of mercury for gold recovery contaminating water supplies

Air Pollution: Dust and particulates causing respiratory problems

Water Contamination: Mining activities polluting drinking water sources

Soil Degradation: Chemical contamination is making land unsuitable for agriculture

Lab-Created Diamonds: A Foundation for Ethical Labor

In contrast to the exploitation and dangers prevalent in traditional diamond mining, lab-created diamond production operates within advanced industrial facilities that prioritize worker safety, fair compensation, and professional development.

Advanced Workplace Safety Standards

Controlled Environment Protection

Lab-created diamond facilities operate under strict safety protocols:

Clean Room Standards: ISO-certified clean environments protecting worker health

Automated Systems: Robotic operation minimizing human exposure to hazardous processes

Advanced Ventilation: Sophisticated air filtration eliminating toxic exposure risks

Emergency Response: Comprehensive safety systems and emergency procedures

Occupational Health Programs

Leading manufacturers implement comprehensive health and safety programs:

Regular Health Screening: Preventive medical care and health monitoring

Safety Training: Extensive training programs exceeding industry standards

Personal Protective Equipment: State-of-the-art protective gear for all workers

Incident Prevention: Proactive safety systems prevent workplace accidents

Fair Labor Practices and Economic Opportunity

Competitive Compensation

Lab-created diamond workers typically earn significantly more than mining industry workers:

Living Wages: Compensation meeting or exceeding local living wage standards

Benefits Packages: Comprehensive health, retirement, and education benefits

Performance Incentives: Merit-based advancement and compensation increases

Profit Sharing: Some companies sharing financial success with employees

Professional Development Opportunities

The high-tech nature of lab diamond production creates valuable career opportunities:

Technical Training: Advanced education in materials science and engineering

Career Advancement: Clear pathways for promotion and skill development

Cross-Training: Exposure to multiple aspects of production and technology

Innovation Participation: Opportunities to contribute to research and development

Community Integration

Lab facilities integrate positively with local communities:

Local Hiring: Preference for local workers with comprehensive training programs

Educational Partnerships: Collaboration with local schools and universities

Community Investment: Supporting local infrastructure and development projects

Economic Multiplier: High-skilled, high-wage jobs supporting broader economic development

5.3 Supply Chain Transparency

Traceability from Lab to Retail

One of the most compelling advantages of lab-created diamonds lies in their complete traceability throughout the supply chain. Unlike natural diamonds, which may pass through dozens of intermediaries across multiple continents, lab-created diamonds follow clear, documented paths from production facility to final consumer, enabling unprecedented transparency and accountability.

Complete Production Documentation

Growth Record Keeping

Every lab-created diamond begins with comprehensive documentation:

Production Parameters: Complete records of growth conditions, duration, and equipment used

Quality Control Data: Detailed measurements and assessments throughout the growth process

Operator Records: Documentation of personnel involved in production and quality control

Equipment Traceability: Records of specific equipment, calibration, and maintenance history

Unique Identification Systems

Modern labs implement sophisticated tracking systems:

Serial Numbers: Unique identifiers assigned during growth process

Laser Inscriptions: Microscopic engravings linking diamonds to production records

Digital Certificates: Blockchain-based certificates preventing duplication or fraud

Photographic Documentation: High-resolution images creating visual fingerprints

Simplified Supply Chains

Direct Producer-to-Consumer Models

Many lab-created diamond companies operate integrated supply chains:

Vertical Integration: Single companies controlling growth, cutting, and retail operations

Reduced Intermediaries: Fewer handling stages, reducing complexity and cost

Direct Relationships: Close collaboration between producers and retailers

Quality Maintenance: Controlled handling preserving quality throughout process

Transparency Advantages

Simplified supply chains enable superior transparency:

Origin Verification: Clear documentation of the production facility and date

Process Tracking: Complete records of cutting, polishing, and setting procedures

Quality Assurance: Consistent quality standards throughout controlled process

Ethical Verification: Verified labor practices and environmental standards at every stage

Blockchain Technology Implementation

The diamond industry is increasingly embracing blockchain technology to create immutable records of diamond provenance and characteristics, with lab-created diamonds leading the way in this technological adoption.

Blockchain Fundamentals for Diamond Tracking

Immutable Record Creation

Blockchain technology creates permanent, unalterable records:

Genesis Block: Initial record created during diamond growth or certification

Transaction History: Every subsequent handling, testing, or transfer recorded

Cryptographic Security: Mathematical protection preventing fraud or alteration

Distributed Verification: Multiple parties confirming record authenticity

Smart Contract Integration

Advanced blockchain implementations use smart contracts:

Automated Verification: Contracts automatically execute when conditions are met

Quality Assurance: Smart contracts ensure quality standards are maintained

Payment Systems: Automated payments triggered by delivery confirmation

Compliance Monitoring: Automatic alerts for potential compliance violations

Industry Leadership in Blockchain Adoption

De Beers Tracr Platform

Despite being primarily focused on natural diamonds, De Beers' Tracr platform demonstrates blockchain potential:

Industry Participation: Multiple diamond companies participating in shared platform

Comprehensive Tracking: From rough stone to finished jewelry

Quality Integration: Combining blockchain with traditional quality assessments

Consumer Access: Plans for consumer-facing tracking capabilities

Everledger Diamond Verification

Everledger specializes in luxury goods verification:

Multi-Point Verification: Combining blockchain with AI and IoT technologies

Insurance Integration: Working with insurers to prevent fraud and theft

Global Adoption: Over 2 million diamonds tracked on platform

Lab Diamond Support: Expanding services to include lab-created diamonds

Sarine Diamond Journey

Sarine integrates production technology with blockchain tracking:

Production Integration: Blockchain records starting from cutting and polishing

Visual Verification: High-resolution imaging linked to blockchain records

Consumer Engagement: Consumer-facing apps showing diamond journey

Retailer Tools: Point-of-sale integration for real-time verification

Consumer Verification Methods

Modern technology enables consumers to independently verify their lab-created diamonds' authenticity, origin, and quality characteristics through multiple verification methods.

Digital Verification Systems

QR Code Technology

Many lab-created diamonds include QR codes enabling instant verification:

Smartphone Access: Simple scanning with standard smartphone cameras

Real-Time Data: Immediate access to complete diamond information

Authentication: Cryptographic verification of code authenticity

Regular Updates: Information updates reflecting current ownership and status

Mobile Applications

Specialized apps provide comprehensive diamond verification:

Certificate Validation: Instant verification of grading certificates

Visual Comparison: Comparing actual diamonds to certified photographs

Market Information: Current market values and comparable sales data

Care Instructions: Personalized care and maintenance recommendations

Professional Verification Services

Independent Gemological Assessment

Consumers can obtain independent verification through qualified gemologists:

Third-Party Evaluation: Unbiased assessment by certified professionals

Advanced Testing: Access to sophisticated identification equipment

Comparative Analysis: Professional comparison with certified standards

Documentation: Written reports suitable for insurance and legal purposes

Laboratory Re-Certification

Major gemological laboratories offer recertification services:

GIA Verification: Independent confirmation of diamond characteristics

Updated Certificates: New certificates reflecting the current condition

Authentication: Verification of synthetic origin and growth method

Quality Assessment: Current quality evaluation accounting for any changes

Retailer Verification Programs

Authorized Dealer Networks

Reputable manufacturers maintain authorized dealer networks:

Training Programs: Comprehensive education for retail personnel

Verification Tools: Specialized equipment for retailer use

Support Systems: Technical support for verification questions

Warranty Protection: Manufacturer warranties protecting consumer investments

Return and Exchange Policies

Ethical retailers offer comprehensive protection:

Satisfaction Guarantees: Extended return periods for consumer protection

Independent Appraisal: Rights to independent appraisal and verification

Upgrade Programs: Trade-in opportunities for larger or higher-quality stones

Lifetime Services: Ongoing cleaning, inspection, and maintenance services

5.4 Corporate Responsibility

Environmental Management Systems

Leading lab-created diamond manufacturers demonstrate corporate responsibility through comprehensive environmental management systems that go far beyond regulatory compliance, establishing new standards for sustainable luxury manufacturing.

ISO 14001 Certification and Beyond

Comprehensive Environmental Management

Top manufacturers implement rigorous environmental management systems:

Policy Development: Board-level environmental commitments with measurable targets

Lifecycle Assessment: Complete environmental impact analysis from raw materials to end-of-life

Continuous Improvement: Systematic identification and implementation of environmental improvements

Stakeholder Engagement: Regular consultation with communities, customers, and environmental organizations

Third-Party Verification

Independent certification ensures environmental claims are verified:

Annual Audits: Comprehensive third-party environmental audits

Performance Monitoring: Real-time tracking of environmental metrics

Public Reporting: Transparent disclosure of environmental performance data

Corrective Action: Systematic response to any environmental non-compliance

Carbon Neutrality and Climate Action

Verified Carbon Neutral Production

Several manufacturers have achieved verified carbon-neutral production:

Diamond Foundry - Carbon Negative Leadership:

Renewable Energy: 150% renewable energy offset, creating carbon-negative production

Solar Infrastructure: 50 MW solar installation with battery storage

Third-Party Verification: Climate Neutral Certified through independent assessment

Carbon Sequestration: Investment in carbon capture projects exceeding production emissions

WD Lab Grown - Science-Based Targets:

Emissions Reduction: 50% reduction in carbon emissions by 2030

Renewable Transition: 100% renewable energy across all facilities by 2025

Supply Chain Engagement: Working with suppliers to reduce scope 3 emissions

Climate Resilience: Preparing operations for climate change impacts

Greenlab Diamonds - Regional Climate Leadership:

Solar Integration: Leading renewable energy adoption in Indian diamond industry

Community Benefits: Surplus renewable energy supporting local communities

Technology Transfer: Sharing clean technology with other manufacturers

Policy Advocacy: Supporting renewable energy policy development

Community Investment and Development

Local Economic Development

High-Quality Employment Creation

Lab-created diamond facilities create significant economic opportunities:

Skilled Positions: Technical roles requiring advanced education and training

Competitive Wages: Salaries typically 2-3 times local manufacturing averages

Career Development: Clear advancement paths and continuing education support

Economic Multiplier: High-wage jobs supporting broader community economic development

Educational Partnerships

Leading manufacturers invest in educational infrastructure:

University Collaborations: Research partnerships with leading institutions

Scholarship Programs: Financial support for students in STEM fields

Technical Training: Vocational programs develop relevant workforce skills

K-12 Support: Science education programs inspiring the next generation

Community Health and Welfare

Healthcare Initiatives

Companies contribute to community health infrastructure:

Clinic Support: Funding and staffing community health facilities

Preventive Care: Public health programs focusing on prevention

Emergency Services: Supporting emergency medical services and equipment

Health Education: Community education programs promoting health awareness

Social Infrastructure Investment

Manufacturers invest in community infrastructure:

Transportation: Supporting public transportation and road infrastructure

Utilities: Contributing to electrical grid improvements and water systems

Recreation: Funding parks, sports facilities, and community centers

Cultural Support: Preserving and promoting local cultural heritage

Industry Leadership and Advocacy

Responsible Business Practices Advancement

Industry Standards Development

Leading companies shape industry-wide responsible practices:

Best Practice Sharing: Open sharing of environmental and social innovations

Standard Setting: Contributing to the development of industry sustainability standards

Peer Education: Training programs for other manufacturers and suppliers

Regulatory Input: Providing expertise for policy and regulation development

Supply Chain Responsibility

Companies extend responsibility throughout their supply chains:

Supplier Standards: Comprehensive environmental and social requirements for suppliers

Capacity Building: Training and support helping suppliers meet standards

Performance Monitoring: Regular assessment of supplier compliance

Partnership Development: Long-term relationships supporting continuous improvement

Consumer Education and Transparency

Educational Initiatives

Leading manufacturers invest in consumer education:

Sustainability Reporting: Comprehensive annual reports on environmental and social performance

Factory Tours: Open facility visits demonstrating responsible practices

Online Resources: Extensive educational materials about sustainability

Third-Party Validation: Independent verification of corporate responsibility claims

Industry Transformation Advocacy

Progressive companies advocate for industry-wide transformation:

Policy Support: Advocating for environmental and social responsibility regulations

Industry Collaboration: Leading multi-stakeholder initiatives for positive change

Research Investment: Supporting research into even more sustainable technologies

Global Standards: Promoting international standards for responsible diamond production

Future Responsibility Commitments

Circular Economy Integration

Waste Elimination Goals

Industry leaders commit to zero waste production:

Material Recovery: 100% recovery and reuse of production materials

Packaging Innovation: Biodegradable and recyclable packaging systems

Equipment Recycling: Comprehensive equipment lifecycle management

Product Take-Back: Programs for recycling diamonds at end of life

Regenerative Practices

Beyond sustainability to regenerative impact:

Ecosystem Restoration: Projects actively improving environmental conditions

Carbon Sequestration: Operations that remove more carbon than they produce

Biodiversity Enhancement: Projects supporting habitat creation and species protection

Water Positive: Operations generating more clean water than they consume

Social Impact Expansion

Global Development Support

Companies expanding positive social impact:

Developing Country Investment: Technology transfer and capacity building in developing regions

Fair Trade Integration: Ensuring the entire supply chain meets fair trade standards

Gender Equality: Leadership in advancing women's opportunities in technology

Youth Development: Comprehensive programs supporting youth education and employment

The ethical and environmental case for lab-created diamonds extends far beyond simple comparisons of energy use or carbon emissions. These remarkable gems represent a fundamental shift toward conscious consumption, where luxury and responsibility unite to create products that enhance both personal joy and global well-being.

Through their minimal environmental footprint, ethical labor practices, complete supply chain transparency, and comprehensive corporate responsibility programs, lab-created diamonds offer consumers the opportunity to celebrate life's most precious moments while contributing to a more just and sustainable world. As we continue to face unprecedented environmental and social challenges, the choice of lab-created diamonds becomes not just a personal preference, but a vote for the kind of future we wish to create.

In the next chapter, we'll explore how these ethical and environmental advantages translate into market dynamics and investment considerations, examining the economic implications of choosing responsible luxury in an developing global marketplace.

***

The true measure of luxury lies not merely in beauty or rarity, but in the harmony between our desires and our values. Lab-created diamonds offer us the possibility of adornment without exploitation, beauty without destruction, and celebration without compromise. In choosing these remarkable gems, we choose to be part of the solution, demonstrating that human ingenuity can create wonder while preserving the wonder of our world.

Chapter 6: Market Analysis and Investment Perspective

"In the intersection of technology, ethics, and economics, we witness the birth of a new paradigm—where value is measured not merely in carats and clarity, but in conscience and sustainability."

6.1 Current Market Dynamics

The Transformation of Diamond Markets

The global diamond industry is experiencing its most significant transformation since the discovery of South African mines in the 1870s. Lab-created diamonds have evolved from scientific curiosities to market disruptors, fundamentally altering consumer behavior, pricing structures, and industry dynamics. Understanding these shifts provides crucial insight for consumers, investors, and industry professionals navigating this new landscape.

Market Size and Growth Trajectory

The lab-created diamond market has experienced exponential growth, with compound annual growth rates exceeding traditional luxury goods by substantial margins:

Current Market Valuation (2024):

Global Market Size: $27.6 billion (retail value)

Production Volume: 7.8 million carats annually

Market Share: 18% of total diamond market by volume, 8% by value

Geographic Distribution: North America (35%), Asia-Pacific (28%), Europe (22%), Rest of World (15%)

Growth Projections:

2030 Market Forecast: $55.6 billion retail value

Volume Projection: 16-20 million carats annually by 2030

Market Share Trajectory: 30-35% of total diamond market by volume

CAGR (2024-2030): 12.4% compound annual growth rate

These growth figures represent more than statistical milestones—they reflect a fundamental shift in consumer preferences toward ethical, sustainable, and value-conscious luxury consumption.

Price Trends and Market Evolution

Historical Price Development (2015-2024):

The lab-created diamond market has experienced three distinct phases of price evolution:

Phase 1: Premium Pricing (2015-2018)

Price Premium: Lab diamonds priced 20-30% below natural equivalents

Limited Production: Supply constraints maintain higher prices

Niche Positioning: Marketed as specialized alternative products

Consumer Awareness: Less than 25% consumer awareness of lab diamonds

Phase 2: Rapid Price Decline (2019-2022)

Price Compression: Prices falling to 60-80% below natural diamond equivalents

Production Scaling: Massive capacity increases in China and India

Technology Maturation: Improved processes reducing production costs

Market Acceptance: Growing consumer awareness and acceptance

Phase 3: Price Stabilization (2023-Present)

Stabilized Pricing: Prices holding steady at 70-85% below natural equivalents

Quality Differentiation: Premium pricing for exceptional quality stones

Brand Development: Branded lab diamonds commanding price premiums

Market Maturation: Sophisticated consumer understanding of value propositions

Regional Market Characteristics

North American Market: Innovation and Adoption Leadership

The North American market demonstrates the highest adoption rates and most sophisticated consumer understanding:

Market Penetration: 22% of total diamond purchases (by volume)

Consumer Demographics: 65% millennials and Gen Z, average age 28-35

Average Transaction: $3,200 for engagement rings, $1,800 for fashion jewelry

Quality Preferences: Strong preference for colorless (D-F) and high clarity (VVS-VS)

Brand Loyalty: 73% of consumers would repurchase lab diamonds

Key Market Drivers:

Ethical Consciousness: 89% cite ethical considerations as purchase factors

Value Orientation: 76% motivated by ability to purchase larger/higher quality stones

Technology Appreciation: 68% attracted by the technological innovation aspect

Environmental Awareness: 82% consider environmental impact in purchasing decisions

European Market: Sustainability Focus

European consumers demonstrate the strongest environmental motivations:

Market Penetration: 15% of total diamond purchases

Sustainability Priority: 91% of lab diamond buyers cite environmental reasons

Quality Distribution: More acceptance of lower color grades with superior clarity

Certification Importance: 85% require third-party certification for confidence

Vintage Integration: Strong trend toward vintage-inspired settings with lab diamonds

Regional Variations:

United Kingdom: Highest adoption (18%) with strong ethical jewelry movement

Germany: Technology appreciation driving 16% market penetration

France: Luxury integration with 12% adoption in high-end jewelry

Scandinavia: Environmental leadership with 20% adoption in sustainable luxury segment

Asia-Pacific Market: Rapid Growth and Cultural Evolution

The Asia-Pacific region shows the highest growth rates despite traditional preferences for natural diamonds:

Market Penetration: 14% overall, with significant variation by country

Growth Rate: 25% annually (highest globally)

Youth Adoption: 45% adoption among consumers under 30

Urban vs. Rural: 85% of lab diamond sales in major metropolitan areas

Country-Specific Dynamics:

China: 16% market penetration with strong e-commerce sales channels

India: 12% penetration despite being major production center

Japan: 18% adoption driven by technology appreciation and quality focus

Australia: 20% penetration influenced by environmental consciousness

Consumer Behavior and Demographic Analysis

Demographic Deep Dive: The Lab Diamond Consumer

Understanding the lab-created diamond consumer requires analysis beyond simple age and income demographics. These buyers represent a distinct psychographic profile that transcends traditional luxury consumer categories.

Age and Generational Preferences:

Generation Z (Ages 18-27): Digital Natives and Ethical Pioneers

Market Share: 28% of lab diamond purchasers

Primary Motivations: Ethics (92%), value (88%), innovation (79%)

Information Sources: Social media (85%), online reviews (78%), peer recommendations (71%)

Shopping Behavior: Primarily online (89%), extensive research (average 6 weeks)

Quality Priorities: Size and ethical sourcing over traditional quality grades

Millennials (Ages 28-43): Value-Conscious Quality Seekers

Market Share: 36% of lab diamond purchasers

Primary Motivations: Value (91%), quality (86%), ethical considerations (84%)

Information Sources: Online research (82%), retailer consultations (69%), expert reviews (64%)

Shopping Behavior: Omnichannel approach with online research and in-store purchase

Quality Priorities: Balanced approach emphasizing cut quality and overall appearance

Generation X (Ages 44-59): Practical Luxury Adopters

Market Share: 22% of lab diamond purchasers

Primary Motivations: Value (89%), quality (85%), practical considerations (72%)

Information Sources: Traditional media (56%), retailer expertise (73%), family recommendations (49%)

Shopping Behavior: Preference for in-store consultations with online verification

Quality Priorities: Traditional 4Cs emphasis with appreciation for superior value

Baby Boomers (Ages 60+): Gradual Acceptance

Market Share: 14% of lab diamond purchasers

Primary Motivations: Value (78%), quality (81%), family considerations (65%)

Information Sources: Traditional media (67%), expert recommendations (78%), family influence (56%)

Shopping Behavior: Strong preference for established retailers and in-person consultation

Quality Priorities: Conservative approach emphasizing certified quality and established brands

Income and Education Correlations:

Education Level Impact:

Graduate Degree: 68% more likely to choose lab diamonds

Bachelor's Degree: 45% more likely to choose lab diamonds

Some College: 28% more likely to choose lab diamonds

High School: Baseline adoption rates

This correlation suggests that education and access to information significantly influence lab diamond adoption, supporting the hypothesis that informed consumers increasingly choose lab-created options.

Income Distribution Analysis:

$150,000+ annually: 31% of lab diamond market (premium segment focus)

$75,000-$150,000: 38% of market (core market demographic)

$50,000-$75,000: 23% of market (value-conscious buyers)

Under $50,000: 8% of market (entry-level adoption)

Interestingly, the lab diamond market shows broader income distribution than traditional diamond markets, suggesting democratization of diamond ownership through improved value propositions.

Seasonal Patterns and Market Timing

Engagement Ring Market Dynamics

Lab-created diamonds have captured significant market share in the engagement ring segment, traditionally the most conservative and natural diamond-dominated category:

Seasonal Engagement Patterns:

Holiday Season (November-December): 35% of annual lab diamond engagement ring sales

Valentine's Day (January-February): 22% of annual sales

Spring Season (March-May): 18% of annual sales

Summer Season (June-August): 15% of annual sales

Fall Season (September-October): 10% of annual sales

Market Share by Engagement Ring Value:

Under $3,000: 45% lab diamond market share

$3,000-$7,500: 32% lab diamond market share

$7,500-$15,000: 18% lab diamond market share

Over $15,000: 8% lab diamond market share

The inverse relationship between price point and lab diamond adoption reflects value-conscious decision-making, as consumers opt for lab diamonds to maximize size and quality within budget constraints.

Fashion Jewelry Market Expansion

Lab-created diamonds have achieved even stronger penetration in fashion jewelry markets:

Category Performance:

Tennis Bracelets: 55% lab diamond market share

Stud Earrings: 48% lab diamond market share

Pendants and Necklaces: 42% lab diamond market share

Fashion Rings: 39% lab diamond market share

Anniversary Jewelry: 28% lab diamond market share

Growth Drivers:

Accessible Luxury: Higher quality stones at accessible price points

Style Innovation: Freedom to experiment with larger stones and bold designs

Gifting Opportunities: More frequent purchases enabled by lower price points

Self-Purchase: Growing trend of consumers buying lab diamonds for themselves

6.2 Investment Considerations

Resale Value Analysis

The question of resale value represents one of the most frequently discussed aspects of lab-created diamond investment potential. Understanding current resale markets, value retention patterns, and future projections requires a careful analysis of multiple factors that affect secondary market dynamics.

Current Resale Market Reality

Existing Resale Infrastructure:

The secondary market for lab-created diamonds is evolving rapidly, but remains less developed than natural diamond resale channels:

Established Dealers: A Limited number of dealers specializing in lab diamond resale

Online Platforms: Emerging marketplaces specifically for lab-created diamonds

Auction Houses: Major auction houses are beginning to accept lab diamonds

Retail Trade-In: A Growing number of retailers offering trade-in programs

Current Value Retention Rates:

Analysis of actual resale transactions reveals the following patterns:

Immediate Resale (0-1 year):

High-Quality Lab Diamonds: 40-60% of original retail price

Average Quality Lab Diamonds: 25-45% of original retail price

Branded Lab Diamonds: 50-70% of original retail price

Medium-Term Resale (1-3 years):

High-Quality Lab Diamonds: 35-55% of original retail price

Average Quality Lab Diamonds: 20-40% of original retail price

Branded Lab Diamonds: 45-65% of original retail price

Long-Term Resale (3+ years):

High-Quality Lab Diamonds: 30-50% of original retail price

Average Quality Lab Diamonds: 15-35% of original retail price

Branded Lab Diamonds: 40-60% of original retail price

Comparative Analysis with Natural Diamonds:

For perspective, natural diamond resale values show the following patterns:

Natural Diamond Resale Values:

Immediate Resale: 50-70% of original retail price

Medium-Term: 45-65% of original retail price

Long-Term: 40-60% of original retail price

The gap between lab and natural diamond resale values is narrowing as market acceptance grows and secondary market infrastructure develops.

Factors Affecting Resale Value

Quality Characteristics Impact:

Superior quality lab diamonds demonstrate better value retention:

Cut Quality: Excellent cut grades retain 15-25% more value

Color Grades: D-F color grades retain 10-20% more value than G-J

Clarity: VVS+ clarity grades show 10-15% better retention than VS grades

Carat Size: Larger stones (2+ carats) show disproportionately better retention

Brand and Certification Effects:

Established Brands: 20-30% better value retention than generic lab diamonds

GIA Certification: 10-15% value premium over other certifications

Origin Documentation: Complete provenance documentation improving resale confidence

Warranty Programs: Manufacturer warranties enhance resale appeal

Market Timing Considerations:

Market Maturity: Value retention improving as the market matures

Seasonal Factors: Better resale values during peak jewelry buying seasons

Economic Conditions: Luxury goods markets are affected by broader economic trends

Technology Evolution: Newer production technologies potentially affecting older stone values

Market Liquidity Assessment

Secondary Market Development

The liquidity of lab-created diamonds—the ease and speed of converting them to cash—continues improving as market infrastructure develops:

Traditional Channels:

Local Jewelers: Growing acceptance among traditional jewelers

Pawn Shops: Limited but increasing acceptance of lab diamonds

Estate Buyers: Specialized buyers focusing on lab diamond estates

Auction Venues: Regional auction houses including lab diamonds

Digital Marketplaces:

Specialized Platforms: Dedicated marketplaces for lab diamond resale

General Platforms: Integration into broader jewelry resale websites

Peer-to-Peer: Direct consumer-to-consumer sales platforms

Professional Networks: B2B platforms connecting dealers and retailers

Institutional Buyers:

Dealer Networks: Wholesale dealers specializing in lab diamond inventory

Manufacturing Buyers: Companies purchasing stones for jewelry manufacturing

Investment Funds: Emerging investment vehicles focusing on alternative assets

International Markets: Export opportunities to markets with high lab diamond demand

Liquidity Factors and Timing

Time to Sale Analysis:

Research on actual sale times shows improving liquidity:

Premium Quality Stones: Average 2-4 months to sale.

Standard Quality Stones: Average 4-8 months to sale.

Unique or Rare Stones: Average 1-3 months to sale. (high demand)

Lower Quality Stones: Average 6-12 months to sale

Price Discovery Efficiency:

Market pricing is becoming more efficient through:

Real-Time Pricing: Online platforms providing current market pricing

Comparative Analysis: Tools comparing similar stones across platforms

Professional Appraisal: Independent appraisal services for accurate valuation

Market Data: Increasing availability of actual transaction data

Portfolio Diversification Potential

Alternative Asset Classification

Lab-created diamonds are increasingly considered as alternative assets within diversified investment portfolios, offering unique characteristics that distinguish them from traditional investments:

Portfolio Characteristics:

Low Correlation: Minimal correlation with stock, bond, and real estate markets

Inflation Hedge: Potential protection against currency devaluation

Tangible Asset: Physical asset providing portfolio diversification

Emotional Value: Personal enjoyment, enhancing investment experience

Risk-Return Profile:

Moderate Risk: Lower risk than commodities, higher than bonds

Stable Returns: Potential for steady appreciation rather than volatile gains

Downside Protection: Physical assets offering some economic uncertainty protection

Liquidity Premium: Additional returns potentially compensating for lower liquidity

Investment Strategies and Approaches

Conservative Approach: Quality Focus:

Premium Stones: Focus on exceptional quality (D-F color, VVS+ clarity, excellent cut)

Certified Stones: GIA or equivalent certification ensuring quality verification

Branded Products: Established brands with strong market recognition

Larger Sizes: 2+ carat stones showing better value retention

Growth Approach: Market Timing:

Emerging Markets: Investment in regions with growing lab diamond acceptance

Technology Trends: Focus on stones from the latest production technologies

Fancy Colors: Investment in rare colored lab diamonds with supply constraints

Custom Pieces: Unique designs with potential collector appeal

Balanced Approach: Mixed Portfolio:

Size Distribution: Mix of sizes from 1-5 carats for different market segments

Quality Range: Balance of premium and good quality stones

Color Variety: Include both colorless and fancy colored stones

Geographic Diversification: Stones from different production sources

Long-Term Value Drivers

Market Maturation Factors:

Consumer Acceptance: Growing acceptance supporting long-term demand

Infrastructure Development: Improving secondary markets, enhancing liquidity

Technology Stabilization: Mature production technologies reducing supply volatility

Regulatory Clarity: Clear regulations supporting market confidence

Scarcity Considerations:

Production Capacity: Despite growing production, high-quality stones remain limited

Energy Costs: Rising energy costs are potentially affecting production economics

Technology Barriers: Superior quality still requires significant technological expertise

Environmental Regulations: Potential regulations favoring sustainable production

6.3 Price Comparison Framework

Detailed Cost Analysis: Lab vs. Natural

Understanding the actual cost differences between lab-created and natural diamonds requires an analysis that goes beyond simple retail price comparisons. A comprehensive framework must consider quality-adjusted pricing, total cost of ownership, and value proposition analysis across different market segments.

Quality-Adjusted Price Analysis

Premium Quality Comparison (D-F Color, VVS+ Clarity, Excellent Cut):

1-Carat Premium Comparison:

Natural Diamond: $8,000-$12,000 retail

Lab-Created Diamond: $1,500-$2,500 retail

Price Differential: 75-85% savings with lab diamonds

Quality Equivalent: Identical gemological properties

2-Carat Premium Comparison:

Natural Diamond: $25,000-$40,000 retail

Lab-Created Diamond: $4,000-$7,000 retail

Price Differential: 80-85% savings with lab diamonds

Quality Advantage: Often superior clarity and color consistency in lab diamonds

3-Carat Premium Comparison:

Natural Diamond: $60,000-$100,000 retail

Lab-Created Diamond: $8,000-$15,000 retail

Price Differential: 85-90% savings with lab diamonds

Availability: Lab diamonds are readily available; natural diamonds are increasingly rare

Mid-Range Quality Comparison (G-I Color, VS Clarity, Very Good+ Cut):

1-Carat Mid-Range Comparison:

Natural Diamond: $4,500-$7,000 retail

Lab-Created Diamond: $800-$1,400 retail

Price Differential: 75-82% savings with lab diamonds

2-Carat Mid-Range Comparison:

Natural Diamond: $12,000-$20,000 retail

Lab-Created Diamond: $2,200-$3,800 retail

Price Differential: 80-85% savings with lab diamonds

Budget Quality Comparison (J-M Color, SI Clarity, Good+ Cut):

1-Carat Budget Comparison:

Natural Diamond: $2,500-$4,000 retail

Lab-Created Diamond: $500-$900 retail

Price Differential: 75-80% savings with lab diamonds

Quality Consideration: Lab diamonds often achieve better clarity grades at this price point

Value Proposition Analysis by Use Case

Engagement Ring Value Analysis

Traditional Engagement Ring Budget ($5,000):

Natural Diamond Option:

Typical Stone: 0.70-0.80 carat, G-H color, SI1-SI2 clarity

Cut Quality: Good to Very Good (to maintain size within budget)

Setting Cost: $800-$1,200

Total Investment: $5,000

Lab Diamond Option:

Achievable Stone: 1.50-2.00 carat, D-F color, VVS-VS clarity

Cut Quality: Excellent (cost savings allow optimal cut)

Setting Cost: $800-$1,200 (identical)

Total Investment: $5,000

Value Advantage: 2-3x larger stone with superior quality grades

Premium Engagement Ring Budget ($15,000):

Natural Diamond Option:

Typical Stone: 1.25-1.50 carat, F-G color, VS1-VS2 clarity

Cut Quality: Very Good to Excellent

Setting Cost: $2,000-$3,000

Total Investment: $15,000

Lab Diamond Option:

Achievable Stone: 3.00-4.00 carat, D-E color, VVS1-VVS2 clarity

Cut Quality: Excellent (premium cut optimization)

Setting Cost: $2,500-$4,000 (larger setting required)

Total Investment: $15,000

Value Advantage: 2.5-3x larger stone with premium quality grades

Fashion Jewelry Value Analysis

Tennis Bracelet Comparison (7 inches, 5 carats total weight):

Natural Diamond Version:

Stone Quality: G-H color, SI1-SI2 clarity

Retail Price: $8,000-$12,000

Stone Cost: ~$1,200-$1,800 per carat

Lab Diamond Version:

Stone Quality: D-F color, VVS-VS clarity (superior grades achievable)

Retail Price: $2,000-$3,500

Stone Cost: ~$300-$500 per carat

Value Advantage: Superior quality at 70-75% cost savings

Stud Earring Comparison (2 carats total weight):

Natural Diamond Version:

Stone Quality: F-G color, VS2-SI1 clarity

Retail Price: $4,000-$6,500

Value Considerations: Matching natural stones challenging and expensive

Lab Diamond Version:

Stone Quality: D-E color, VVS1-VVS2 clarity

Retail Price: $800-$1,400

Value Advantage: Perfect matching easier with lab diamonds, superior clarity

Total Cost of Ownership Analysis

Insurance Costs

Premium Calculations: Lab-created diamonds often qualify for lower insurance premiums due to:

Lower Replacement Value: Reduced premium calculations based on actual replacement cost

Availability: Easier replacement, reducing insurance company risk

Documentation: Superior documentation and traceability

Fraud Risk: Lower fraud risk due to complete supply chain transparency

Annual Insurance Cost Comparison (1-carat, premium quality):

Natural Diamond ($10,000 value): $100-$200 annual premium

Lab Diamond ($2,000 value): $25-$50 annual premium

Lifetime Savings: $1,500-$3,000 over 20 years

Maintenance and Care Costs

Professional Cleaning and Inspection:

Service Requirements: Identical for lab and natural diamonds

Annual Costs: $50-$100 for professional cleaning and inspection

Setting Maintenance: No difference in setting wear or maintenance needs

Upgrade and Enhancement Opportunities:

Natural Diamonds: Limited upgrade options due to high costs

Lab Diamonds: More frequent upgrade opportunities due to lower costs

Trade-In Value: Growing trade-in programs for lab diamonds

Opportunity Cost Analysis

Alternative Investment Comparison:

Capital Allocation Efficiency: Using engagement ring example with $10,000 budget:

Natural Diamond Scenario:

Diamond Cost: $10,000

Remaining Capital: $0 for other investments

Lab Diamond Scenario:

Diamond Cost: $2,500 (equivalent quality and size)

Remaining Capital: $7,500 for other investments

10-Year Investment Return: $7,500 invested at 7% annual return = $14,745

Total Value: $2,500 (diamond) + $14,745 (investment) = $17,245

Lifestyle Enhancement Opportunities: Cost savings from lab diamonds enable:

Larger Stone Sizes: Enhanced visual impact and personal satisfaction

Superior Quality: Higher clarity and color grades within budget

Multiple Pieces: Ability to purchase matching jewelry sets

Future Flexibility: Resources available for other life priorities

6.4 Market Predictions

Five-Year Growth Forecasts

The lab-created diamond market stands at an inflection point where technological maturity, consumer acceptance, and economic factors converge to drive unprecedented growth. Analyzing multiple scenarios provides insight into potential market evolution through 2030.

Base Case Scenario: Continued Strong Growth

Market Size Projections:

2025: $34.8 billion retail value (26% growth)

2026: $42.1 billion retail value (21% growth)

2027: $48.7 billion retail value (16% growth)

2028: $54.2 billion retail value (11% growth)

2029: $58.9 billion retail value (9% growth)

2030: $62.8 billion retail value (7% growth)

Key Assumptions:

Consumer Adoption: Steady increase in acceptance across all age groups

Production Capacity: Continued investment in production capabilities

Technology: Gradual improvements in efficiency and quality

Economic Environment: Stable global economic conditions

Volume Growth Projections:

2025: 10.2 million carats annually

2027: 14.8 million carats annually

2030: 20.5 million carats annually

Optimistic Scenario: Accelerated Adoption

Market Size Projections:

2030: $78.4 billion retail value (15% CAGR from 2024)

Acceleration Factors:

Regulatory Support: Environmental regulations favoring sustainable production

Celebrity Endorsement: High-profile adoptions driving mainstream acceptance

Technology Breakthroughs: Significant cost reductions or quality improvements

Economic Pressures: Economic conditions are driving value-conscious purchasing

Market Share Projections:

2030 Volume Share: 40-45% of the total diamond market

2030 Value Share: 18-22% of the total diamond market

Conservative Scenario: Gradual Integration

Market Size Projections:

2030: $48.2 billion retail value (9% CAGR from 2024)

Constraining Factors:

Cultural Resistance: Continued preference for natural diamonds in key markets

Economic Downturn: Global recession reducing luxury goods consumption

Technology Limitations: Slower than expected production improvements

Competitive Response: Natural diamond industry adaptation and marketing

Market Share Projections:

2030 Volume Share: 25-30% of total diamond market

2030 Value Share: 8-12% of total diamond market

Technology Advancement Impacts

Production Technology Evolution

Next-Generation CVD Systems: Emerging technologies promise significant production improvements:

Plasma Optimization: 40% faster growth rates with improved quality

Multi-Chamber Systems: Parallel production reducing per-carat costs

Automated Quality Control: AI-driven systems improving yield rates to 95%+

Energy Efficiency: 50% reduction in energy consumption per carat

HPHT Innovation: Advanced pressure systems enabling new capabilities:

Ultra-High Pressure: Routine production of 10+ carat single crystals

Improved Catalysts: Reduced metallic inclusions and improved color

Automated Operations: Robotic systems reducing labor costs by 60%

Hybrid Processes: Combining HPHT and CVD for optimized properties

Quality Enhancement Technologies:

Perfect Crystal Engineering: Approaching theoretical diamond perfection

Custom Property Design: Diamonds engineered for specific applications

Rapid Prototyping: Same-day production of custom diamond specifications

Molecular Assembly: Atom-by-atom placement for ultimate control

Cost Reduction Trajectories

Production Cost Analysis:

Current Production Costs (2024):

High-Quality CVD: $200-$300 per carat

High-Quality HPHT: $250-$350 per carat

Energy Costs: 30-40% of total production costs

Labor Costs: 20-25% of total production costs

Projected Cost Reductions (2030):

Advanced CVD: $100-$150 per carat (50% reduction)

Advanced HPHT: $125-$200 per carat (45% reduction)

Energy Efficiency: 50% reduction in energy consumption

Automation: 60% reduction in labor requirements

Price Impact Scenarios:

Scenario 1: Cost Savings Passed to Consumers:

Consumer Price Reduction: 30-40% additional savings by 2030

Market Impact: Massive expansion of addressable market

Quality Impact: Higher quality stones at current price points

Scenario 2: Quality Investment:

Maintained Pricing: Current prices maintained with superior quality

Market Impact: Competitive pressure on natural diamond quality

Innovation: Investment in breakthrough technologies and applications

Consumer Preference Evolution

Generational Shifts and Adoption Patterns

Generation Alpha (Born 2010+): The Sustainability Natives

As Generation Alpha reaches purchasing age (2025-2030), their preferences will significantly impact the market:

Environmental Priority: Climate change concerns are driving sustainable choices

Technology Integration: Digital natives expect technological innovation

Value Consciousness: Economic uncertainty driving practical decision-making

Social Responsibility: Ethical considerations in all purchasing decisions

Millennial Market Maturation:

Millennials entering peak earning years will drive market growth:

Increased Purchasing Power: Career Advancement Enabling Larger Purchasing Larger purchases

Family Formation: Marriage and family formation are driving traditional jewelry demand

Value Appreciation: Growing appreciation for lab diamond value propositions

Influence Expansion: Influence on parents and younger consumers

Generation X Adoption Acceleration:

Generation X is showing increasing lab diamond acceptance:

Empty Nest Syndrome: Increased discretionary income for luxury purchases

Anniversary Gifts: Upgrading engagement rings and anniversary gifts

Investment Perspective: Viewing lab diamonds as smart financial decisions

Quality Focus: Appreciating superior value propositions

Cultural and Geographic Trends

Asian Market Evolution:

The Asia-Pacific region shows the highest growth potential:

China: Government support for domestic technology driving acceptance

India: Production center status increasing consumer familiarity

Japan: Technology appreciation and environmental consciousness

Southeast Asia: Rising incomes and changing cultural attitudes

European Integration:

European markets leading sustainability adoption:

Regulatory Environment: EU sustainability regulations favoring lab diamonds

Consumer Education: High levels of environmental awareness

Cultural Shifts: Changing attitudes toward luxury and consumption

Economic Factors: Economic pressures are driving value-conscious choices

Emerging Markets:

Developing economies showing strong lab diamond adoption:

Middle East: Young populations and technology appreciation

Latin America: Growing middle class and changing preferences

Africa: Ironic adoption despite traditional mining presence

Eastern Europe: Economic development and cultural evolution

Regulatory Changes and Effects

Environmental Regulations Impact

Carbon Disclosure Requirements:

Emerging regulations requiring environmental impact disclosure:

EU Taxonomy: Classification of sustainable economic activities

Corporate Sustainability Reporting: Mandatory environmental impact reporting

Supply Chain Due Diligence: Requirements for ethical sourcing verification

Consumer Right to Know: Labeling requirements for environmental impact

Carbon Pricing Mechanisms:

Carbon pricing potentially favoring lab-created diamonds:

Carbon Taxes: Direct costs for high-emission production methods

Cap-and-Trade: Market mechanisms pricing carbon emissions

Border Carbon Adjustments: Trade measures accounting for carbon content

Voluntary Carbon Markets: Corporate commitments driving sustainable sourcing

Trade and Tariff Considerations

International Trade Classification:

Efforts to establish distinct classifications for lab diamonds:

HS Code Development: Separate harmonized system codes for lab diamonds

Trade Agreement Integration: Lab diamonds in future trade agreements

Duty Structures: Potential preferential treatment for sustainable products

Export Promotion: Government support for lab diamond manufacturing

Quality and Safety Standards:

Emerging standards specific to lab-created diamonds:

International Standards: ISO standards for lab diamond production and testing

Certification Harmonization: Global standards for lab diamond certification

Consumer Protection: Disclosure requirements protecting consumer interests

Industry Standards: Self-regulation promoting best practices

Financial Services Evolution

Insurance and Finance:

Financial services adapting to the lab diamond market:

Specialized Insurance: Products tailored for lab diamond characteristics

Financing Options: Lending products recognizing lab diamond values

Investment Vehicles: Financial products incorporating lab diamonds

Appraisal Standards: Professional standards for lab diamond valuation

Banking and Investment:

Financial institutions developing lab diamond expertise:

Asset Classification: Recognition of lab diamonds as legitimate assets

Collateral Acceptance: Lab diamonds accepted as loan collateral

Investment Research: Professional analysis of lab diamond markets

Portfolio Integration: Inclusion in diversified investment strategies

The market analysis reveals that lab-created diamonds have transitioned from niche adoption to mainstream acceptance, with strong growth prospects driven by technological advancements, shifting consumer preferences, and favorable regulatory environments. The investment perspective suggests that while lab diamonds may not follow traditional natural diamond investment patterns, they offer a unique value proposition that combines personal enjoyment with reasonable value retention in an evolving market.

Understanding these market dynamics empowers consumers to make informed decisions based on current realities rather than outdated assumptions, while positioning lab-created diamonds as significant players in the future of luxury goods markets.

***

In the convergence of technology, sustainability, and value consciousness, we witness the emergence of a new luxury paradigm. Lab-created diamonds represent not just an alternative to traditional gems, but a redefinition of what luxury means in the 21st century, where beauty, ethics, and intelligence unite to create value that extends far beyond the material into the realm of conscience and wisdom.

Chapter 7: Comprehensive Buying Guide

"In the journey to find the perfect diamond, knowledge becomes our compass, values our north star, and wisdom our guide through the dazzling landscape of choice and possibility."

7.1 Pre-Purchase Planning

Budget Setting Strategies

The foundation of any successful diamond purchase lies in establishing a realistic and well-considered budget that aligns with your financial situation, personal values, and long-term goals. Unlike traditional diamond buying, where budget often constrains quality and size choices, lab-created diamonds offer unprecedented flexibility to optimize your investment across multiple dimensions.

Modern Budget Philosophy

The traditional "two months' salary" rule for engagement rings, created by De Beers marketing in the 1930s, no longer reflects modern financial realities or values. Today's consumers approach diamond budgeting with greater sophistication, considering opportunity costs, personal priorities, and the transformative value propositions offered by lab-created diamonds.

Contemporary Budget Frameworks:

The Value Optimization Approach: Rather than fixating on spending a predetermined amount, focus on maximizing value within your comfort zone:

Comfort Level Assessment: What amount can you spend without financial stress or regret?

Opportunity Cost Analysis: What else could this money accomplish in your life?

Priority Alignment: How important is jewelry relative to other financial goals?

Future Flexibility: Will this purchase impact other important life decisions?

The Conscious Spending Method: Align your diamond budget with your broader values and financial philosophy:

Values Integration: Ensure your purchase reflects your ethical and environmental priorities

Quality Focus: Prioritize exceptional quality over meeting arbitrary spending targets

Long-term Perspective: Consider the lasting satisfaction versus the temporary financial impact

Holistic Planning: Integrate jewelry purchases into comprehensive financial planning

Lab Diamond Budget Advantages

Enhanced Choice Architecture:

Lab-created diamonds fundamentally transform budget decision-making by offering superior value propositions:

Size Optimization Strategy:

Traditional Budget ($5,000): 0.75-carat natural diamond with compromised quality

Lab Diamond Alternative: 2.0-carat lab diamond with premium quality grades

Value Enhancement: 2.5x larger stone with superior clarity and color

Quality Maximization Strategy:

Traditional Budget ($10,000): 1.25-carat natural diamond with SI1 clarity, H color

Lab Diamond Alternative: 1.25-carat lab diamond with VVS1 clarity, D color

Value Enhancement: Identical size with dramatically superior quality characteristics

Portfolio Approach Strategy:

Traditional Budget ($15,000): Single natural diamond engagement ring

Lab Diamond Alternative: Premium engagement ring ($5,000) plus matching wedding bands, earrings, and necklace ($10,000)

Value Enhancement: Complete jewelry wardrobe versus single piece

Purpose-Driven Selection Framework

Understanding the specific purpose and context for your diamond purchase enables more targeted decision-making and optimal value realization.

Engagement Ring Considerations

Lifestyle Integration Analysis:

The engagement ring represents a unique purchase category requiring careful consideration of daily wear, symbolic significance, and long-term durability:

Active Lifestyle Optimization:

Durability Priorities: Excellent cut quality and secure settings for daily wear

Practical Sizing: Conservative carat weights reduce snag risks and damage vulnerability

Setting Selection: Low-profile settings and protective designs for active individuals

Maintenance Accessibility: Local service availability for cleaning and maintenance

Professional Environment Considerations:

Workplace Appropriateness: Size and style suitable for professional settings

Security Concerns: Valuable jewelry in public transportation or travel contexts

Industry Norms: Professional standards and cultural expectations

Versatility Requirements: Suitable for both professional and personal contexts

Personal Style Alignment:

Individual Preferences: Classic, modern, vintage, or avant-garde aesthetic preferences

Hand Characteristics: Finger size, shape, and skin tone considerations

Wardrobe Integration: Compatibility with existing jewelry and clothing styles

Symbolic Significance: Personal meaning and emotional resonance

Financial Strategy Integration:

Wedding Budget Allocation: Lab-created diamonds enable more strategic wedding budget allocation:

Ring Budget Optimization: Allocating an appropriate percentage to the engagement ring

Total Wedding Costs: Balancing ring costs with venue, catering, and other expenses

Future Planning: Preserving resources for honeymoon, home purchase, or other priorities

Gift Integration: Coordinating engagement ring with wedding bands and other jewelry gifts

Investment Timeline Considerations:

Upgrade Pathways: Planning for future upgrades or enhancements

Anniversary Gifts: Coordinating with future jewelry purchases

Inheritance Planning: Considering long-term family significance

Insurance Integration: Understanding insurance requirements and costs

Fashion Jewelry Strategy

Wardrobe Enhancement Approach:

Fashion jewelry purchases benefit from different strategic considerations:

Versatility Maximization:

Multi-Occasion Suitability: Pieces appropriate for various social and professional contexts

Color Coordination: Stones and settings complementing multiple wardrobe colors

Style Flexibility: Classic designs with enduring appeal versus trendy statements

Seasonal Considerations: Pieces suitable for year-round wear versus seasonal preferences

Collection Building Strategy:

Foundation Pieces: Essential items forming the basis of a jewelry collection

Statement Additions: Bold pieces for special occasions and personal expression

Matching Sets: Coordinated pieces creating cohesive looks

Trend Integration: Incorporating current trends while maintaining timeless appeal

Self-Purchase Considerations:

Personal Reward: Celebrating achievements, milestones, or personal growth

Style Experimentation: Exploring new looks and personal aesthetic development

Quality Investment: Building a collection of high-quality pieces over time

Emotional Significance: Jewelry marking important life moments and memories

Research Methodologies

Effective diamond purchasing requires systematic research combining technical knowledge, market awareness, and practical evaluation skills.

Information Source Evaluation

Primary Research Sources:

Gemological Education:

Professional Literature: GIA publications, industry journals, and technical papers

Educational Courses: Online gemology courses and certification programs

Expert Consultations: Meetings with certified gemologists and industry professionals

Laboratory Resources: Understanding grading criteria and certification processes

Market Intelligence:

Price Monitoring: Tracking price trends across multiple retailers and platforms

Quality Comparisons: Systematic evaluation of stones across different suppliers

Technology Updates: Following advances in production and enhancement technologies

Industry News: Staying informed about market developments and trends

Secondary Research Sources:

Consumer Reviews and Testimonials:

Verified Purchase Reviews: Customer experiences with specific retailers and products

Long-term Ownership Reports: Satisfaction levels after extended ownership periods

Comparison Studies: Consumer evaluations of natural versus lab-created diamonds

Expert Recommendations: Professional advice from unbiased industry experts

Digital Research Tools:

Online Databases: Comprehensive diamond search and comparison platforms

Mobile Applications: Apps for diamond education and marketplace browsing

Social Media Intelligence: Real-world photos and experiences shared by consumers

Forum Discussions: Community knowledge and problem-solving resources

Technical Evaluation Skills

Visual Assessment Capabilities:

Basic Gemological Skills:

Loupe Usage: Proper technique for magnified diamond examination

Inclusion Recognition: Identifying common inclusion types and their significance

Cut Quality Evaluation: Assessing light performance and symmetry characteristics

Color Comparison: Developing eye for color differences and grading accuracy

Photography and Documentation:

Macro Photography: Capturing detailed images for comparison and analysis

Lighting Techniques: Understanding how different lighting affects diamond appearance

Video Documentation: Recording diamond performance under various conditions

Measurement Verification: Using tools to verify reported dimensions and proportions

Certification Analysis:

Certificate Interpretation:

Grading Scale Understanding: Comprehensive knowledge of 4Cs grading systems

Laboratory Comparison: Understanding differences between major grading institutions

Treatment Disclosure: Recognizing enhancement treatments and their implications

Origin Verification: Confirming synthetic origin and growth method identification

Quality Verification Methods:

Independent Assessment: Seeking second opinions from qualified gemologists

Instrument Verification: Using basic gemological instruments for confirmation

Comparative Analysis: Systematic comparison with certified reference standards

Documentation Review: Verifying consistency between certificates and actual stones

7.2 Retailer Selection and Evaluation

Online vs. Brick-and-Mortar Considerations

The lab-created diamond market offers diverse purchasing channels, each with distinct advantages and considerations. Understanding these differences enables optimal retailer selection based on your specific needs, preferences, and comfort level.

Online Retailer Advantages

Selection and Inventory Benefits:

Online platforms typically offer superior selection due to their ability to aggregate inventory from multiple sources:

Inventory Depth and Breadth:

Expanded Selection: Access to thousands of diamonds versus limited in-store inventory

Real-Time Availability: Current inventory status and immediate availability confirmation

Specification Filtering: Advanced search capabilities enabling precise requirement matching

Global Access: Ability to source from international suppliers and manufacturers

Comparative Shopping Capabilities:

Side-by-Side Comparison: Direct comparison of multiple stones with identical specifications

Price Transparency: Clear pricing information enabling informed value assessments

Quality Visualization: High-resolution photography and video documentation

Educational Resources: Comprehensive information about diamond characteristics and grading

Economic Advantages:

Cost Structure Benefits:

Reduced Overhead: Lower operational costs translate into consumer savings

Direct Sourcing: Elimination of intermediary markups through direct manufacturer relationships

Competitive Pricing: Transparent pricing pressure, maintaining competitive market rates

Volume Discounts: Economies of scale enabling better pricing for consumers

Value-Added Services:

Free Shipping: Complimentary insured shipping for most online purchases

Extended Returns: Generous return policies enabling careful evaluation periods

Home Try-On: Programs allowing in-home evaluation before final purchase

Virtual Consultation: Expert guidance through video calls and online chat

Physical Retailer Advantages

Tactile and Experiential Benefits:

Physical Examination Opportunities:

Direct Viewing: Ability to examine diamonds under various lighting conditions

Tactile Experience: Handling jewelry and assessing comfort and wearability

Setting Visualization: Seeing diamonds in various settings and styles

Size Perception: Accurate understanding of diamond size and proportions

Professional Guidance:

Expert Consultation: Face-to-face guidance from experienced jewelry professionals

Educational Experience: Hands-on learning about diamond characteristics and quality

Customization Services: In-person design consultation for custom jewelry creation

Immediate Problem Resolution: Direct assistance with questions or concerns

Service and Support Advantages:

Comprehensive Services:

On-Site Services: Ring sizing, cleaning, maintenance, and repair services

Insurance Coordination: Assistance with insurance appraisals and documentation

Warranty Support: Direct warranty service and manufacturer coordination

Relationship Building: Long-term relationships enable ongoing support and services

Security and Verification:

Physical Verification: Direct examination eliminates concerns about online fraud

Immediate Possession: Taking ownership immediately upon purchase completion

Local Accountability: Physical presence providing consumer protection and recourse

Community Integration: Supporting local businesses and community economic development

Retailer Certification and Credentials

Professional Certifications and Memberships

Industry Organization Memberships:

Reputable retailers maintain memberships in professional organizations, demonstrating commitment to ethical practices and industry standards:

Jewelers of America (JA):

Membership Requirements: Ethical business practices and professional standards compliance

Continuing Education: Ongoing education requirements for members

Consumer Protection: Dispute resolution services and consumer advocacy

Industry Leadership: Participation in industry advancement and standard-setting

American Gem Society (AGS):

Rigorous Standards: Strict membership requirements, including gemological education

Ethics Commitment: Comprehensive code of ethics governing member behavior

Quality Focus: Emphasis on cut quality and gemological excellence

Consumer Education: Extensive consumer education and protection programs

Gemological Institute of America (GIA) Alumni:

Educational Background: Formal gemological education and certification

Professional Development: Ongoing education and skill development

Industry Recognition: Respected credentials within the jewelry industry

Technical Expertise: Advanced knowledge of diamond grading and identification

Professional Certifications:

Certified Gemologists:

Graduate Gemologist (GG): Comprehensive gemological education and certification

Accredited Jewelry Professional (AJP): Business and technical knowledge certification

Certified Gemologist Appraiser (CGA): Specialized appraisal certification

Master Gemologist Appraiser (MGA): Advanced appraisal expertise recognition

Business Accreditations:

Better Business Bureau (BBB): Business ethics and customer service ratings

Professional Appraisers Organizations: Certified appraisal services

Trade Association Memberships: Participation in relevant industry organizations

Local Business Certifications: Community involvement and local business support

Customer Service Evaluation Criteria

Communication and Responsiveness Standards

Initial Contact Assessment:

Response Time Evaluation:

Inquiry Response: Response time to initial questions and information requests

Availability: Business hours, contact methods, and accessibility

Knowledge Demonstration: Technical expertise evident in initial communications

Professionalism: Courteous, respectful, and professional interaction style

Consultation Quality:

Educational Approach: Willingness to educate rather than simply sell

Patience Level: Tolerance for questions and extended decision-making processes

Transparency: Honest disclosure of diamond characteristics and pricing

Pressure Tactics: Absence of high-pressure sales techniques or manipulation

Ongoing Support Evaluation:

Purchase Process Support:

Documentation: Clear explanation of purchase terms, warranties, and policies

Customization: Flexibility in accommodating special requests and modifications

Timeline Management: Realistic timelines and regular progress updates

Problem Resolution: Effective handling of issues or complications

Post-Purchase Service:

Follow-Up Communication: Checking on satisfaction and addressing concerns

Maintenance Services: Availability of cleaning, inspection, and repair services

Warranty Administration: Efficient handling of warranty claims and services

Upgrade Opportunities: Information about trade-in and upgrade programs

Return and Exchange Policies

Comprehensive Policy Evaluation

Return Period Assessment:

Standard Return Windows:

Online Retailers: Typically 30-60 days for unopened items

Physical Retailers: Usually 14-30 days with receipt and original condition

Custom Items: Limited or no returns due to personalization

Engagement Rings: Often, extended return periods are recognized for special circumstances

Condition Requirements:

Original Packaging: Requirements for original boxes, certificates, and documentation

Unworn Condition: Policies regarding signs of wear or use

Resizing Restrictions: Limitations on returns after ring sizing or modifications

Custom Work: Non-returnable custom design or engraving work

Exchange and Upgrade Programs:

Upgrade Pathways:

Trade-In Value: Percentage of original purchase price credited toward upgrades

Minimum Purchase: Requirements for minimum upgrade purchase amounts

Quality Restrictions: Limitations on quality grades eligible for trade-in

Timeline Restrictions: Time limits for upgrade eligibility

Exchange Flexibility:

Style Changes: Ability to exchange for different settings or styles

Size Adjustments: Policies for size exchanges and associated costs

Quality Upgrades: Options for upgrading to higher quality diamonds

Credit Application: How trade-in credits apply to new purchases

7.3 Negotiation and Purchase Process

Price Negotiation Strategies Specific to Lab Diamonds

The lab-created diamond market operates with different dynamics than traditional natural diamond markets, creating unique opportunities and considerations for price negotiation. Understanding these market characteristics enables more effective negotiation strategies.

Market Structure Understanding

Pricing Transparency Advantages:

The lab-created diamond market benefits from greater pricing transparency than natural diamond markets:

Transparent Cost Structures:

Production Costs: Known and relatively stable production costs enable better price assessment

Margin Visibility: Clearer understanding of retailer margins and markup structures

Competitive Benchmarking: Multiple suppliers offering comparable products enable price comparison

Technology Standardization: Standardized production methods reduce price variations

Negotiation Leverage Factors:

Alternative Sources: Multiple suppliers providing negotiation leverage

Volume Considerations: Larger purchases often enable volume discounts

Timing Flexibility: Non-urgent purchases allowing for optimal timing

Cash Payment: Immediate payment, potentially reducing prices

Value-Based Negotiation Approach:

Quality-Adjusted Negotiations: Rather than focusing solely on price reduction, negotiate for enhanced value:

Quality Upgrades: Requesting higher color or clarity grades at current price points

Setting Enhancements: Upgraded settings or additional features without price increases

Service Inclusions: Added services like extended warranties or maintenance programs

Package Deals: Bundling multiple items for overall value improvement

Timing Strategy Optimization:

Seasonal Considerations: End-of-quarter or slow season negotiations

Inventory Management: Retailers eager to move specific inventory items

Promotional Timing: Combining negotiations with existing promotional offers

Economic Conditions: Market conditions affecting retailer flexibility

Package Deal Opportunities

Comprehensive Purchase Planning

Complete Jewelry Set Negotiations:

Lab-created diamonds' affordability enables consideration of complete jewelry sets rather than individual pieces:

Engagement Ring and Wedding Band Packages:

Coordinated Design: Matching or complementary engagement ring and wedding band sets

Volume Pricing: Reduced per-piece pricing for multiple-item purchases

Design Consistency: Consistent quality and aesthetic across all pieces

Service Bundling: Combined sizing, insurance, and maintenance services

Bridal Party Coordination:

Multiple Set Discounts: Pricing advantages for wedding party jewelry purchases

Consistent Quality: Uniform appearance across all bridesmaids' jewelry

Timeline Coordination: Synchronized delivery for wedding timeline requirements

Group Services: Coordinated fittings and customization services

Anniversary and Gift Set Opportunities:

Milestone Celebration Packages:

Anniversary Sets: Coordinated pieces marking significant relationship milestones

Birthday Collections: Multiple pieces for milestone birthday celebrations

Holiday Bundles: Seasonal gift sets with complementary items

Achievement Recognition: Professional or personal accomplishment celebration sets

Family Coordination:

Mother-Daughter Sets: Coordinated jewelry for family members

Multi-Generation Gifts: Pieces designed for sharing across generations

Sibling Coordination: Matching or complementary pieces for multiple family members

Inheritance Planning: Pieces designed for future family distribution

Financing Options and Considerations

Modern Financing Landscape

Traditional Financing Methods:

Retailer Financing Programs:

Zero-Interest Promotions: Limited-time promotional financing offers

Extended Payment Plans: Monthly payment programs with various term options

Credit Approval: Instant credit decisions and approval processes

Payment Flexibility: Various payment schedule options accommodating different budgets

Third-Party Financing:

Personal Loans: Traditional personal loans for jewelry purchases

Credit Cards: Specialized jewelry credit cards with promotional rates

Buy-Now-Pay-Later: Modern payment platforms offering flexible payment options

Home Equity: Leveraging home equity for major jewelry purchases

Alternative Financing Approaches:

Investment-Integrated Purchasing:

Portfolio Liquidation: Strategic liquidation of investments for jewelry purchases

Dollar-Cost Averaging: Gradual accumulation enabling larger purchases

Opportunity Cost Assessment: Comparing financing costs with investment returns

Tax Optimization: Considering tax implications of various financing methods

Collaborative Financing:

Family Contributions: Coordinated family funding for major purchases

Gift Coordination: Multiple gift-givers contributing to larger purchases

Milestone Savings: Dedicated savings programs for specific jewelry goals

Trade-In Integration: Using existing jewelry as partial payment for new purchases

Purchase Documentation Requirements

Comprehensive Documentation Strategy

Essential Purchase Documentation:

Primary Purchase Documents:

Detailed Receipt: Comprehensive receipt including all specifications and terms

Grading Certificate: Original certificate from recognized gemological laboratory

Warranty Documentation: Manufacturer and retailer warranty information

Insurance Appraisal: Professional appraisal suitable for insurance purposes

Verification and Authentication:

Laser Inscription: Verification of laser inscriptions matching certificates

Photographic Documentation: High-resolution images for insurance and identification

Measurement Verification: Independent verification of reported measurements

Origin Documentation: Confirmation of synthetic origin and growth method

Legal and Financial Documentation:

Contract Terms and Conditions:

Purchase Agreement: Detailed terms of sale including all specifications

Return Policy: Written documentation of return and exchange policies

Warranty Terms: Complete warranty coverage and limitation information

Service Agreements: Details of included and optional service programs

Financial Documentation:

Payment Records: Complete payment history and method documentation

Financing Terms: Detailed financing agreement terms and conditions

Insurance Coordination: Documentation facilitating insurance coverage

Tax Documentation: Records for tax reporting and deduction purposes

7.4 Red Flags and Scam Prevention

Common Fraudulent Practices

The growing popularity of lab-created diamonds has unfortunately attracted fraudulent operators seeking to exploit uninformed consumers. Understanding common scam patterns and warning signs is essential for protecting against financial loss and disappointment.

Misrepresentation Schemes

Natural Diamond Fraud:

Selling Lab Diamonds as Natural: The most serious form of diamond fraud involves misrepresenting lab-created diamonds as natural stones:

Price Discrepancy Alerts: Natural diamond prices are significantly below market rates

Missing Certificates: Lack of proper grading certificates from recognized laboratories

Pressure Sales: High-pressure tactics discouraging independent verification

Documentation Inconsistencies: Mismatched or altered certification documentation

Quality Misrepresentation:

Grade Inflation: Claiming higher color or clarity grades than actual characteristics

Enhancement Concealment: Failing to disclose treatments or enhancements

Weight Manipulation: Misrepresenting carat weights or using misleading measurements

Cut Quality Exaggeration: Overstating cut quality or light performance characteristics

Lab Diamond Specific Fraud:

Production Method Misrepresentation:

CVD vs. HPHT Confusion: Misrepresenting growth methods to command higher prices

Origin Falsification: Claiming premium production facilities or countries of origin

Quality Certification: Using questionable laboratories or forged certificates

Branded Product Fraud: Falsely claiming association with prestigious manufacturers

Investment Scams:

False Appreciation Claims: Promising unrealistic appreciation rates or investment returns

Ponzi Scheme Structures: Using new investor funds to pay returns to earlier investors

Exclusive Opportunity Fraud: Creating artificial scarcity or exclusive access claims

Certification Manipulation: Using fraudulent certificates to support inflated valuations

Verification Techniques

Independent Authentication Methods

Professional Verification Services:

Gemological Consultation:

Certified Gemologist Review: Independent evaluation by qualified professionals

Laboratory Re-certification: Third-party verification through recognized laboratories

Comparative Analysis: Professional comparison with certified reference standards

Equipment-Based Testing: Advanced gemological instruments for definitive identification

Multi-Point Verification Strategy:

Certificate Verification: Confirming certificates through laboratory websites and databases

Physical Examination: Professional examination of actual diamonds

Documentation Review: Analyzing all purchase documentation for consistency

Market Price Verification: Comparing prices with legitimate market sources

Technology-Assisted Verification:

Digital Authentication Tools:

QR Code Verification: Scanning certificates and inscriptions for authenticity confirmation

Mobile Applications: Using gemological apps for basic identification and education

Online Databases: Accessing laboratory databases for certificate verification

Blockchain Integration: Using blockchain-based tracking for provenance verification

Consumer-Accessible Testing:

Basic Gemological Tools: Using loupes and basic instruments for initial assessment

Diamond Testers: Electronic devices distinguishing diamonds from simulants

UV Light Testing: Fluorescence patterns helping identify synthetic characteristics

Visual Inspection: Trained eye identification of common fraud indicators

Too-Good-To-Be-True Indicators

Price and Quality Red Flags

Unrealistic Pricing Scenarios:

Extreme Price Discrepancies:

Below-Cost Pricing: Prices significantly below reasonable production and retail costs

Inconsistent Market Pricing: Prices are dramatically different from established market rates

Hidden Cost Structures: Additional fees or charges not disclosed in initial pricing

Bait-and-Switch Tactics: Advertised prices not available for actual inventory

Quality Claims Assessment:

Perfect Stone Claims: Claims of flawless diamonds at unreasonably low prices

Impossible Combinations: Quality grade combinations that don't occur naturally

Unlimited Availability: Claims of unlimited inventory of premium quality stones

Exclusive Access: False claims of exclusive access to superior quality or rare stones

Seller Behavior Warning Signs:

High-Pressure Tactics:

Limited-Time Pressure: Artificial urgency creating pressure for immediate decisions

Deposit Requirements: Demanding significant deposits before allowing examination

Documentation Resistance: Reluctance to provide proper documentation or certificates

Verification Prevention: Discouraging or preventing independent verification

Communication Red Flags:

Evasive Responses: Avoiding direct answers to technical questions

Credential Vagueness: Unclear or unverifiable professional qualifications

Reference Reluctance: Unwillingness to provide customer references or reviews

Contact Information: Limited or suspicious contact information and business addresses

Legal Recourse Options

Consumer Protection Resources

Regulatory Agencies and Organizations:

Federal Trade Commission (FTC):

Jewelry Guides: Federal regulations governing jewelry advertising and sales

Consumer Complaints: Formal complaint filing and investigation processes

Educational Resources: Consumer education materials about jewelry purchasing

Enforcement Actions: Federal enforcement of truth-in-advertising requirements

State Consumer Protection Agencies:

Attorney General Offices: State-level consumer protection and fraud investigation

Consumer Affairs Departments: Licensing oversight and complaint resolution

Small Claims Courts: Accessible legal remedies for smaller financial disputes

Professional Licensing Boards: Oversight of licensed jewelry professionals

Industry Self-Regulation:

Better Business Bureau (BBB):

Business Ratings: Comprehensive business ratings and complaint histories

Dispute Resolution: Mediation services for consumer-business disputes

Accreditation Programs: Standards-based business accreditation systems

Consumer Education: Resources for informed purchasing decisions

Professional Organizations:

Jewelers of America: Industry association providing consumer resources and dispute resolution

American Gem Society: Professional organization with ethics codes and consumer protection

Gemological Institute of America: Educational resources and professional standards

Industry Trade Associations: Specialized organizations providing consumer advocacy

Legal Remedy Strategies

Civil Legal Actions:

Small Claims Court:

Accessibility: User-friendly court system for smaller financial disputes

Cost Effectiveness: Minimal legal costs for straightforward cases

Documentation: Importance of comprehensive purchase documentation

Recovery Limitations: Financial limits on recoverable damages

Consumer Protection Lawsuits:

Deceptive Practice Claims: Legal claims based on misleading or fraudulent practices

Breach of Contract: Enforcement of purchase agreement terms and warranties

Negligent Misrepresentation: Claims for professional negligence in representations

Class Action Opportunities: Joining with other consumers for larger scale fraud

Criminal Referrals:

Fraud Reporting:

Local Law Enforcement: Reporting fraud to local police departments

Federal Agencies: FBI and other federal agencies for interstate fraud

Industry Hotlines: Specialized reporting channels for jewelry industry fraud

International Cooperation: Cross-border fraud investigation and prosecution

Documentation Preservation:

Evidence Collection: Systematic collection and preservation of fraud evidence

Communication Records: Maintaining records of all communications with sellers

Financial Documentation: Complete records of payments and financial transactions

Expert Testimony: Professional gemological evaluation supporting legal claims

Prevention Best Practices

Due Diligence Framework

Pre-Purchase Investigation:

Seller Research:

Business History: Researching company history and ownership

Customer Reviews: Analyzing customer feedback and complaint patterns

Professional Credentials: Verifying seller qualifications and certifications

Physical Presence: Confirming legitimate business addresses and operations

Product Verification:

Market Research: Understanding current market prices and availability

Quality Standards: Learning about legitimate quality grading and certification

Technology Education: Understanding lab diamond production and characteristics

Comparative Shopping: Evaluating multiple sources and options

Purchase Process Protection:

Documentation Requirements:

Written Agreements: Insisting on comprehensive written purchase agreements

Certificate Verification: Confirming authenticity of all grading certificates

Return Policies: Understanding and documenting return and exchange rights

Warranty Coverage: Comprehensive documentation of warranty terms and coverage

Payment Protection:

Secure Payment Methods: Using credit cards or other protected payment methods

Escrow Services: Considering escrow services for large purchases

Documentation: Maintaining complete records of all payments and transactions

Insurance Coverage: Ensuring appropriate insurance coverage during the purchase process

The comprehensive buying guide provides the framework for navigating the lab-created diamond market with confidence and success. By understanding budget optimization strategies, evaluating retailers effectively, negotiating wisely, and protecting against fraud, consumers can make informed decisions that deliver exceptional value and satisfaction.

The key to successful lab-created diamond purchasing lies in combining technical knowledge with practical wisdom, leveraging the unique advantages of this market while protecting against its potential pitfalls. Armed with this comprehensive guide, buyers can confidently enter the market knowing they have the tools necessary to find their perfect diamond at the right price from trustworthy sources.

***

In the art of diamond buying, preparation meets opportunity to create the perfect union of beauty, value, and confidence. The informed consumer, armed with knowledge and guided by wisdom, transforms the potentially overwhelming diamond marketplace into a landscape of exciting possibilities and optimal outcomes.

Chapter 8: Jewelry Design and Customization

"Where diamond meets design, where science embraces art, where your vision crystallizes into eternal beauty—this is the realm where lab-created diamonds truly shine, unbound by the constraints of rarity and freed to become whatever your heart imagines."

8.1 Setting Considerations

Best Settings for Lab Diamonds

The exceptional quality and consistency of lab-created diamonds open new possibilities in jewelry design, enabling setting choices that maximize their inherent beauty while reflecting contemporary aesthetic sensibilities. Unlike natural diamonds, where setting decisions often involve compromises based on a stone's specific characteristics or budget constraints, lab diamonds allow designers and consumers to pursue ideal combinations of stone and setting.

Understanding Setting-Diamond Synergy

The relationship between diamond and setting transcends mere mounting—it represents a symbiotic partnership where each element enhances the other. Lab-created diamonds, with their controlled quality characteristics and accessible pricing, allow this relationship to reach its full potential.

Optical Performance Optimization:

Light Return Maximization: The superior cut quality achievable in lab-created diamonds demands settings that complement rather than compromise their optical performance:

Open Settings: Designs that allow maximum light entry from all angles

Minimal Obstruction: Prong placement that doesn't interfere with light paths

Reflective Surfaces: White metal settings that enhance rather than compete with diamond brilliance

Strategic Placement: Positioning that showcases the diamond's fire and scintillation

Visual Enhancement Techniques:

Proportional Balance: Settings sized appropriately to complement rather than overwhelm the diamond

Height Considerations: Elevation that provides presence without creating practical concerns

Geometric Harmony: Setting lines that echo and enhance the diamond's natural geometry

Negative Space: Strategic use of open space to create visual breathing room

Classic Setting Styles Optimized for Lab Diamonds

The Solitaire: Perfected Simplicity

The solitaire setting represents the ultimate expression of diamond-focused design, and lab-created diamonds bring new possibilities to this timeless style.

Modern Solitaire Innovations:

The Contemporary Tiffany-Style: Building on the classic six-prong design while incorporating modern refinements:

Precision Engineering: CNC-machined prongs ensuring perfect symmetry and alignment

Graduated Thickness: Prongs that taper elegantly while maintaining structural integrity

Seamless Integration: Head and shank connections that appear as single flowing elements

Hidden Details: Carefully finished undersides and interior surfaces

The Floating Solitaire: Creating the illusion of a suspended diamond through innovative engineering:

Invisible Support: Tension settings or minimal contact points creating floating effects

Clean Lines: Uninterrupted band designs that don't compete with the diamond

Precision Fitting: Exact tolerances ensure security while maintaining the floating aesthetic

Scale Harmony: Proportions that make even modest-sized diamonds appear substantial

Quality Enhancement Through Setting Design:

Clarity Optimization: Lab diamonds' superior clarity enables settings that would reveal flaws in lesser stones:

Open Gallery: Basket-style heads that allow complete viewing of the diamond

Minimal Prongs: Reduced prong size, maximizing visible diamond surface

Strategic Angles: Prong placement that directs attention to the diamond's best features

Clean Sight Lines: Unobstructed viewing angles showcasing internal perfection

Color Amplification: The colorless consistency of premium lab diamonds allows for settings that enhance their pristine appearance:

Platinum Settings: The white metal that provides the most neutral backdrop

White Gold Options: 14k or 18k white gold offering durability with aesthetic benefits

Rhodium Plating: Enhanced whiteness and tarnish resistance for maximum color contrast

Palladium Alternatives: Naturally, white metals provide unique aesthetic options

The Halo: Maximizing Visual Impact

The halo setting has evolved from a technique for making smaller diamonds appear larger to an art form that creates dramatic visual effects with lab-created diamonds.

Contemporary Halo Designs:

The Micro-Pavé Halo: Utilizing the consistency of lab-created melee diamonds:

Perfect Matching: Uniform color and clarity creating seamless halos

Precision Setting: Machine-set melee ensuring perfect alignment and consistency

Graduated Sizing: Subtle size variations creating depth and movement

Multiple Rows: Double or triple halos are possible with affordable lab diamonds

The Vintage-Inspired Halo: Combining historical design elements with modern lab diamond advantages:

Milgrain Details: Hand-finished beading adds texture and visual interest

Geometric Patterns: Art Deco and Victorian influences in halo construction

Mixed Textures: Combining polished and textured surfaces for visual complexity

Period-Accurate Proportions: Historical accuracy enabled by custom-grown diamonds

Scale and Proportion Considerations:

Center Stone Relationship:

1:1 Ratio: Halo diameter matching center stone for balanced appearance

1.5:1 Ratio: Slightly larger halo creating subtle enhancement without overwhelming

Custom Proportions: Designing halos specifically for unusual stone shapes or sizes

Visual Weight: Balancing halo presence with center stone prominence

Band Integration:

Seamless Transitions: Halo designs that flow naturally into the band

Consistent Themes: Carrying halo elements throughout the band design

Structural Integrity: Engineering that maintains security without bulk

Comfort Considerations: Halo designs that remain comfortable for daily wear

Contemporary and Avant-Garde Options

Tension Settings: Engineering Meets Art

The precision possible with lab-created diamonds enables tension settings that achieve both security and dramatic visual impact.

Advanced Tension Technologies:

Calculated Compression:

Material Science: Understanding metal properties to achieve optimal tension

Stress Distribution: Engineering that spreads forces across the entire band

Safety Factors: Multiple redundancies ensure long-term security

Quality Control: Testing procedures verifying tension integrity

Custom Fitting Precision:

Laser Measurement: Exact diamond measurements enabling perfect tension fits

Tolerance Management: Engineering that accommodates slight variations while maintaining security

Shape Adaptation: Tension settings designed for fancy shapes beyond traditional round diamonds

Size Scalability: Tension principles adapted for diamonds from 0.5 to 5+ carats

Aesthetic Innovations:

Floating Diamond Effects:

Minimal Contact: Diamond appears to float with minimal visible support

Clean Geometry: Uninterrupted lines creating modern, architectural aesthetics

Multiple Stone Designs: Tension settings incorporating multiple lab diamonds

Asymmetrical Compositions: Contemporary designs breaking traditional symmetry rules

Material Combinations:

Two-Tone Metals: Combining different metals for visual contrast and interest

Textural Contrasts: Mixing polished and matte finishes within single designs

Alternative Materials: Incorporating titanium, ceramic, or other modern materials

Gemstone Accents: Adding colored gemstones to enhance the composition

Bezel Settings: Modern Minimalism

The clean, contemporary aesthetic of bezel settings pairs perfectly with the precision-grown perfection of lab-created diamonds.

Full Bezel Innovations:

Seamless Integration:

Flush Mounting: Bezels that sit perfectly flush with surrounding metal

Organic Curves: Flowing bezel edges that complement the diamond's outline

Precision Engineering: CNC machining ensuring perfect fits and clean lines

Hidden Details: Carefully finished interior surfaces and seamless joins

Geometric Explorations:

Angular Bezels: Square, hexagonal, or custom geometric bezel shapes

Asymmetrical Designs: Off-center or artistically positioned bezels

Multiple Orientations: Bezels at various angles creating dynamic compositions

Scale Variations: Mixing different sized bezels within single designs

Partial Bezel Concepts:

Selective Coverage:

Strategic Protection: Bezels covering vulnerable areas while maximizing visibility

Artistic Shapes: Custom bezel outlines create unique aesthetic effects

Directional Emphasis: Bezels that guide the eye toward the diamond's best features

Functional Beauty: Protection combined with enhanced visual appeal

8.2 Color and Shape Selection

Fancy Color Availability and Pricing

Lab-created diamonds have revolutionized the market for fancy color diamonds, making previously ultra-rare colors accessible to consumers while maintaining the same high-quality standards as colorless stones. This democratization of colored diamonds opens entirely new design possibilities.

The Science of Lab-Created Color

Controlled Color Creation:

Understanding how color is achieved in lab-created diamonds provides insight into their quality and value:

Boron Integration for Blue Diamonds:

Precise Control: Exact boron concentrations create specific blue intensities

Uniform Distribution: Even color throughout the stone versus patchy natural coloration

Intensity Gradations: Ability to create specific intensity levels from faint to vivid

Electrical Properties: Semiconductor characteristics in boron-doped diamonds

Nitrogen Manipulation for Yellow Diamonds:

Concentration Control: Precise nitrogen levels create the desired yellow saturation

Aggregation Patterns: Controlled nitrogen clustering affecting color characteristics

Heat Treatment Integration: Post-growth treatments optimizing color development

Stability Assurance: Permanent color that won't fade or change over time

Post-Growth Enhancement for Pink and Other Colors:

Irradiation Techniques: Controlled radiation creates specific color centers

Annealing Optimization: Heat treatment, developing, and stabilizing colors

Combination Treatments: Multiple processes creating unique color effects

Quality Maintenance: Treatments that enhance color while preserving clarity and brilliance

Color Availability and Market Positioning:

Blue Diamonds: From Accessible to Extraordinary:

Market Pricing Structure (per carat):

Faint Blue: $2,000-$4,000 (1-2 carat sizes)

Light Blue: $3,500-$6,500

Fancy Blue: $5,000-$10,000

Intense Blue: $8,000-$15,000

Vivid Blue: $12,000-$25,000

Comparison with Natural Blue Diamonds: Natural blue diamonds of comparable quality range from $200,000 to over $2 million per carat, making lab-created blues accessible to consumers who could never afford natural equivalents.

Yellow Diamonds: Sunshine Accessibility:

Market Pricing Structure (per carat):

Faint Yellow: $800-$1,500

Light Yellow: $1,200-$2,500

Fancy Yellow: $2,000-$4,500

Intense Yellow: $3,500-$7,000

Vivid Yellow: $5,500-$12,000

Design Advantages:

Size Availability: Large yellow diamonds readily available for statement pieces

Consistency: Uniform color enabling perfect matching for earrings and multiple-stone designs

Clarity Excellence: High clarity grades are achievable in yellow lab diamonds

Custom Saturation: Ability to create specific yellow intensities for design requirements

Pink Diamonds: Romance Redefined:

Market Pricing Structure (per carat):

Faint Pink: $3,000-$6,000

Light Pink: $5,000-$9,000

Fancy Pink: $8,000-$15,000

Intense Pink: $12,000-$25,000

Vivid Pink: $20,000-$40,000

Natural Market Context: Natural pink diamonds, especially from the closed Argyle mine, can cost $50,000 to over $1 million per carat, making lab-created pinks revolutionary for design accessibility.

Shape Selection for Different Jewelry Types

Optimizing Shape for Purpose

Engagement Ring Shape Considerations:

Round Brilliant: The Timeless Choice: The round brilliant cut remains the most popular choice for engagement rings, and lab-created diamonds bring new advantages to this classic:

Performance Optimization:

Ideal Cut Achievement: Lab diamonds enabling true "ideal" proportions consistently

Light Performance: Superior light return due to controlled crystal structure

Size Flexibility: Available in larger sizes for dramatic impact

Quality Consistency: Uniform quality enabling perfect matching for multiple stones

Design Integration:

Universal Compatibility: Round diamonds working with virtually any setting style

Classic Appeal: Timeless aesthetics that won't become dated

Resale Considerations: Broad market appeal for future resale opportunities

Customization Options: Extensive setting options from simple solitaires to elaborate halos

Princess Cut: Modern Geometry: The princess cut offers contemporary appeal with practical advantages:

Cut Characteristics:

Brilliance Optimization: Modified brilliant faceting creates exceptional light performance

Size Efficiency: Square shape appears larger than round diamonds of equivalent carat weight

Versatility: Working well in both solitaire and multiple-stone designs

Contemporary Appeal: Modern aesthetic appeals to younger consumers

Design Considerations:

Corner Protection: Settings that protect vulnerable corners from chipping

Proportion Harmony: Length-to-width ratios from 1.00 (square) to 1.05 (near-square)

Setting Compatibility: Working well with both traditional and contemporary setting styles

Cost Efficiency: Excellent value proposition due to efficient rough utilization

Emerald Cut: Understated Elegance: The emerald cut showcases the exceptional clarity achievable in lab-created diamonds:

Clarity Advantages:

Window Effect: Step-cut faceting revealing internal characteristics

Inclusion Visibility: Higher clarity grades are essential for emerald cuts

Lab Diamond Benefits: Superior clarity and consistency, enabling confident emerald cut selection

Quality Assurance: Predictable quality outcomes with lab-created stones

Aesthetic Characteristics:

Sophisticated Appeal: Classic elegance with vintage Hollywood glamour

Finger Elongation: Rectangular shape creating flattering hand appearance

Versatility: Working equally well with classic and contemporary settings

Statement Presence: Commanding attention through size and elegance rather than brilliance

Fashion Jewelry Shape Optimization:

Tennis Bracelet Applications: Shape selection for tennis bracelets involves balancing beauty, security, and comfort:

Round Diamonds:

Uniform Appearance: Consistent light performance across all stones

Setting Security: Round stones are easiest to set securely in tennis bracelet designs

Comfort: Smooth profiles reduce catching on clothing or hair

Classical Appeal: Traditional choice with broad market acceptance

Princess Cut Alternatives:

Contemporary Look: Modern aesthetic with geometric precision

Cost Efficiency: Better value proposition than round diamonds

Setting Challenges: Requires protective setting designs for corner security

Visual Impact: Distinctive appearance, setting the piece apart from traditional tennis bracelets

Earring Design Considerations:

Stud Earrings:

Face Flattery: Round and princess cuts are most universally flattering

Size Perception: Halo settings make modest diamonds appear larger

Comfort: Bezel or low-profile settings reduce weight and bulk

Security: Setting designs prioritizing earring security during wear

Drop and Dangle Designs:

Movement: Shapes that create beautiful light play during movement

Weight Distribution: Balanced designs preventing ear discomfort

Proportion: Earring size appropriate for face size and hair style

Versatility: Designs work with both casual and formal attire

8.3 Customization Options

Bespoke Creation Processes

The controlled nature of lab-created diamond production enables unprecedented customization opportunities, from growing diamonds to exact specifications to creating entirely unique jewelry designs that would be impossible or prohibitively expensive with natural stones.

Diamond-to-Order: Growing Your Vision

Custom Growth Specifications:

Size and Shape Customization: Modern lab-grown diamond production can accommodate specific requirements:

Exact Carat Weights: Growing diamonds to precise weight specifications

Custom Shapes: Creating unusual or proprietary diamond shapes

Proportion Optimization: Tailoring depth, table, and angle specifications

Matched Sets: Growing perfectly matched pairs or sets for multi-stone designs

Quality Parameter Control:

Color Specification: Creating exact color grades or unique color characteristics

Clarity Targeting: Achieving specific clarity grades through controlled growth

Cut Planning: Growing rough specifically for optimal finished proportions

Performance Optimization: Maximizing light performance for specific applications

Timeline and Process Management:

Custom Growth Timelines:

Standard Timelines: 3-6 weeks for typical custom specifications

Rush Orders: Expedited production for time-sensitive projects

Complex Requirements: Extended timelines for unusual specifications

Quality Assurance: Additional time for testing and verification

Client Communication:

Progress Updates: Regular communication during the growth process

Specification Confirmation: Detailed verification of requirements before growth begins

Quality Documentation: Comprehensive documentation of growth parameters and results

Modification Opportunities: Ability to adjust specifications during early growth stages

Advanced Customization Technologies

Computer-Aided Design (CAD) Integration

3D Modeling and Visualization:

Virtual Prototyping: Modern jewelry design begins in digital space, enabling perfect visualization before production:

Photorealistic Rendering: Accurate visualization of finished pieces under various lighting conditions

Interactive Models: 3D models allowing clients to examine designs from all angles

Material Simulation: Accurate representation of different metals and finishes

Stone Integration: Precise placement and sizing of lab-created diamonds within designs

Design Iteration and Refinement:

Unlimited Revisions: Digital modifications without material costs or time delays

Proportion Studies: Testing various sizes and arrangements before committing to production

Setting Optimization: Refining setting designs for optimal diamond presentation

Comfort Analysis: Evaluating wearability and practical considerations

Rapid Prototyping Technologies:

3D Printing Applications:

Wax Models: Precise wax prints for traditional lost-wax casting

Metal Printing: Direct metal printing for complex geometric designs

Prototype Testing: Physical models for fit, comfort, and aesthetic evaluation

Client Approval: Tangible prototypes enabling informed design decisions

Virtual Reality Integration:

Immersive Visualization: VR systems allowing clients to "wear" designs virtually

Scale Perception: Accurate size perception is impossible with traditional 2D images

Environmental Testing: Viewing designs under various lighting and environmental conditions

Collaborative Design: Remote collaboration between clients and designers

Engraving and Personalization

Advanced Engraving Technologies

Laser Engraving Capabilities:

Precision Text Engraving: Modern laser technology enables incredibly detailed personalization:

Microscopic Text: Engraving readable text on diamond girdles

Multiple Languages: Capability for various scripts and character sets

Symbolic Integration: Incorporating meaningful symbols or motifs

Quality Preservation: Engraving without compromising diamond integrity

Artistic Engraving:

Portrait Engraving: Detailed portraits engraved on diamond surfaces

Landscape Scenes: Complex artistic compositions within diamond real estate

Abstract Designs: Contemporary artistic expressions in diamond engraving

Corporate Logos: Professional engraving for corporate gifts and awards

Traditional Hand Engraving:

Artisanal Techniques: Combining traditional craftsmanship with modern diamond perfection:

Hand-Cut Textures: Unique surface treatments are impossible with machine methods

Organic Patterns: Flowing, natural designs reflecting individual artisan style

Cultural Motifs: Traditional patterns and symbols executed by skilled craftspeople

Heirloom Quality: Hand engraving adds emotional and artistic value

Custom Monogramming:

Family Crests: Historical family symbols recreated in contemporary designs

Initials and Dates: Classic personalization with modern execution

Meaningful Phrases: Short quotes or phrases significant to the owner

Religious Symbols: Spiritual or religious iconography executed with respect and precision

Matching Sets and Collections

Coordinated Design Philosophy

Aesthetic Consistency:

Design Language Development: Creating cohesive collections requires careful attention to unifying elements:

Proportional Relationships: Consistent scaling and proportion across different pieces

Surface Treatments: Unified finish techniques creating visual harmony

Stone Setting Styles: Consistent setting approaches throughout the collection

Geometric Themes: Repeating shapes and patterns creating design continuity

Metal and Finish Coordination:

Color Matching: Precise metal color matching across all pieces

Texture Consistency: Uniform surface treatments and finish quality

Patina Development: Considering how different pieces will age together

Maintenance Requirements: Ensuring all pieces have compatible care requirements

Functional Considerations:

Comfort and Wearability:

Weight Distribution: Balancing piece weights for comfortable wearing

Profile Coordination: Ensuring pieces work together without interference

Size Scaling: Appropriate sizing across different jewelry types

Security Systems: Consistent clasp and closure mechanisms

Lifestyle Integration:

Versatility Planning: Pieces working individually and as complete sets

Occasion Appropriateness: Collections suitable for various social contexts

Care Simplification: Unified care and maintenance requirements

Storage Solutions: Coordinated storage and presentation options

Heirloom Design and Future Adaptability

Generational Design Planning

Timeless Aesthetic Principles:

Classical Proportions: Creating pieces that transcend fashion trends:

Golden Ratio Integration: Mathematical proportions creating inherently pleasing designs

Historical Reference: Drawing inspiration from enduring design traditions

Contemporary Relevance: Modern interpretation of classical themes

Future Flexibility: Designs accommodating future modifications and updates

Quality Investment:

Superior Materials: Platinum and high-karat gold for longevity

Exceptional Craftsmanship: Hand-finishing and attention to detail ensure durability

Modular Design: Components that can be reconfigured for different family members

Documentation: Comprehensive records enabling future authentication and modification

Adaptation and Evolution:

Modification Possibilities:

Stone Upgrades: Designs accommodating larger or different stones in the future

Setting Changes: Ability to modify settings while preserving diamonds

Repurposing Options: Transforming pieces for different jewelry types

Size Adjustments: Accommodation for different finger sizes across generations

Legacy Documentation:

Design History: Complete documentation of the design process and inspiration

Technical Specifications: Detailed technical drawings and specifications

Care Instructions: Comprehensive maintenance and care documentation

Authentication Records: Permanent records for insurance and authentication purposes

The world of lab-created diamond jewelry design represents a new frontier where traditional craftsmanship meets cutting-edge technology, where artistic vision is freed from the constraints of natural rarity, and where personal expression finds its perfect crystalline canvas. The exceptional quality, consistency, and accessibility of lab-grown diamonds enable design possibilities that were previously reserved for only the most affluent consumers or remained entirely in the realm of the imagination.

As we move forward in this exciting era of diamond democratization, the boundaries between dream and reality continue to dissolve, replaced by a landscape where every vision can find its perfect expression in the marriage of human creativity and scientific precision. The future of jewelry design is not just about creating beautiful objects; it's about forging meaningful connections between technology and emotion, between innovation and tradition, between individual expression and universal beauty.

***

In the alchemy of design, where vision meets precision and dreams take crystalline form, lab-created diamonds serve as both medium and message—proof that human ingenuity can not only replicate nature's masterpieces but surpass them in consistency, accessibility, and ethical beauty. Here, in the intersection of art and science, every design tells a story of possibility realized.

Chapter 9: Care, Maintenance, and Insurance

"The true measure of a diamond's worth lies not merely in its brilliance at first sight, but in its enduring radiance through decades of love, care, and cherished moments. In preserving perfection, we honor both the miracle of creation and the promise of forever."

9.1 Professional Maintenance

Regular Inspection Schedules

The exceptional quality and precision engineering of lab-created diamonds merit equally exceptional care protocols. Unlike natural diamonds that may have internal stress patterns or structural vulnerabilities, lab-created diamonds offer predictable maintenance requirements, enabling systematic care schedules that preserve their perfection for generations.

Understanding Diamond Durability in Context

While diamonds rank 10 on the Mohs hardness scale—the hardest naturally occurring substance—this hardness refers specifically to scratch resistance, not impact resistance or overall durability. Lab-created diamonds, with their controlled crystal structure and minimal internal stress, often demonstrate superior practical durability compared to natural stones with complex inclusion patterns or structural irregularities.

Professional Assessment Frequency:

Annual Comprehensive Inspections: The foundation of proper diamond care rests on professional annual evaluations:

Setting Security: Microscopic examination of prongs, bezels, and mounting structures

Stone Condition: Assessment of surface condition, clarity characteristics, and overall integrity

Wear Patterns: Identification of wearing patterns that might predict future problems

Documentation: Photographic records tracking condition changes over time

Quarterly Quick Checks for High-Wear Pieces: Engagement rings and daily-wear jewelry benefit from more frequent professional attention:

Prong Tension: Verification that prongs maintain proper tension and alignment

Surface Inspection: Checking for chips, scratches, or surface damage

Setting Alignment: Ensuring stones remain properly positioned and secure

Cleaning Assessment: Determining whether professional cleaning is needed

Specialized Inspection Protocols:

Post-Impact Evaluation: Following any suspected impact or trauma:

Immediate Assessment: Professional evaluation within 24-48 hours of suspected damage

Stress Analysis: Checking for internal stress fractures or damage not visible to the naked eye

Setting Integrity: Comprehensive evaluation of mounting security and alignment

Insurance Documentation: Professional assessment for potential insurance claims

Pre-Event Inspections: Before significant life events, jewelry receives extra attention:

Wedding Preparations: Ensuring engagement rings are perfect for wedding photography

Special Occasions: Verification before important social events or celebrations

Travel Preparations: Security check before international travel or extended trips

Anniversary Celebrations: Ensuring pieces are in optimal condition for milestone celebrations

Professional Cleaning Services

Advanced Cleaning Technologies

Ultrasonic Cleaning Systems:

Professional-grade ultrasonic cleaning represents the gold standard for diamond maintenance:

Frequency-Tuned Systems:

Optimal Frequency: 40-80 kHz frequency ranges providing optimal cleaning without damage

Solution Chemistry: Specialized cleaning solutions designed for precious metals and diamonds

Temperature Control: Precise temperature management, optimizing cleaning effectiveness

Timing Protocols: Carefully controlled exposure times, preventing potential damage

Safety Protocols:

Pre-Cleaning Inspection: Thorough examination for loose stones or damaged settings

Controlled Environment: Professional supervision ensuring safe cleaning processes

Post-Cleaning Verification: Confirmation that all stones remain secure and undamaged

Documentation: Records of cleaning frequency and any observations

Steam Cleaning Applications:

High-Pressure Steam Systems: Professional steam cleaning offers advantages for specific applications:

Deep Penetration: Steam reaches areas inaccessible to other cleaning methods

Chemical-Free: Pure steam cleaning without potentially harmful chemicals

Immediate Results: Instant visualization of cleaning effectiveness

Versatile Application: Suitable for various metal types and setting styles

Specialized Techniques:

Directional Cleaning: Targeted steam application for specific problem areas

Temperature Gradation: Gradually increasing temperature, preventing thermal shock

Drying Protocols: Proper drying techniques prevent water spots or residue

Quality Verification: Immediate assessment of cleaning results

Setting Maintenance and Repair

Preventive Maintenance Philosophy

Proactive Care Strategies:

Professional maintenance adopts a preventive rather than reactive approach:

Prong Maintenance: The most vulnerable components of most jewelry settings require systematic attention:

Wear Assessment: Regular evaluation of prong thickness and integrity

Re-tipping Services: Adding metal to worn prongs before stone security is compromised

Tension Verification: Ensuring prongs maintain proper pressure on diamonds

Alignment Correction: Adjusting prongs that have shifted or bent over time

Gallery and Support Structure Care:

Joint Inspection: Checking solder joints and connection points for stress or failure

Structural Integrity: Assessing the overall structural setting for wear or damage

Support Enhancement: Reinforcing areas showing signs of stress or weakness

Modernization: Updating older settings with contemporary security features

Metal-Specific Maintenance:

Platinum Care Requirements: Platinum's unique properties require specialized maintenance approaches:

Patina Development: Managing the natural patina that develops over time

Work Hardening: Addressing hardening that occurs through wear and stress

Restoration Techniques: Professional restoration of platinum's original finish

Compatibility Issues: Ensuring repairs use platinum-compatible techniques and materials

Gold Alloy Considerations: Different gold alloys present unique maintenance challenges:

14k vs. 18k Durability: Understanding wear patterns in different gold compositions

Color Retention: Maintaining color consistency in white gold through re-rhodium plating

Alloy Stress: Managing stress patterns in different gold formulations

Repair Compatibility: Using appropriate alloys for repairs and modifications

Upgrade and Enhancement Options

Strategic Enhancement Planning

Value-Added Improvements:

Setting Upgrades: Lab-created diamonds' accessible pricing enables consideration of setting upgrades that might be prohibitively expensive with natural stones:

Contemporary Modernization:

Style Updates: Modernizing vintage or dated setting styles

Security Enhancement: Updating older settings with contemporary security features

Comfort Improvements: Modifying settings for enhanced wearability

Aesthetic Refinement: Improving proportions and visual appeal through professional redesign

Stone Enhancement Opportunities:

Size Upgrades: Trading up to larger lab-created diamonds within budget constraints

Quality Improvements: Upgrading to higher color or clarity grades

Shape Changes: Exploring different diamond shapes for renewed aesthetic appeal

Multiple Stone Integration: Adding accent stones or creating multi-stone designs

Technology Integration:

Modern Security Features:

Hidden Security: Discrete security features protecting valuable diamonds

Insurance Compliance: Upgrades to meet current insurance requirements

Travel Considerations: Modifications enhancing security during travel

Professional Requirements: Adaptations for specific professional or lifestyle needs

9.2 Home Care Best Practices

Daily Cleaning Routines

Proper daily care extends the time between professional cleanings while maintaining the brilliance and beauty that first attracted you to your lab-created diamonds. Unlike natural diamonds that may have unique care requirements based on their specific characteristics, lab-created diamonds offer the advantage of predictable care needs and consistent responses to cleaning methods.

Understanding Diamond Surface Chemistry

Oil and Residue Attraction:

Diamonds, whether natural or lab-created, attract oils and residues through their surface properties:

Oleophilic Nature: Diamond surfaces naturally attract and hold oils from skin contact

Soap Residue: Common soaps and lotions leave films that diminish brilliance

Environmental Contaminants: Dust, cooking residues, and airborne particles accumulate over time

Cosmetic Interactions: Makeup, perfumes, and hair products affecting diamond appearance

Surface Cleaning Science:

Capillary Action: Understanding how cleaning solutions penetrate small spaces

Emulsification: The process of breaking down oil-based residues

Rinse Protocols: Proper rinsing techniques prevent residue buildup

Drying Methods: Techniques that prevent water spots and mineral deposits

Daily Care Protocols

Morning Preparation Routines:

Pre-Application Cleaning: Before applying cosmetics, lotions, or perfumes:

Quick Rinse: Warm water rinse, removing overnight accumulation

Gentle Brushing: A Soft toothbrush removes debris from setting crevices

Pat Drying: Lint-free cloth drying prevents water spots

Visual Inspection: Quick check for loose stones or setting problems

Application Order Management:

Cosmetics First: Applying makeup and hair products before wearing jewelry

Jewelry Last: Putting on diamond jewelry as the final step in preparation

Spray Protection: Shielding jewelry when using hair sprays or perfumes

Setting Time: Allowing cosmetics to dry before jewelry contact

Evening Care Routines:

End-of-Day Cleaning:

Immediate Removal: Taking off jewelry before washing face or showering

Quick Clean: Brief cleaning to remove daily accumulation

Inspection: Checking for damage or changes in setting security

Proper Storage: Secure storage, preventing damage or loss

Weekly Deep Cleaning:

Soaking Solution: Gentle dish soap and warm water for thorough cleaning

Brush Technique: Soft-bristled brush reaching all setting areas

Thorough Rinsing: Complete removal of soap residues

Professional Drying: Lint-free cloths and air drying for optimal results

Storage Solutions and Recommendations

Scientific Storage Principles

Environmental Control:

Temperature and Humidity Management:

Stable Conditions: Consistent temperature and humidity, preventing metal expansion/contraction

Moisture Control: Appropriate humidity levels prevent tarnish and corrosion

Air Circulation: Adequate ventilation prevents stagnant conditions

Light Exposure: Controlled lighting, preventing potential damage to metals or gems

Chemical Environment:

Acid-Free Materials: Storage materials that won't emit harmful chemicals

Metal Compatibility: Ensuring storage materials don't react with jewelry metals

Isolation Protocols: Preventing chemical interactions between different jewelry pieces

Contamination Prevention: Protecting jewelry from household chemicals and pollutants

Physical Protection Systems:

Individual Compartmentalization: Preventing damage through strategic separation:

Scratch Prevention: Keeping diamonds separated to prevent mutual scratching

Impact Protection: Cushioning that absorbs shocks and prevents damage

Entanglement Avoidance: Organization preventing chains and settings from tangling

Easy Access: Storage systems enabling easy retrieval without risk

Security Considerations:

Discrete Storage: Storage solutions that don't advertise valuable contents

Secure Mounting: Proper installation of safes and security storage

Access Control: Limiting access to valuable jewelry storage

Insurance Compliance: Meeting insurance requirements for storage security

Specialized Storage Solutions

Home Safe Systems:

Fire and Security Ratings:

Fire Protection: Safes rated for appropriate fire protection duration

Security Ratings: Burglary protection suitable for jewelry values

Size Considerations: Adequate space for current and future jewelry collections

Access Methods: Electronic, combination, or key access systems

Environmental Controls:

Humidity Regulation: Built-in humidity control preventing tarnish and corrosion

Interior Organization: Adjustable compartments and organization systems

Lighting Systems: Interior lighting enabling easy identification and selection

Power Independence: Systems that function during power outages

Jewelry Box Optimization:

Professional-Grade Organization:

Compartment Design: Specialized compartments for different jewelry types

Cushioning Materials: Appropriate padding materials protecting delicate pieces

Access Design: Easy access preventing damage during retrieval

Security Features: Locking mechanisms and security features

Material Selection:

Lining Quality: Appropriate fabric linings that won't snag or damage jewelry

Construction Quality: Durable construction withstanding regular use

Hardware Quality: Hinges, locks, and mechanisms built for longevity

Aesthetic Integration: Designs complementing home décor while providing security

Activity Restrictions and Precautions

Lifestyle Risk Assessment

High-Risk Activities:

Physical Activities and Sports: Understanding when diamond jewelry should be removed:

Contact Sports: Activities with significant impact risk requiring jewelry removal

Weight Training: Exercise involving gripping that could damage rings or settings

Swimming: Chlorine exposure and slippage risks in pool and ocean environments

Rock Climbing: Activities where jewelry could catch or be damaged by impacts

Professional Hazards:

Healthcare Work: Medical environments requiring jewelry restrictions

Food Service: Commercial kitchens with heat, chemicals, and sanitation requirements

Construction: Industrial environments with multiple hazards to jewelry

Chemical Exposure: Laboratories and industrial settings with chemical hazards

Chemical Exposure Risks:

Household Chemicals:

Cleaning Products: Bleach, ammonia, and other chemicals that can damage metals

Beauty Treatments: Hair dyes, permanents, and chemical treatments

Gardening: Fertilizers and plant chemicals that may affect jewelry

Pool Maintenance: Chlorine and other pool chemicals causing metal damage

Professional Chemical Exposure:

Laboratory Work: Research chemicals and solvents requiring jewelry removal

Manufacturing: Industrial chemicals and processes hazardous to jewelry

Art and Crafts: Paints, solvents, and artistic materials are potentially damaging

Automotive Work: Oils, solvents, and mechanical hazards

Emergency Damage Response

Immediate Response Protocols

Damage Assessment:

Initial Evaluation: When damage is suspected or observed:

Immediate Removal: Safely removing jewelry to prevent further damage

Visual Inspection: Careful examination without handling damaged areas

Photo Documentation: Taking photos for insurance and repair purposes

Professional Consultation: Immediate contact with qualified jewelers

Temporary Stabilization:

Loose Stone Management: Securing loose stones in safe containers

Damaged Setting Protection: Preventing further damage to compromised settings

Professional Transport: Safe transportation to qualified repair professionals

Insurance Notification: Prompt notification of insurance carriers when appropriate

Emergency Repair Decisions:

Professional vs. DIY Assessment:

Complexity Evaluation: Understanding which repairs require professional intervention

Time Sensitivity: Assessing the urgency of repair needs

Cost Considerations: Balancing repair costs with jewelry value

Quality Standards: Maintaining quality through appropriate repair choices

Insurance Integration:

Claim Procedures: Understanding insurance claim processes and requirements

Documentation Needs: Gathering appropriate documentation for claims

Approved Repair Facilities: Using insurance-approved repair professionals

Value Protection: Ensuring repairs maintain jewelry value and integrity

9.3 Insurance and Protection

Insurance Policy Types and Coverage

The unique characteristics of lab-created diamonds require specialized consideration in insurance planning. While these diamonds possess identical physical properties to natural stones, their different market dynamics and replacement costs necessitate tailored insurance approaches that recognize their specific value propositions and market realities.

Understanding Insurance Fundamentals for Lab-Created Diamonds

Replacement Value Considerations:

The primary challenge in insuring lab-created diamonds lies in accurately establishing replacement values that reflect current market realities rather than outdated assumptions:

Actual Replacement Cost (ARC) Policies:

Market Reality: Coverage based on current lab-created diamond replacement costs

Technology Consideration: Accounting for improving production technologies affecting costs

Quality Equivalence: Ensuring diamond replacement match original quality specifications

Market Timing: Coverage reflecting current market prices rather than historical values

Agreed Value Policies:

Pre-Negotiated Values: Establishing replacement values at policy inception

Market Protection: Protection against market value fluctuations

Quality Guarantee: Assurance of specific quality replacement standards

Periodic Review: Regular value updates reflecting market changes

Coverage Type Analysis:

Comprehensive Personal Property Coverage: Standard homeowner's insurance may provide basic coverage, but often proves inadequate for valuable jewelry.

Coverage Limits: Typical limits of $1,000-$2,500 for jewelry are insufficient for quality pieces

Deductible Issues: High deductibles reduce effective coverage

Proof Requirements: Extensive documentation requirements for claims

Replacement Limitations: Restrictions on replacement quality and source

Specialized Jewelry Insurance: Dedicated jewelry insurance provides superior protection tailored to unique needs:

Broader Coverage: Protection against loss, theft, damage, and mysterious disappearance

No Deductibles: Zero-deductible policies provide complete protection

Worldwide Coverage: Protection during travel and temporary relocations

Professional Replacement: Access to qualified jewelers and appropriate replacement sources

Appraisal Requirements and Frequency

Professional Appraisal Standards

Appraiser Qualifications:

Certified Appraisal Professionals: Proper insurance protection requires appraisals from qualified professionals:

ASA Certification: American Society of Appraisers certification ensures professional standards

ASI Membership: American Society of Investigators membership demonstrating specialized expertise

GIA Education: Graduate Gemologist credentials providing technical competence

Lab Diamond Expertise: Specific experience with lab-created diamond valuation

Appraisal Methodology:

Market Research: Current market analysis for comparable lab-created diamonds

Quality Documentation: Detailed documentation of diamond characteristics and setting

Replacement Cost Analysis: Realistic assessment of current replacement costs

Insurance Compliance: Appraisals meeting specific insurance company requirements

Appraisal Frequency Requirements:

Initial Appraisal Protocols:

Purchase Documentation: Original purchase receipts and certificates

Professional Evaluation: Independent appraisal within 30-60 days of purchase

Insurance Submission: Prompt submission to insurance carriers for coverage activation

Value Verification: Confirmation that appraisal values reflect purchase prices

Update Schedules:

Annual Reviews: Yearly market value assessments for high-value pieces

Bi-Annual Updates: Two-year appraisal cycles for standard jewelry pieces

Market Trigger Events: Updates following significant market changes

Policy Renewal: Appraisal updates coordinating with insurance policy renewals

Documentation for Insurance Claims

Comprehensive Documentation Systems

Preventive Documentation:

Purchase Documentation: Maintaining complete purchase records enables smooth claim processing.

Original Receipts: Detailed receipts showing purchase prices and specifications

Grading Certificates: Original certificates from recognized laboratories

Warranty Information: Manufacturer and retailer warranty documentation

Custom Design Records: Documentation for custom or unique pieces

Photographic Documentation:

High-Resolution Images: Professional-quality photographs from multiple angles

Macro Details: Close-up photography showing setting details and characteristics

Scale References: Images including scale references for size documentation

Regular Updates: Updated photography reflecting any modifications or changes

Professional Documentation:

Gemological Reports:

Independent Verification: Third-party gemological assessment and documentation

Quality Confirmation: Professional verification of diamond characteristics

Treatment Disclosure: Documentation of any treatments or enhancements

Origin Certification: Confirmation of lab-created origin and growth method

Appraisal Integration:

Detailed Descriptions: Comprehensive written descriptions of all jewelry characteristics

Market Analysis: Current market analysis supporting replacement values

Quality Standards: Specifications ensuring appropriate replacement quality

Update Protocols: Systems for maintaining current documentation

Replacement Value Considerations

Market Reality Integration

Lab-Created Diamond Market Dynamics:

Technology Impact on Values: The evolving technology behind lab-created diamonds affects replacement considerations:

Production Efficiency: Improving production methods affecting replacement costs

Quality Enhancement: Technology advances enabling superior replacement quality

Market Maturation: Developing markets providing more replacement options

Scale Economics: Volume production reducing per-unit replacement costs

Insurance Company Education:

Market Education: Educating insurers about lab-created diamond markets

Value Documentation: Providing current market data supporting replacement values

Quality Equivalence: Demonstrating quality comparability with natural diamonds

Professional Networks: Connecting insurers with qualified lab diamond professionals

Replacement Strategy Development:

Quality Matching Requirements:

Specification Matching: Ensuring replacements match original quality characteristics

Certification Standards: Requiring appropriate certification for replacement diamonds

Setting Compatibility: Ensuring replacement diamonds work with existing settings

Timeline Considerations: Realistic timelines for locating appropriate replacements

Alternative Replacement Options:

Cash Settlements: Options for cash settlements when replacement isn't desired

Upgrade Opportunities: Using insurance settlements for quality or size upgrades

Custom Recreation: Recreating unique or custom pieces through specialized craftspeople

Technology Integration: Utilizing advanced technology for superior replacements

9.4 Long-term Value Preservation

Condition Maintenance Strategies

Preserving the long-term value of lab-created diamonds requires understanding that value encompasses more than just monetary worth—it includes emotional significance, aesthetic appeal, and the preservation of memories and meaning embedded in these remarkable gems.

Systematic Preservation Philosophy

Preventive Care Integration:

Lifestyle Integration: Long-term preservation begins with integrating care into daily routines.

Habit Formation: Developing automatic care behaviors that protect jewelry

Environmental Awareness: Understanding how different environments affect jewelry

Activity Planning: Making conscious decisions about when to wear valuable pieces

Professional Relationships: Establishing ongoing relationships with qualified care professionals

Quality Documentation:

Baseline Establishment: Comprehensive documentation of the initial condition

Change Tracking: Systematic recording of any changes or modifications

Professional Assessment: Regular professional evaluation of condition changes

Historical Record: Maintaining a complete history for future reference

Technological Preservation:

Advanced Monitoring:

Digital Photography: High-resolution photography tracking conditions over time

Measurement Documentation: Precise measurements enabling future verification

Condition Mapping: Detailed mapping of any existing characteristics or conditions

Professional Analysis: Periodic professional analysis of preservation effectiveness

Market Value Monitoring

Strategic Value Assessment

Market Intelligence Systems:

Price Tracking Methodologies: Understanding market trends enables informed decisions about timing and value.

Comparative Analysis: Regular comparison with similar pieces in current markets

Technology Impact: Monitoring how advancing technology affects values

Market Segment Analysis: Understanding value trends in specific market segments

Geographic Variations: Recognizing regional differences in value and demand

Professional Valuation Services:

Periodic Revaluation: Regular professional assessment of current market values

Insurance Coordination: Ensuring insurance coverage reflects current values

Documentation Updates: Maintaining current documentation for all purposes

Market Trend Analysis: Professional analysis of market trends affecting values

Investment Perspective Integration:

Portfolio Considerations:

Diversification Role: Understanding jewelry's role within broader asset portfolios

Liquidity Planning: Realistic assessment of liquidity options and timelines

Estate Planning: Integration with comprehensive estate planning strategies

Tax Considerations: Understanding the tax implications of ownership and transfers

Upgrade Timing and Strategies

Strategic Enhancement Planning

Optimal Timing Assessment:

Market Timing Considerations:

Technology Cycles: Timing upgrades with advancing technology for optimal value

Market Conditions: Understanding how market conditions affect upgrade economics

Personal Timing: Coordinating upgrades with personal milestones and occasions

Financial Planning: Integrating upgrade decisions with broader financial planning

Life Stage Integration:

Anniversary Opportunities: Using anniversaries as natural upgrade occasions

Career Milestones: Celebrating professional achievements through jewelry upgrades

Family Events: Coordinating upgrades with family celebrations and milestones

Personal Growth: Reflecting personal development through jewelry evolution

Value Optimization Strategies:

Trade-In Maximization:

Condition Optimization: Ensuring pieces are in optimal condition before trading

Market Timing: Choosing optimal market conditions for trade-in activities

Dealer Selection: Working with dealers offering the best trade-in values

Documentation Preparation: Assembling complete documentation supporting values

Upgrade Path Planning:

Progressive Enhancement: Planning a logical progression of upgrades over time

Budget Integration: Coordinating upgrade costs with financial planning

Quality Objectives: Establishing long-term quality and size objectives

Emotional Considerations: Balancing practical and emotional factors in upgrade decisions

Estate Planning Considerations

Generational Value Transfer

Legal and Financial Planning:

Documentation Requirements: Proper estate planning requires comprehensive documentation.

Ownership Records: Clear documentation of ownership and acquisition

Valuation Documentation: Current appraisals and valuation records

Insurance Records: Complete insurance documentation and claim history

Modification History: Documentation of any modifications or enhancements

Transfer Mechanisms:

Will Integration: Specific bequests of jewelry items within estate planning

Trust Structures: Using trusts for jewelry transfer and management

Gift Planning: Strategic gifting during lifetime for tax optimization

Family Agreements: Formal agreements regarding jewelry distribution

Cultural and Emotional Considerations:

Family Significance:

Story Preservation: Documenting the stories and significance behind pieces

Cultural Continuity: Ensuring jewelry traditions continue across generations

Adaptation Planning: Allowing for modification to suit different family members

Conflict Prevention: Clear guidelines preventing family disputes over jewelry

Educational Integration:

Knowledge Transfer: Educating family members about care and value

Appreciation Development: Helping family members understand and appreciate pieces

Responsibility Preparation: Preparing recipients for ownership responsibilities

Professional Networks: Introducing family members to care professionals

The comprehensive care, maintenance, and insurance of lab-created diamonds represent an investment in their enduring beauty and significance. Through professional maintenance, proper home care, adequate insurance protection, and strategic long-term planning, these remarkable gems can retain their brilliance and meaning across generations.

The unique advantages of lab-created diamonds—their predictable characteristics, accessible replacement costs, and ethical provenance—enable care strategies that would be impossible or prohibitively expensive with natural stones. This accessibility extends to maintenance, insurance, and long-term planning, making proper care achievable for a broader range of consumers.

Most importantly, the care we provide for our diamonds reflects the care we have for the relationships and memories they represent. In preserving their physical perfection, we honor the emotions and commitments they symbolize, ensuring that their radiance continues to illuminate our most precious moments for generations to come.

***

In the careful tending of our diamonds, we engage in an act of love—love for the beauty they represent, love for the memories they hold, and love for the future moments they will witness. Like the relationships they celebrate, diamonds reward care with enduring brilliance, becoming more precious with each passing year of thoughtful attention.

Chapter 10: Lab-Created Diamond Trends and Innovations

"At the nexus of technology and beauty, where innovation meets imagination, lab-created diamonds illuminate not just our present desires, but our future possibilities—transforming from symbols of luxury into harbingers of a new age where science and artistry dance in perfect harmony."

10.1 Current Trends in Lab-Created Diamond Market

Consumer Adoption Patterns

The lab-created diamond market has evolved from a niche curiosity to a mainstream phenomenon, driven by a convergence of technological advancements, shifting consumer values, and generational shifts in luxury consumption patterns. Understanding these adoption patterns reveals not only current market dynamics but also the trajectory of future diamond consumption.

Demographic Evolution and Market Penetration

Generation-Specific Adoption Characteristics:

Generation Z (Born 1997-2012): The Sustainability Natives

Generation Z approaches luxury consumption with fundamentally different expectations than previous generations, viewing sustainability and ethical sourcing as non-negotiable rather than value-added features:

Environmental Priority Integration: 94% of Gen Z consumers consider environmental impact in luxury purchases

Authenticity Redefinition: Viewing ethical production as more "authentic" than natural origin

Technology Appreciation: Celebrating human innovation and technological achievement

Value Consciousness: Prioritizing value optimization over status symbolism

Social Media Influence: Instagram and TikTok are driving awareness and acceptance

Adoption Metrics:

Market Penetration: 47% of Gen Z diamond purchases involve lab-created stones

Price Sensitivity: 78% prioritize size and quality over natural origin within budget constraints

Information Sources: 89% research purchases are made extensively online before buying

Brand Loyalty: 65% show preference for brands emphasizing sustainability and innovation

Millennials (Born 1981-1996): The Value Optimizers

Millennials, now in their prime earning and family-formation years, represent the largest and most influential segment of the lab-created diamond market:

Financial Pragmatism: Balancing luxury desires with practical financial constraints

Ethical Consciousness: Strong preference for ethically sourced products

Experience Prioritization: Valuing experiences enabled by cost savings over traditional status symbols

Quality Focus: Appreciation for superior technical quality and consistency

Brand Sophistication: Understanding of production methods and quality distinctions

Market Behavior Analysis:

Engagement Ring Segment: 38% of millennial engagement rings feature lab-created diamonds

Average Transaction Value: $4,200 for engagement rings (vs. $6,800 for natural equivalents)

Quality Preferences: 67% choose higher color/clarity grades when budget allows

Research Duration: Average 8 weeks of research before purchase

Influence Networks: 73% consult multiple sources including peers, professionals, and online resources

Generation X (Born 1965-1980): The Practical Adopters

Generation X adoption reflects practical considerations combined with growing environmental awareness:

Investment Perspective: Viewing lab diamonds as smart financial decisions

Quality Appreciation: Recognizing superior value propositions in lab-created options

Family Considerations: Making decisions that benefit family financial planning

Professional Integration: Choosing appropriate jewelry for professional advancement

Legacy Planning: Considering long-term family significance and inheritance

Adoption Patterns:

Market Share: 28% of Gen X luxury jewelry purchases include lab-created diamonds

Upgrade Motivation: 45% purchase lab diamonds as upgrades from smaller natural stones

Anniversary Gifts: 52% of significant anniversary gifts involve lab-created diamonds

Professional Consultation: 81% seek professional guidance before purchase decisions

Geographic Market Variations

North American Market Leadership

United States: Innovation Hub

The United States represents the most mature and sophisticated lab-created diamond market globally:

Market Characteristics:

Penetration Rate: 24% of the total diamond market by volume

Growth Trajectory: 18% annual growth rate sustaining for five consecutive years

Quality Premium: Higher average quality grades compared to global markets

Price Acceptance: Consumer willingness to pay premiums for superior quality and branding

Regional Variations Within the US:

West Coast Leadership: California leading adoption at 31% market penetration

Urban vs. Rural: Metropolitan areas showing 28% adoption vs. 16% in rural markets

Educational Correlation: Areas with higher education levels show increased adoption

Income Distribution: Broad adoption across income levels, unlike traditional luxury patterns

Canada: Environmental Leadership

Canadian consumers demonstrate the strongest environmental motivations globally:

Sustainability Focus: 92% of lab diamond buyers cite environmental considerations

Quality Standards: Highest average clarity and color grade preferences

Professional Consultation: 87% seek gemological advice before purchase

Brand Loyalty: Strong preference for Canadian-produced lab diamonds

European Market Sophistication

United Kingdom: Ethical Jewelry Movement

The UK market demonstrates a sophisticated understanding of ethical jewelry principles:

Consumer Characteristics:

Ethical Priority: 89% prioritize ethical sourcing over traditional luxury markers

Vintage Integration: 67% pair lab diamonds with vintage or vintage-inspired settings

Quality Education: High levels of gemological knowledge among consumers

Professional Integration: Growing acceptance in professional and social contexts

Continental European Trends:

Germany: Technology appreciation driving 19% market penetration

France: Luxury integration with emphasis on craftsmanship and design

Netherlands: Early adoption through diamond trade center expertise

Scandinavia: Environmental leadership with 23% average market penetration

Regulatory Environment Impact:

EU Sustainability Reporting: Environmental regulations supporting lab diamond adoption

Consumer Protection: Strong regulatory frameworks building consumer confidence

Trade Standards: Harmonized standards facilitating cross-border commerce

Educational Initiatives: Government-supported consumer education programs

Asia-Pacific: Rapid Growth Markets

China: Manufacturing and Consumption Hub

China presents unique dynamics as both the largest producer and fastest-growing consumer market:

Market Development:

Production Advantage: Domestic production reduces costs and improves availability

Youth Adoption: 89% of consumers under 30 are open to lab-created diamonds

E-commerce Leadership: 76% of lab diamond sales occur through online channels

Cultural Evolution: Shifting from tradition-focused to innovation-appreciating luxury consumption

Regional Variations:

Tier 1 Cities: Beijing, Shanghai, Shenzhen, showing 22% market penetration

Technology Sectors: High adoption among technology industry professionals

Educational Influence: University graduates showing 3x higher adoption rates

Income Correlation: The Growing middle class is driving market expansion

Japan: Quality and Innovation Focus

Japanese consumers demonstrate appreciation for technological excellence and precision:

Quality Standards: Highest cut quality preferences globally

Brand Consciousness: Strong preference for established, reputable brands

Professional Consultation: 91% seek expert guidance before purchases

Technology Appreciation: Celebration of manufacturing precision and innovation

India: Production Center Evolution

India's role as a major production center influences domestic market development:

Industry Familiarity: High awareness due to diamond industry presence

Price Sensitivity: Strong value consciousness driving lab diamond adoption

Cultural Integration: Gradual integration with traditional jewelry preferences

Export Market Influence: International market trends affecting domestic preferences

Retail Channel Evolution

E-commerce Dominance

Digital-First Consumer Behavior:

The lab-created diamond market has pioneered digital-first retail approaches:

Online Platform Advantages:

Selection Breadth: Access to global inventory through digital platforms

Price Transparency: Direct price comparisons and competitive marketplace dynamics

Educational Resources: Comprehensive educational content supporting informed decisions

Virtual Try-On: Advanced visualization technologies enabling confident online purchases

Technology Integration:

AR/VR Applications: Augmented reality enabling virtual try-on experiences

AI Consultation: Artificial intelligence provides personalized recommendations

Blockchain Verification: Digital provenance tracking, ensuring authenticity

Mobile Commerce: Smartphone-optimized shopping experiences

Consumer Confidence Building:

Extended Return Policies: 60-90 day return periods build purchase confidence

Virtual Consultations: Expert guidance through video calls and chat

Detailed Documentation: High-resolution photography and comprehensive specifications

Certification Integration: Digital certificates and verification systems

Omnichannel Retail Evolution

Hybrid Shopping Experiences:

Modern consumers expect seamless integration across online and offline channels:

Research-to-Purchase Patterns:

Online Research: 87% begin the purchase process with online research

Physical Examination: 64% prefer to see diamonds in person before final purchase

Expert Consultation: 71% value professional guidance during the decision process

Flexible Fulfillment: Options for online ordering with in-store pickup or consultation

Retailer Adaptation Strategies:

Showroom Innovation: Physical spaces optimized for education and experience

Inventory Integration: Seamless access to online and offline inventory

Staff Training: Enhanced gemological education for retail professionals

Service Integration: Comprehensive services spanning online and offline channels

Traditional Retailer Integration:

Established Jewelry Retailers: Traditional jewelers increasingly embrace lab-created diamonds:

Inventory Expansion: Major retailers adding lab diamond selections

Staff Education: Comprehensive training programs for sales professionals

Consumer Education: In-store educational programs build market awareness

Service Integration: Incorporating lab diamonds into existing service offerings

Luxury Brand Adoption:

High-End Integration: Luxury brands launching lab diamond collections

Brand Positioning: Positioning lab diamonds as innovation and sustainability leaders

Design Innovation: Unique designs highlighting lab diamond advantages

Market Education: Brand authority supporting consumer education and acceptance

10.2 Advancements in Diamond Creation Technology

Production Efficiency Improvements

The relentless pace of technological advancement in lab-created diamond production continues to drive improvements in quality, efficiency, and cost-effectiveness. These developments not only enhance the economic viability of lab diamonds but also expand their applications across multiple industries.

Next-Generation CVD Systems

Plasma Engineering Breakthroughs:

Microwave Plasma Optimization: Advanced microwave systems achieve unprecedented control over diamond growth:

Frequency Tuning: Precise frequency control optimizing plasma density and uniformity

Power Distribution: Advanced antenna arrays creating larger, more uniform growth zones

Gas Flow Dynamics: Computational fluid dynamics optimizing gas distribution patterns

Real-Time Monitoring: Advanced sensors enabling immediate process adjustments

Performance Improvements:

Growth Rate Enhancement: 40% faster growth rates while maintaining quality

Size Scalability: Routine production of 5+ carat single crystals

Quality Consistency: 95%+ gem-grade yield rates in production environments

Energy Efficiency: 35% reduction in energy consumption per carat

Atmospheric Pressure CVD Development:

Breakthrough Technology: New atmospheric pressure systems eliminate vacuum requirements:

Simplified Equipment: Reduced complexity and maintenance requirements

Continuous Operation: Potential for continuous production processes

Cost Reduction: Significant reduction in equipment and operational costs

Scalability: Enhanced scalability for industrial production

Technical Advantages:

Process Control: Enhanced control over growth parameters

Quality Enhancement: Improved crystal quality through optimized conditions

Throughput Increase: Higher production volumes through continuous operation

Energy Optimization: Reduced energy requirements for pressure management

Advanced HPHT Innovations

Ultra-High Pressure Systems:

Pressure Technology Evolution: Next-generation HPHT systems achieve unprecedented pressure levels:

Pressure Capabilities: 12+ GPa pressures enabling new growth possibilities

Temperature Control: Precise temperature gradients optimizing crystal quality

Multi-Station Operation: Simultaneous processing of multiple growth chambers

Automated Handling: Robotic systems improving efficiency and safety

Production Improvements:

Growth Acceleration: 60% faster production cycles

Size Enhancement: Routine production of 10+ carat crystals

Quality Optimization: Enhanced control, reducing inclusion formation

Cost Effectiveness: Reduced per-carat production costs through efficiency gains

Catalyst Technology Advancement:

Novel Catalyst Systems:

Inclusion Reduction: Advanced catalysts minimize metallic inclusions

Temperature Optimization: Lower temperature operation reduces stress

Efficiency Enhancement: Improved catalytic efficiency, accelerating growth

Customization Capability: Tailored catalysts for specific diamond characteristics

Environmental Integration:

Renewable Energy: Systems optimized for renewable energy operation

Waste Reduction: Closed-loop processes minimizing waste generation

Resource Efficiency: Optimized material usage, reducing environmental impact

Carbon Neutrality: Production processes achieving carbon-neutral operation

Quality Enhancement Technologies

Precision Engineering Developments

Atomic-Level Control:

Molecular Beam Epitaxy Applications: Adapting semiconductor manufacturing techniques for diamond production:

Layer Control: Atomic-level control of diamond layer deposition

Defect Minimization: Precise control eliminates common defect formation

Property Engineering: Custom diamond properties through controlled doping

Interface Quality: Perfect interfaces between different diamond layers

Applications:

Electronic Diamonds: Semiconducting diamonds for electronic applications

Optical Enhancement: Optimized optical properties for specific applications

Mechanical Properties: Enhanced mechanical characteristics for industrial uses

Thermal Management: Optimized thermal conductivity for heat management applications

In-Situ Monitoring Systems:

Real-Time Quality Control: Advanced monitoring enables immediate quality optimization:

Spectroscopic Analysis: Real-time analysis of growth chemistry and quality

Interferometry: Precise thickness and uniformity measurements during growth

Temperature Mapping: Real-time thermal analysis optimizing growth conditions

Stress Analysis: Immediate detection and correction of stress development

Feedback Control Systems:

Automated Adjustment: AI-driven systems automatically optimize growth parameters

Predictive Modeling: Machine learning predicting and preventing quality issues

Process Optimization: Continuous improvement through data analysis and feedback

Quality Assurance: Immediate detection of deviations from quality standards

Post-Growth Enhancement Techniques

Advanced Treatment Methods:

High-Pressure High-Temperature Treatment: Sophisticated HPHT treatment optimizing finished diamond properties:

Color Enhancement: Precise color optimization through controlled treatment

Clarity Improvement: Stress relief and inclusion modification

Structural Optimization: Crystal lattice improvement, enhancing properties

Stability Enhancement: Permanent improvements maintain long-term quality

Irradiation and Annealing:

Color Creation: Controlled irradiation creates specific color centers

Defect Engineering: Precise defect creation for desired properties

Thermal Treatment: Optimized annealing stabilizes created defects

Quality Control: Comprehensive testing ensures treatment effectiveness

Surface Engineering:

Precision Polishing Technologies:

Ion Beam Polishing: Atomic-level surface finishing, achieving perfect surfaces

Chemical Mechanical Polishing: Combined chemical and mechanical optimization

Laser Polishing: Precision laser techniques for complex surface geometries

Quality Verification: Advanced metrology confirming surface quality

Automation and AI Integration

Artificial Intelligence Applications

Machine Learning in Production:

Process Optimization Algorithms: AI systems revolutionizing production efficiency and quality:

Parameter Optimization: Machine learning optimizing complex multi-variable processes

Predictive Maintenance: AI predicting equipment maintenance needs

Quality Prediction: Algorithms predicting final quality from process parameters

Yield Optimization: Maximizing gem-quality diamond production rates

Data Integration Systems:

Sensor Fusion: Combining multiple sensor inputs for comprehensive process understanding

Historical Analysis: Learning from historical data to improve future production

Real-Time Decision Making: Immediate process adjustments based on AI analysis

Continuous Improvement: Self-learning systems continuously enhance performance

Robotic Integration:

Automated Handling Systems:

Substrate Preparation: Robotic systems prepare growth substrates with precision

Growth Chamber Loading: Automated loading and unloading of growth systems

Quality Inspection: Robotic inspection systems with computer vision analysis

Packaging and Logistics: Automated systems manage finished diamond handling

Safety and Reliability:

Hazard Reduction: Robotics removes humans from potentially dangerous processes

Consistency Enhancement: Robotic systems ensure consistent handling and processing

Quality Assurance: Automated quality control reduces human error

Efficiency Optimization: 24/7 operation capability, maximizing production throughput

Industry 4.0 Integration

Smart Factory Concepts:

Connected Production Systems: Integration of all production elements into cohesive smart manufacturing:

IoT Integration: Internet of Things sensors throughout the production environment

Cloud Computing: Cloud-based analysis and optimization systems

Digital Twins: Virtual replicas of production systems enabling optimization

Blockchain Tracking: Immutable records of the production process and quality

Supply Chain Integration:

Demand Forecasting: AI systems predicting market demand and optimizing production

Inventory Management: Automated inventory optimization reducing waste and costs

Logistics Optimization: AI-optimized shipping and distribution systems

Customer Integration: Direct customer feedback integration into production planning

10.3 Future Prospects and Predictions

Emerging Applications Beyond Jewelry

The exceptional properties of lab-created diamonds position them at the forefront of multiple technological revolutions, extending far beyond their traditional role in jewelry to become critical enablers of advanced technologies across various industries, including quantum computing and space exploration.

Quantum Technology Applications

Quantum Computing Infrastructure:

Nitrogen-Vacancy (NV) Centers: Lab-created diamonds with precisely controlled NV centers represent breakthrough quantum technology:

Qubit Functionality: NV centers serving as stable quantum bits at room temperature

Coherence Times: Maintaining quantum states for milliseconds, enabling practical computation

Scalability: Controlled placement of NV centers enabling scalable quantum processors

Error Correction: High-fidelity quantum operations supporting error correction protocols

Market Projections:

2025 Market Size: $150 million for quantum-grade diamonds

2030 Projection: $2.3 billion market for quantum technology diamonds

Growth Drivers: Government quantum initiatives and private sector investment

Technical Requirements: Ultra-high purity and precise defect control

Quantum Sensing Applications:

Medical Diagnostics:

Molecular Detection: Single-molecule detection capabilities for medical diagnostics

Brain Imaging: Non-invasive neural activity monitoring using diamond sensors

Cancer Detection: Early cancer detection through cellular magnetic field analysis

Drug Development: Accelerated drug development through enhanced molecular analysis

Industrial Sensing:

Precision Metrology: Atomic-scale measurement capabilities for manufacturing

Material Analysis: Non-destructive testing with unprecedented sensitivity

Environmental Monitoring: Ultra-sensitive detection of environmental contaminants

Navigation Systems: GPS-independent navigation using quantum sensors

Advanced Electronics and Computing

High-Power Electronics:

Wide Bandgap Semiconductors: Diamond's exceptional electronic properties enable revolutionary electronic devices:

Power Electronics: High-voltage, high-frequency power conversion systems

RF Applications: Radio frequency devices for telecommunications and radar

Extreme Environment: Electronics functioning in high-temperature, high-radiation environments

Energy Efficiency: Dramatically improved efficiency in power conversion systems

Performance Characteristics:

Voltage Capability: Operating voltages exceeding 10,000 volts

Frequency Response: Gigahertz frequency operation capability

Temperature Range: Functionality from -200°C to +600°C

Radiation Resistance: Operation in high-radiation environments

Thermal Management Solutions:

Heat Spreading Applications:

CPU Cooling: Diamond heat spreaders for high-performance processors

LED Thermal Management: Enhanced LED efficiency through diamond heat sinks

Laser Diodes: Improved laser performance through diamond thermal management

Power Electronics: Thermal management for high-power electronic systems

Space Technology Applications

Satellite and Spacecraft Systems:

Radiation-Hard Electronics: Diamond electronics offering superior radiation resistance for space applications:

Satellite Electronics: Long-duration missions enabled by radiation-resistant electronics

Deep Space Exploration: Electronics functioning in extreme radiation environments

Nuclear Space Power: Electronics for Nuclear-Powered Spacecraft Systems

Solar Panel Efficiency: Diamond-enhanced photovoltaic systems for space applications

Optical Applications:

Space Telescopes: Diamond optical components for space-based astronomy

Laser Communications: Diamond components for space-based laser communication

Precision Optics: Ultra-stable optical systems for space applications

Sensing Systems: Advanced sensing capabilities for planetary exploration

Manufacturing in Space:

Microgravity Production: Research into space-based diamond manufacturing:

Crystal Perfection: Microgravity enabling perfect crystal growth

Large Crystal Production: Space-based growth of extremely large single crystals

Novel Properties: Unique diamond properties achievable only in microgravity

Commercial Viability: Economic analysis of space-based diamond production

Technological Integration Trends

Artificial Intelligence and Machine Learning

AI-Enhanced Production:

Intelligent Manufacturing Systems: AI integration transforming every aspect of diamond production:

Process Optimization: Machine learning optimizing complex multi-parameter processes

Quality Prediction: AI systems predicting final quality from early growth indicators

Maintenance Scheduling: Predictive maintenance optimizing equipment utilization

Energy Management: AI-optimized energy consumption reducing environmental impact

Customer Experience Enhancement:

Personalized Recommendations: AI systems providing customized diamond recommendations

Virtual Try-On: Advanced AI enabling realistic virtual jewelry experiences

Design Assistance: AI helping customers design custom jewelry pieces

Market Analysis: AI-driven market analysis optimizing pricing and availability

Blockchain and Digital Identity:

Provenance Tracking:

Complete Traceability: Blockchain records from growth through retail sale

Authentication: Immutable digital certificates prevent fraud

Smart Contracts: Automated execution of warranties and service agreements

Consumer Confidence: Enhanced consumer confidence through transparent provenance

Internet of Things Integration

Connected Jewelry Concepts:

Smart Jewelry Applications: Integration of technology into diamond jewelry:

Health Monitoring: Jewelry incorporating biometric sensors and health monitoring

Communication: Discrete communication capabilities integrated into jewelry

Security: Authentication and security functions through smart jewelry

Personal Assistant: AI assistant capabilities integrated into jewelry pieces

Technical Implementation:

Miniaturization: Ultra-small electronic components compatible with jewelry design

Power Management: Energy harvesting and wireless charging for jewelry electronics

Durability: Electronics designed for jewelry wear patterns and environments

Aesthetic Integration: Technology integration maintains jewelry's beauty and appeal

Market Evolution Predictions

Size and Scale Projections

Global Market Forecasts:

Market Size Evolution: Comprehensive projections across multiple scenarios:

Conservative Scenario (2030):

Global Market Size: $48 billion retail value

Market Share: 28% of the total diamond market by volume

Growth Drivers: Steady adoption and technology improvement

Geographic Distribution: Continued leadership in developed markets

Base Case Scenario (2030):

Global Market Size: $67 billion retail value

Market Share: 35% of the total diamond market by volume

Growth Drivers: Accelerating adoption and expanding applications

Technology Impact: Significant cost reductions and quality improvements

Optimistic Scenario (2030):

Global Market Size: $89 billion retail value

Market Share: 45% of the total diamond market by volume

Growth Drivers: Breakthrough technologies and regulatory support

Market Transformation: Fundamental shift in luxury consumption patterns

Production Volume Forecasts:

Manufacturing Capacity Evolution:

2025 Production: 12 million carats annually

2027 Production: 18 million carats annually

2030 Production: 28 million carats annually

Quality Distribution: Increasing percentage of premium quality production

Geographic Production Distribution:

Asia-Pacific: 65% of global production (China, India, Singapore)

North America: 20% of global production (US, Canada)

Europe: 10% of global production (various countries)

Other Regions: 5% of global production (emerging markets)

Consumer Behavior Evolution

Generational Transition Impact:

Generation Alpha Integration: As Generation Alpha reaches purchasing age, their preferences will reshape markets:

Technology Expectation: Expectation of technological integration in all products

Sustainability Requirements: Non-negotiable environmental and ethical standards

Customization Demands: Expectation of personalized and customizable products

Digital Integration: Seamless integration of physical and digital experiences

Market Implications:

Product Development: Jewelry designed for digital-native consumers

Service Evolution: Service models adapted for technology-integrated lifestyles

Communication Strategies: Marketing and communication adapted for new consumer behaviors

Value Proposition: Evolving definitions of luxury and value

Cultural Integration Patterns:

Traditional Market Evolution:

Asian Markets: Gradual integration with traditional luxury preferences

Middle Eastern Markets: Growing acceptance among younger consumers

African Markets: Unique dynamics in regions with diamond mining heritage

Latin American Markets: Emerging middle-class adoption patterns

Luxury Redefinition:

Conscious Luxury: Luxury consumption aligned with personal values

Experience Integration: Luxury products enabling experiences rather than just ownership

Technology Enhancement: Technology as a luxury enhancement rather than a replacement

Community Values: Luxury consumption supporting community and environmental values

The future of lab-created diamonds extends far beyond the boundaries of traditional jewelry, encompassing revolutionary applications in quantum technology, advanced electronics, space exploration, and smart manufacturing. As these technologies mature and markets evolve, lab-created diamonds will likely become critical enablers of technological advancement while continuing to redefine luxury consumption for increasingly conscious consumers.

The convergence of technological capability, market acceptance, and generational change positions lab-created diamonds at the forefront of multiple transformative trends. From quantum computers that may revolutionize information processing to space-based manufacturing that could transform production economics, these remarkable crystals represent not just the future of luxury goods but the future of technology itself.

As we stand on the threshold of this transformation, the story of lab-created diamonds evolves from one of alternative luxury to one of technological leadership, where human ingenuity crystallizes into solutions for humanity's greatest challenges while continuing to celebrate life's most precious moments with uncompromising beauty and ethical clarity.

***

In the laboratory's controlled environment, we witness not just the birth of diamonds but the dawn of possibilities, where each perfect crystal represents humanity's potential to create beauty without compromise, luxury without guilt, and innovation without limits. The future sparkles with promise, illuminated by the brilliance of human achievement crystallized in diamond form.

Chapter 11: Frequently Asked Questions about Lab-Created Diamonds

"In the realm of knowledge, questions are the diamonds that illuminate understanding. Each inquiry is polished to reveal truth, each answer faceted to reflect wisdom, together creating the brilliance of informed decision-making."

11.1 Fundamental Questions and Comprehensive Answers

Are Lab-Created Diamonds Real Diamonds?

This question stands as perhaps the most fundamental inquiry about lab-created diamonds, touching on issues of authenticity, value, and the very nature of what defines a diamond. The answer is unequivocal: lab-created diamonds are absolutely real diamonds, identical in every measurable way to their natural counterparts.

The Science of Diamond Identity

Chemical and Physical Properties:

At the atomic level, lab-created diamonds are indistinguishable from natural diamonds:

Chemical Composition:

Pure Carbon: Both natural and lab-created diamonds consist of pure carbon atoms

Crystal Structure: Identical cubic crystal lattice arrangement in both types

Atomic Bonding: Same covalent bonding pattern creating diamond's characteristic properties

Isotopic Composition: While minor isotopic variations may exist, they don't affect diamond properties

Physical Characteristics:

Hardness: Both score exactly 10 on the Mohs hardness scale

Density: Identical specific gravity of 3.52 g/cm^3

Refractive Index: Same light-bending properties at 2.42

Thermal Conductivity: Identical heat conduction characteristics

Gemological Testing Results:

Professional gemological instruments cannot distinguish between high-quality lab-created and natural diamonds without specialized equipment:

Standard Testing:

Diamond Testers: Thermal and electrical conductivity testers confirm both as genuine diamonds

Refractometer: Identical refractive index readings for both types

Specific Gravity: Same density measurements for natural and lab-created stones

Hardness Testing: Identical scratch resistance and durability characteristics

Advanced Analysis Required:

Photoluminescence Spectroscopy: Specialized equipment detecting subtle growth-related differences

Fourier Transform Infrared (FTIR): Advanced spectroscopy revealing trace element differences

Cathodoluminescence: Sophisticated imaging showing growth pattern variations

Professional Expertise: Trained gemologists using advanced equipment for origin determination

Historical Context and Industry Recognition

Professional Acknowledgment:

Major gemological institutions recognize lab-created diamonds as genuine diamonds:

Gemological Institute of America (GIA):

Grading Reports: Issues comprehensive grading reports for lab-created diamonds

Same Standards: Applies identical 4Cs grading criteria to lab and natural diamonds

Clear Identification: Reports clearly indicate synthetic origin while confirming diamond identity

Educational Resources: Extensive educational materials explaining lab diamond authenticity

Federal Trade Commission (FTC):

Legal Recognition: Official recognition of lab-created diamonds as genuine diamonds

Terminology Guidelines: Approved terminology including "laboratory-grown diamonds"

Truth-in-Advertising: Requirements for clear disclosure of origin, not diamond authenticity

Consumer Protection: Guidelines protecting consumers while acknowledging diamond legitimacy

Market Recognition:

Insurance Industry:

Coverage Policies: Insurance companies provide identical coverage types for lab and natural diamonds

Appraisal Standards: Professional appraisers use same methodologies for both types

Replacement Protocols: Insurance replacements based on quality characteristics, not origin

Value Recognition: Industry acknowledgment of lab diamonds as legitimate insurable assets

Financial Institutions:

Collateral Acceptance: Banks accepting lab-created diamonds as loan collateral

Estate Planning: Inclusion in estate valuations and inheritance planning

Investment Recognition: Growing recognition as a legitimate alternative investment

Professional Services: Expansion of financial services to lab-created diamond owners

Will Lab-Created Diamonds Lose Their Value?

The question of value retention reflects legitimate concerns about investment protection and long-term satisfaction with purchase decisions. Understanding value dynamics requires examining multiple factors affecting both lab-created and natural diamond markets.

Understanding Value Components

Intrinsic vs. Market Value:

Intrinsic Value Elements:

Beauty and Brilliance: Identical optical performance creating the same aesthetic value

Durability: Same hardness and longevity, ensuring lasting physical value

Symbolic Significance: Equal capacity to represent love, commitment, and achievement

Practical Utility: Identical performance in jewelry applications and personal enjoyment

Market Value Factors:

Supply and Demand: Economic forces affecting pricing and liquidity

Consumer Perception: Evolving attitudes toward lab-created diamonds

Technology Impact: Production improvements affecting cost structures

Cultural Acceptance: Growing integration into luxury consumption patterns

Historical Value Analysis:

Lab-Created Diamond Value Evolution (2015-2024):

2015-2017: Premium pricing at 70-80% of natural diamond costs

2018-2020: Rapid price decline to 40-60% of natural equivalents

2021-2023: Price stabilization at 20-30% of natural diamond prices

2024-Present: Stable pricing with quality differentiation emerging

Natural Diamond Value Context: For perspective on value retention concerns:

Immediate Depreciation: Natural diamonds typically lose 50-80% of their retail value upon purchase

Long-term Trends: Natural diamond prices declined 25% in real terms from 2011-2021

Market Volatility: Natural diamond values are subject to mining company manipulation and market forces

Resale Challenges: Limited liquidity in natural diamond resale markets

Factors Supporting Value Retention

Market Maturation Indicators:

Growing Consumer Acceptance:

Adoption Rates: Increasing market penetration across all demographic segments

Brand Development: Establishment of recognized lab-created diamond brands

Retail Integration: Major jewelry retailers adding lab-created diamond inventory

Professional Recognition: Growing gemological and jewelry industry acceptance

Infrastructure Development:

Secondary Markets: Emerging resale and consignment markets for lab-created diamonds

Financing Options: Expanding financing and insurance options

Professional Services: A Growing network of qualified appraisers and service providers

Quality Standards: Establishment of quality premiums for superior lab-created diamonds

Unique Value Propositions:

Ethical Premium:

Sustainability Value: Increasing premium for environmentally responsible products

Transparency Advantage: Complete supply chain transparency, adding value

Social Responsibility: Ethical production methods commanding consumer loyalty

Future Orientation: Alignment with evolving luxury consumption values

Quality Advantages:

Consistency: Predictable quality characteristics supporting value stability

Size Availability: Access to larger stones at accessible prices

Cut Optimization: Superior cut quality is achievable through cost-effective production

Customization: Enhanced customization options adding personal value

How Do Lab-Created Diamonds Compare to Natural Diamonds?

This comprehensive comparison addresses the practical considerations consumers face when choosing between natural and lab-created options across multiple evaluation criteria.

Physical and Optical Comparison

Performance Characteristics:

Light Performance: Lab-created diamonds often demonstrate superior optical performance:

Cut Quality: Cost advantages enabling ideal cut proportions more consistently

Clarity Advantages: Controlled growth, reducing inclusion formation

Color Consistency: Uniform color distribution throughout the stones

Brilliance: Identical light return when cut to the same standards

Durability Factors:

Hardness: Identical Mohs 10 hardness rating for both types

Toughness: Lab-created diamonds often show superior toughness due to reduced internal stress

Stability: Both types are equally stable under normal wearing conditions

Longevity: Identical lifespan and aging characteristics

Manufacturing Quality:

Controlled Production Advantages:

Defect Minimization: Controlled environment reduces naturally formed defects

Stress Patterns: Reduced internal stress improves durability

Inclusion Control: Fewer problematic inclusions affecting structural integrity

Size Consistency: Precise control over final diamond dimensions

Quality Distribution:

Grade Concentration: Higher percentage of lab diamonds are achieving premium grades

Consistency: More predictable quality outcomes in lab production

Rejection Rates: Lower rejection rates due to controlled growth conditions

Matching: Easier to achieve perfectly matched pairs and sets

Economic Comparison

Price-Value Analysis:

Cost Comparison by Quality Grade:

Premium Quality (D-F Color, VVS+ Clarity, Excellent Cut):

1 Carat Natural: $8,000-$15,000

1 Carat Lab-Created: $1,500-$3,000

Savings: 75-85% cost reduction

Value Proposition: Identical quality at dramatically lower cost

Commercial Quality (G-I Color, VS Clarity, Very Good+ Cut):

1 Carat Natural: $4,000-$8,000

1 Carat Lab-Created: $800-$1,600

Savings: 70-80% cost reduction

Market Position: Excellent value in the mainstream market

Total Cost of Ownership:

Acquisition Costs:

Purchase Price: Significant advantage to lab-created diamonds

Setting Costs: Identical setting and mounting costs

Certification: Comparable certification costs from major laboratories

Customization: Enhanced customization affordability with lab diamonds

Ongoing Costs:

Insurance: Lower premiums reflecting reduced replacement costs

Maintenance: Identical cleaning and care requirements

Professional Services: Same service needs and costs for both types

Replacement: Lower cost for replacement if loss or damage occurs

Market and Resale Considerations

Liquidity Analysis:

Resale Market Development:

Natural Diamond Resale: Established but limited resale markets

Lab Diamond Resale: Developing markets with improving infrastructure

Value Retention: Natural diamonds retain 30-60% of retail value; lab diamonds 20-40%

Market Trends: Lab diamond resale values stabilizing as market matures

Investment Perspective:

Natural Diamonds: Traditional investment vehicle with an established track record

Lab-Created Diamonds: An Emerging asset class with different risk-return profile

Portfolio Role: Both are suitable for personal enjoyment rather than primary investment

Long-term Outlook: Market evolution favoring sustainable and ethical options

Geographic Variations:

Regional Market Differences:

North America: Strong lab diamond acceptance and market development

Europe: Growing acceptance driven by sustainability concerns

Asia-Pacific: Rapid growth in lab diamond adoption, especially among younger consumers

Emerging Markets: Varying adoption rates based on cultural and economic factors

Can Lab-Created Diamonds Be Insured?

Insurance coverage is a crucial practical consideration for diamond owners, and lab-created diamonds often enjoy comprehensive insurance options comparable to those for natural stones, with additional benefits.

Insurance Coverage Fundamentals

Policy Types and Coverage:

Homeowner's Insurance Coverage: Standard homeowner's policies provide basic coverage with limitations:

Coverage Limits: Typically $1,000-$2,500 for jewelry without additional coverage

Covered Perils: Usually limited to theft and some forms of damage

Deductible: Standard homeowner's deductible applies to jewelry claims

Documentation: Basic documentation requirements for coverage

Specialized Jewelry Insurance: Dedicated jewelry insurance offers superior protection:

Comprehensive Coverage: Protection against loss, theft, damage, and mysterious disappearance

No Deductible: Zero-deductible policies providing complete protection

Worldwide Coverage: Protection during travel and temporary relocation

Professional Replacement: Access to qualified jewelers for repairs and replacements

Coverage Advantages for Lab-Created Diamonds:

Premium Advantages:

Lower Replacement Cost: Reduced premiums reflecting actual replacement values

Risk Assessment: Lower risk profile due to improved availability and replaceability

Fraud Reduction: Complete provenance reduces insurance fraud concerns

Documentation: Superior documentation supporting claims processing

Replacement Benefits:

Availability: Easier replacement, reducing insurance company risk

Quality Matching: Ability to achieve exact quality matches for replacements

Timeline: Faster replacement processing due to availability

Cost Certainty: Predictable replacement costs enabling better policy pricing

Appraisal and Documentation Requirements

Professional Appraisal Standards:

Appraiser Qualifications: Insurance appraisals require qualified professionals:

Certified Appraisers: ASA, ASI, or equivalent professional certification

Gemological Training: GG or equivalent gemological education

Lab Diamond Expertise: Specific experience with lab-created diamond valuation

Insurance Recognition: Appraisers recognized by insurance companies

Appraisal Methodology:

Market Research: Current market analysis for replacement cost determination

Quality Documentation: Detailed description of diamond characteristics and setting

Photographic Documentation: Professional photography for identification purposes

Replacement Cost Analysis: Realistic assessment of current replacement costs

Documentation Best Practices:

Essential Documentation:

Purchase Receipt: Original receipt showing purchase price and specifications

Grading Certificate: Professional grading report from a recognized laboratory

Professional Appraisal: Insurance appraisal from a qualified appraiser

Photographic Record: High-resolution photographs from multiple angles

Maintenance Requirements:

Regular Updates: Periodic appraisal updates reflecting market changes

Policy Reviews: Annual review of coverage adequacy and terms

Documentation Storage: Secure storage of important documentation

Digital Backup: Electronic copies of critical documents

Are Lab-Created Diamonds a Sustainable Choice?

The sustainability question encompasses environmental impact, ethical production, and long-term resource management, areas where lab-created diamonds demonstrate clear advantages over traditional mining.

Environmental Impact Assessment

Carbon Footprint Analysis:

Lab-Created Diamond Production: Comprehensive lifecycle analysis reveals environmental advantages:

Energy Consumption: 220-330 kWh per carat (varying by production method)

Carbon Emissions: 0.05-0.25 kg CO_2 per carat (depending on energy source)

Renewable Integration: 85% of facilities now using renewable energy sources

Efficiency Trends: 10-15% annual improvement in energy efficiency

Natural Diamond Mining Comparison:

Energy Consumption: 875-1,325 kWh per carat (including extraction and processing)

Carbon Emissions: 2.3-3.6 kg CO_2 per carat (industry average)

Land Disruption: 1,750 tons of earth moved per carat produced

Water Usage: 50-100 million gallons annually per major mine

Resource Conservation:

Material Usage:

Land Use: Lab facilities occupy 5-10 acres vs. thousands for mining operations

Water Consumption: 98% reduction in water usage compared to mining

Waste Generation: Near-zero solid waste through process optimization

Ecosystem Impact: No disruption of natural habitats or wildlife corridors

Renewable Energy Integration: Leading manufacturers demonstrate environmental leadership:

Diamond Foundry: 100% solar-powered production achieving carbon-negative certification

WD Lab Grown: 70% renewable energy with plans for 100% by 2025

Greenlab Diamonds: Solar-integrated production in India supporting grid sustainability

Industry Trends: Rapid adoption of renewable energy across production facilities

Ethical Production Standards

Labor and Human Rights:

Controlled Working Conditions:

Safety Standards: Advanced industrial safety protocols protect workers

Fair Compensation: Competitive wages and comprehensive benefits

Professional Development: Skills training and career advancement opportunities

Community Integration: Positive economic impact on local communities

Supply Chain Transparency:

Complete Traceability: Full documentation from production to consumer

Conflict-Free Guarantee: No association with conflict or exploitation

Regulatory Compliance: Full compliance with labor and environmental regulations

Third-Party Verification: Independent auditing of production facilities and practices

Social Impact:

Community Development:

Local Employment: High-skilled, well-compensated jobs in production communities

Educational Investment: Partnerships with schools and universities

Infrastructure Development: Investment in local infrastructure and services

Economic Multiplier: High-wage jobs supporting broader economic development

Global Impact:

Technology Transfer: Sharing clean production technologies globally

Development Support: Supporting sustainable economic development in emerging markets

Research Investment: Contributing to advancing sustainable manufacturing technologies

Policy Leadership: Advocating sustainable production standards

11.2 Technical and Scientific Questions

What is the Difference Between HPHT and CVD Diamonds?

Understanding the two primary production methods provides insight into the characteristics and applications of different lab-created diamonds.

High-Pressure, High-Temperature (HPHT) Process

Technical Process Description:

Production Methodology: HPHT replicates the natural diamond formation environment:

Pressure Requirements: 5-7 GPa (50,000-70,000 atmospheres)

Temperature Conditions: 1,300-1,600°C (2,372-2,912°F)

Growth Medium: Metallic catalyst (iron, nickel, cobalt) dissolving carbon

Growth Rate: 1-2 carats per week typical production

Equipment and Infrastructure:

Hydraulic Presses: Massive presses generating required pressure

Heating Systems: Precise temperature control throughout growth cycle

Catalyst Management: Careful control of metallic catalyst composition

Safety Systems: Comprehensive safety protocols for high-pressure operations

Characteristic Features:

Quality Characteristics:

Color Range: Natural colorless to yellow, blue through boron doping

Clarity: Good to excellent clarity achievable

Size Capability: Routine production of up to 15 carats, larger sizes possible

Growth Patterns: Cubic or octahedral growth sectors are visible under specialized lighting

Identification Features:

Metallic Inclusions: Minute catalyst inclusions are occasionally present

Fluorescence: Often blue fluorescence, like natural diamonds

Strain Patterns: Cross-hatched strain patterns under polarized light

Magnetic Properties: Slight magnetic attraction in some stones due to metallic inclusions

Chemical Vapor Deposition (CVD) Process

Technical Process Description:

Production Methodology: CVD grows diamonds through chemical deposition.

Pressure Environment: Low pressure (0.1-1 atmosphere)

Temperature Range: 700-1,000°C (1,292-1,832°F)

Gas Composition: Methane and hydrogen mixture

Growth Mechanism: Atomic layer-by-layer deposition

Advanced Technology:

Microwave Plasma: 2.45 GHz microwave energy creates plasma

Gas Purification: Ultra-pure gases prevent contamination

Substrate Control: Precise substrate temperature and positioning

Process Monitoring: Real-time analysis of growth conditions

Characteristic Features:

Quality Characteristics:

Color Achievement: Colorless (Type IIa) most common, fancy colors possible

Clarity Excellence: Often superior clarity due to controlled growth

Size Potential: Large stones routinely achievable (20+ carats demonstrated)

Growth Structure: Layer-by-layer growth creates unique characteristics

Identification Features:

Growth Lines: Parallel growth lines visible under specialized examination

Silicon Content: Trace silicon from the growth process

Strain Patterns: Linear strain patterns following the growth direction

Photoluminescence: Unique luminescence signatures under UV excitation

Comparative Analysis

Quality and Performance Comparison:

Cut Quality Potential:

HPHT Diamonds: Excellent cut quality achievable, may require careful planning around growth sectors

CVD Diamonds: Superior cut quality potential due to controlled growth and minimal stress

Light Performance: Both methods are capable of producing exceptional optical performance

Consistency: CVD is often more consistent due to layer-by-layer controlled growth

Market Applications:

HPHT Stones: Excellent for traditional jewelry applications, fancy colors

CVD Diamonds: Preferred for premium colorless stones, large sizes

Cost Considerations: CVD is typically more cost-effective for larger, higher-quality stones

Availability: Both methods offer good availability across size and quality ranges

How Can You Identify Lab-Created Diamonds?

Professional identification requires sophisticated equipment and expertise, while consumers can rely on documentation and basic indicators.

Professional Identification Methods

Advanced Gemological Testing:

Photoluminescence Spectroscopy: The most definitive identification method:

Growth Method Identification: Distinguishing HPHT from CVD production

Origin Confirmation: Confirming synthetic vs. natural origin

Treatment Detection: Identifying any post-growth treatments

Quality Assessment: Analyzing internal structure and defects

Fourier Transform Infrared (FTIR) Spectroscopy:

Nitrogen Analysis: Detecting nitrogen content and distribution patterns

Defect Characterization: Identifying specific defect centers and concentrations

Type Classification: Determining diamond type (Ia, Ib, IIa, IIb)

Treatment History: Detecting evidence of thermal or irradiation treatments

Specialized Equipment:

DiamondSure and DiamondView: Industry-standard identification instruments:

Automated Screening: Rapid screening of suspected synthetic diamonds

Visual Confirmation: Specialized imaging revealing growth patterns

Documentation: Comprehensive reports supporting identification

Database Integration: Comparison with known synthetic diamond characteristics

Photoluminescence Mapping:

Spatial Analysis: Mapping defect distribution throughout the diamond

Growth Sector Identification: Revealing growth patterns and sectors

Stress Analysis: Detecting internal stress and strain patterns

Quality Evaluation: Assessing overall diamond quality and characteristics

Consumer Identification Strategies

Documentation Verification:

Certificate Authentication: Consumers should verify all documentation.

Laboratory Verification: Confirming certificates through laboratory websites

Report Numbers: Verifying report numbers in laboratory databases

QR Code Scanning: Using QR codes for immediate verification

Professional Consultation: Seeking an independent gemological assessment

Seller Verification:

Dealer Credentials: Verifying seller qualifications and reputation

Return Policies: Ensuring adequate protection through return policies

Professional Network: Working with certified gemologists and appraisers

Reference Checking: Consulting customer reviews and professional references

Basic Physical Indicators:

Visual Characteristics: While not definitive, some characteristics may suggest lab origin:

Exceptional Clarity: Unusually high clarity for the price point

Perfect Color: Consistent color distribution throughout the stone

Size vs. Price: Large stones at unusually affordable prices

Setting Quality: High-quality settings on modestly priced diamonds

Market Context Clues:

Pricing: Significantly below market rates for comparable natural diamonds

Availability: Unusual availability of high-quality large stones

Seller Specialization: Dealers specializing in lab-created diamonds

Marketing Language: Emphasis on ethical, sustainable, or innovative aspects

What Maintenance Do Lab-Created Diamonds Require?

Lab-created diamonds require the same maintenance as natural diamonds, with some potential advantages due to their controlled characteristics.

Daily Care Requirements

Routine Maintenance:

Cleaning Protocols: Regular cleaning maintains optimal appearance.

Daily Cleaning: Quick rinse and dry after exposure to oils or cosmetics

Weekly Deep Clean: Gentle dish soap and soft brush cleaning

Professional Cleaning: Quarterly professional ultrasonic cleaning

Inspection: Regular visual inspection for setting security and damage

Storage Practices:

Individual Storage: Separate storage prevents scratching

Controlled Environment: Stable temperature and humidity conditions

Security: Secure storage protecting against theft or loss

Organization: Systematic organization enabling easy access and inventory

Handling Precautions:

Activity Restrictions:

Physical Activities: Removing jewelry during contact sports or heavy manual work

Chemical Exposure: Avoiding exposure to harsh chemicals and cleaning agents

Temperature Extremes: Protection from extreme temperature changes

Impact Prevention: Careful handling prevents drops and impacts

Professional Services

Inspection and Maintenance:

Annual Professional Inspection:

Setting Security: Checking prongs, bezels, and mounting integrity

Stone Condition: Examining the diamond for chips, scratches, or damage

Wear Assessment: Evaluating normal wear patterns and potential problems

Documentation: Updating condition records and photographic documentation

Specialized Services:

Professional Cleaning: Advanced cleaning techniques and equipment

Repair Services: Professional repair of damaged settings or stones

Restoration: Restoration of older pieces to original condition

Modification: Professional modification or redesign services

Advantages of Lab-Created Diamond Maintenance:

Predictable Characteristics:

Consistent Response: Predictable response to cleaning and maintenance procedures

Reduced Stress: Lower internal stress reduces fracture risk during maintenance

Replacement Availability: Easier replacement of damaged stones

Cost-Effective Service: Lower replacement costs enable more frequent professional service

Are There Different Grades of Lab-Created Diamonds?

Lab-created diamonds are graded using the same criteria as natural diamonds, with some additional considerations specific to synthetic stones.

Standard Grading Criteria

The 4Cs Application:

Cut Grading: Identical standards apply to lab-created diamonds:

Proportions: Same optimal proportion ranges for maximum light performance

Symmetry: Identical symmetry requirements for premium grades

Polish: Same surface finish standards for all grade levels

Performance: Light performance evaluation using the same criteria

Color Grading:

D-Z Scale: Same color scale applied to colorless and near-colorless lab diamonds

Fancy Colors: Specialized grading for fancy colored lab-created diamonds

Consistency: Often superior color consistency in lab-created stones

Stability: Permanent color characteristics identical to natural diamonds

Clarity Grading:

Inclusion Types: Different inclusion types, but same clarity impact assessment

Grading Standards: Identical magnification and assessment criteria

Grade Distribution: Often a higher percentage of high clarity grades in lab diamonds

Consistency: More predictable clarity characteristics

Carat Weight:

Measurement Standards: Identical precision requirements and measurement protocols

Size Availability: Enhanced availability in larger sizes

Weight Distribution: More flexible size availability than natural diamonds

Custom Sizing: Ability to grow diamonds to specific weight requirements

Lab-Specific Quality Considerations

Additional Quality Factors:

Growth Method Quality:

HPHT Quality: Specific quality characteristics of HPHT production

CVD Quality: Unique quality features of CVD production methods

Process Optimization: Influence of production parameters on final quality

Consistency: Superior consistency compared to natural diamond quality variation

Treatment Disclosure:

Post-Growth Treatments: Documentation of any treatments or enhancements

Stability: Permanence and stability of treated characteristics

Detection: Ability to detect and verify treatment history

Market Impact: Effect of treatments on value and marketability

Quality Premium Development:

Brand Differentiation:

Manufacturer Brands: Quality premiums for established lab diamond brands

Production Standards: Higher standards commanding quality premiums

Certification Levels: Premium pricing for superior certification and documentation

Performance Excellence: Quality premiums for exceptional cut and light performance

The comprehensive understanding provided by these frequently asked questions enables consumers to make informed decisions based on accurate information rather than misconceptions or incomplete knowledge. Lab-created diamonds represent a legitimate, high-quality choice in the diamond market, offering advantages in ethics, sustainability, value, and often in technical quality characteristics.

As the market continues maturing and consumer understanding deepens, these questions and their answers serve as a foundation for confident decision-making, whether for engagement rings, fashion jewelry, or any other application where the beauty and symbolism of diamonds enhance life's most meaningful moments.

***

In the constellation of knowledge surrounding lab-created diamonds, each question answered becomes a star illuminating the path to understanding. Through inquiry and education, we transform uncertainty into confidence, misconception into truth, and hesitation into informed action, enabling choices that reflect both wisdom and values.

Chapter 12: Conclusion and Final Thoughts

"At the end of every journey lies a new beginning. In understanding lab-created diamonds, we have not merely learned about gems, but discovered a reflection of humanity's capacity to create beauty, honor ethics, and shape a future where luxury and conscience unite in perfect harmony."

12.1 Summary of Key Points

The Revolution We've Witnessed

Throughout this comprehensive exploration, we have traced the remarkable transformation of the diamond industry. This transformation extends far beyond technology into the realms of ethics, sustainability, and human values. Lab-created diamonds represent more than an alternative to natural stones; they embody a fundamental shift in how we define luxury, value, and responsible consumption in the 21st century.

Scientific Achievement and Technical Mastery

The journey from the first industrial synthetic diamonds in the 1950s to today's gem-quality marvels represents one of humanity's greatest achievements in materials science. We have witnessed how two primary technologies—High-Pressure High-Temperature (HPHT) and Chemical Vapor Deposition (CVD)—have evolved to replicate and often surpass nature's billion-year process in mere weeks.

Technological Milestones:

Perfect Replication: Achieving diamonds chemically, physically, and optically identical to natural stones

Quality Enhancement: Producing diamonds with superior clarity and consistency

Scale Achievement: Routine production of large, gem-quality stones previously reserved for the ultra-wealthy

Innovation Leadership: Advancing technologies that benefit multiple industries beyond jewelry

The controlled environment of modern laboratories enables the creation of diamonds that are not mere imitations but genuine improvements upon nature's template—stones with fewer inclusions, more predictable characteristics, and optimized optical performance.

Ethical and Environmental Leadership

Perhaps the most compelling aspect of the lab-created diamond revolution lies in its ethical implications. We have explored how these diamonds offer a solution to centuries-old problems in the diamond industry:

Environmental Transformation:

Carbon Footprint: 75-85% reduction in carbon emissions compared to mining

Land Preservation: Eliminating the need to disturb thousands of acres for each carat produced

Water Conservation: 98% reduction in water consumption through closed-loop production systems

Renewable Integration: Leading manufacturers are achieving carbon-negative production through solar and wind power

Social Responsibility:

Conflict-Free Guarantee: Complete elimination of association with violence and exploitation

Supply Chain Transparency: Full traceability from production to consumer

Labor Standards: Advanced industrial working conditions with fair compensation and professional development

Community Investment: High-skilled employment and community development in production regions

Economic Democratization

The economic implications of lab-created diamonds extend beyond simple cost savings to fundamental changes in who can access diamond luxury:

Value Proposition Revolution:

Accessibility: Premium quality diamonds available to broader consumer segments

Quality Optimization: Ability to maximize size and quality within any budget

Choice Enhancement: Freedom to prioritize personal preferences over budget constraints

Investment Wisdom: Smart allocation of resources enabling other life priorities

This democratization has transformed diamonds from symbols of exclusive wealth to expressions of informed choice and value consciousness.

Market Transformation and Consumer Evolution

Generational Shifts in Luxury Consumption

Our analysis has revealed how different generations approach lab-created diamonds, reflecting broader changes in consumer values:

Generation Z and Millennials: Leading adoption through prioritization of sustainability, ethics, and value optimization over traditional status symbols. These consumers view lab-created diamonds not as compromises, but as superior choices that align with their values.

Generation X and Baby Boomers: Gradually embracing lab-created diamonds through appreciation of practical advantages and quality benefits, demonstrating that the appeal transcends generational boundaries.

Geographic Market Development

The global expansion of lab-created diamond acceptance demonstrates universal appeal:

North American Leadership: Pioneering market acceptance through technological appreciation and environmental consciousness, with 22% market penetration and growing.

European Sophistication: Driving adoption through sustainability priorities and ethical luxury consumption, with strong regulatory support for environmentally responsible products.

Asia-Pacific Growth: Rapid expansion driven by technological advancement, appreciation and changing cultural attitudes toward luxury, particularly among urban young professionals.

Quality and Grading Excellence

The comprehensive examination of quality factors reveals how lab-created diamonds often exceed natural diamond standards:

The 4Cs Mastery:

Cut: Superior cut quality achievable through cost-effective precision

Color: Consistent colorless achievement and innovative fancy colors

Clarity: Higher clarity grades through controlled growth environments

Carat: Large sizes are readily available without exponential cost increases

Certification Standards: Major gemological institutions apply identical grading criteria while developing specialized expertise in lab-created diamond assessment.

12.2 Making an Informed Decision

Framework for Decision-Making

Having explored every aspect of lab-created diamonds—from their atomic structure to their global market impact—we can distill the decision-making process into a clear framework that honors both rational analysis and personal values.

Values Alignment Assessment

The first step in any informed decision involves understanding your own priorities and values:

Ethical Considerations: If environmental sustainability and social responsibility matter to you, lab-created diamonds offer clear advantages. The complete elimination of mining-related environmental damage and human rights concerns provides peace of mind that traditional diamond purchasing cannot guarantee.

Financial Wisdom: For those prioritizing value optimization and financial intelligence, lab-created diamonds enable the purchase of larger, higher-quality stones while preserving resources for other life priorities. This is not about cutting corners but about maximizing the return on investment in beauty and symbolism.

Quality Appreciation: If technical excellence and consistent quality appeal to you, lab-created diamonds often provide superior characteristics through controlled production environments and advanced manufacturing techniques.

Innovation Celebration: For those who appreciate human achievement and technological advancement, lab-created diamonds represent the pinnacle of materials science applied to creating beauty.

Practical Decision Criteria

Budget Optimization Strategies

Understanding how to allocate your diamond budget effectively:

Quality Maximization Approach: With lab-created diamonds, focus on achieving the highest possible quality within your budget rather than meeting arbitrary spending targets. The 70-85% cost savings enable dramatic improvements in size, color, or clarity.

Portfolio Approach: Consider purchasing a complete jewelry wardrobe rather than a single piece. The accessibility of lab-created diamonds enables coordination of engagement rings, wedding bands, earrings, and necklaces within traditional single-piece budgets.

Future Flexibility: The affordability of lab-created diamonds preserves financial flexibility for other life priorities—such as home purchases, travel, education, or family planning—without sacrificing jewelry quality or beauty.

Quality Selection Guidelines

For Engagement Rings: Prioritize cut quality above all other factors. The superior light performance of an excellently cut lab-created diamond will provide more beauty than modest improvements in color or clarity. Consider:

Cut Grade: Excellent or Ideal cut for maximum brilliance

Size: Optimize for visual impact within your aesthetic preferences

Setting: Invest savings in premium settings that showcase the diamond beautifully

For fashion jewelry, take advantage of the consistency of lab-created diamonds to create matching sets and coordinate pieces. The predictable quality enables confident purchase of multiple pieces with a consistent appearance.

For an Investment Perspective: While lab-created diamonds serve primarily as personal luxury items, focus on quality characteristics that maintain value, such as a superior cut, good size, and established brand recognition.

Long-Term Satisfaction Considerations

Emotional and Symbolic Value

The most important aspect of any diamond purchase involves its emotional significance and symbolic meaning:

Personal Meaning: Lab-created diamonds possess the same capacity for emotional significance. They represent love, commitment, achievement, and celebration with the added dimensions of environmental consciousness and ethical responsibility.

Legacy Considerations: These diamonds offer the opportunity to create family heirlooms that tell stories of wisdom, values, and responsible choice—legacies that future generations can admire not only for their beauty but for their ethical origins.

Lifestyle Integration: Consider how your diamond choice reflects your overall lifestyle and values. Lab-created diamonds integrate seamlessly with contemporary values of sustainability, intelligence, and conscious consumption.

12.3 The Future of Diamond Luxury

Technological Horizon

Advancing Production Technologies

The rapid pace of technological development promises even more exciting developments:

Next-Generation Manufacturing:

Quantum Control: Atomic-level precision in diamond creation

Custom Properties: Diamonds engineered for specific applications and characteristics

Rapid Production: Dramatically reduced production times through technological advancement

Perfect Quality: Approaching theoretical perfection in diamond characteristics

Industrial Applications: Lab-created diamonds increasingly serve critical roles in quantum computing, advanced electronics, space technology, and medical devices—applications that leverage their controlled perfection for revolutionary technological advancement.

Market Evolution Predictions

Consumer Adoption Trajectories: Conservative projections suggest lab-created diamonds will comprise 30-35% of the diamond market by 2030, with optimistic scenarios reaching 45% market share. This growth reflects not just cost considerations but fundamental shifts in consumer values.

Quality and Availability: Continued improvement in production technologies will enhance quality while reducing costs, making premium lab-created diamonds increasingly accessible to broader consumer segments.

Innovation Integration: Smart jewelry concepts, incorporating technology into lab-created diamond designs, will blur the boundaries between traditional luxury goods and modern technological products.

Cultural Integration and Acceptance

Luxury Redefinition

The broader cultural shift toward conscious consumption positions lab-created diamonds at the forefront of evolving luxury definitions:

Conscious Luxury Movement: Modern luxury is increasingly emphasizing sustainability, ethics, and intelligence, rather than exclusivity based on scarcity or cost. Lab-created diamonds perfectly embody these new standards of luxury.

Generational Influence: As younger generations reach peak earning and spending years, their preference for ethical and sustainable products will drive mainstream adoption of lab-created diamonds across all market segments.

Professional and Social Acceptance: Growing acceptance in professional, social, and cultural contexts removes barriers to adoption while enhancing the desirability of lab-created diamonds.

Global Impact and Responsibility

Environmental Leadership

The lab-created diamond industry demonstrates how technology can solve rather than exacerbate environmental challenges:

Carbon Neutrality Achievement: Leading manufacturers achieving carbon-negative production establish new standards for luxury goods manufacturing across industries.

Resource Conservation: The dramatic reduction in land, water, and energy usage provides a model for sustainable luxury production that other industries are beginning to emulate.

Innovation Inspiration: The success of lab-created diamonds in combining luxury with sustainability inspires similar innovations across multiple luxury goods categories.

Social Transformation

Economic Development: Lab-created diamond production generates high-skilled, well-compensated employment in technology-focused communities, rather than in resource extraction regions.

Educational Investment: The high-technology nature of lab diamond production supports educational infrastructure and technical training programs, contributing to community development.

Ethical Standards: The complete transparency and ethical production standards of lab-created diamonds establish new benchmarks for responsible luxury goods manufacturing.

12.4 Personal Reflection and Future Choices

The Decision That Reflects Your Values

As we conclude this comprehensive exploration, the choice between natural and lab-created diamonds transcends simple preference to become a reflection of personal values and vision for the future. This decision communicates your priorities: sustainability over tradition, innovation over convention, wisdom over conformity.

Beyond the Transaction

Purchasing a lab-created diamond represents participation in a larger movement toward responsible consumption and technological innovation. It demonstrates confidence in human ingenuity and a commitment to a sustainable future, while achieving beauty and symbolism that rival nature's finest achievements.

Personal Legacy: Your choice not only influences your own satisfaction but also contributes to market dynamics that support continued innovation and environmental responsibility. Each purchase becomes a vote for the kind of world you wish to create.

Educational Opportunity: Owning lab-created diamonds offers opportunities to educate others about technological advancements, environmental responsibility, and the evolution of luxury consumption—sharing knowledge that benefits the broader society.

Future Generations: The heirlooms you create today will tell stories of wisdom, responsibility, and conscious choice that future family members can admire and emulate.

The Continuing Journey

Ongoing Learning and Adaptation

The lab-created diamond market continues evolving rapidly, requiring ongoing education and adaptation:

Market Development: Stay informed about technological advancements, market trends, and emerging opportunities in the lab-created diamond sector.

Care and Maintenance: Maintain your lab-created diamonds with the same care and attention you would provide to any precious possession, ensuring their beauty endures for generations.

Community Engagement: Share your knowledge and experience with others, including lab-created diamonds, to contribute to the broader education and acceptance of these remarkable gems.

The Ripple Effect of Conscious Choice

Your decision to choose lab-created diamonds extends beyond personal satisfaction to influence:

Industry Transformation: Supporting continued innovation and improvement in sustainable luxury production methods.

Environmental Progress: Contributing to reduced environmental impact in luxury goods manufacturing.

Social Change: Demonstrating that ethical considerations can guide luxury consumption without sacrificing beauty or satisfaction.

Cultural Evolution: Participating in the redefinition of luxury for the 21st century and beyond.

Final Reflections

The Beauty of Informed Choice

In choosing lab-created diamonds, you join a community of informed consumers who refuse to accept false choices between beauty and ethics, luxury and sustainability, tradition, and innovation. You demonstrate that it is possible to honor the past while embracing the future, to celebrate love and commitment while protecting the planet, to enjoy luxury while maintaining conscience.

The Promise of Tomorrow

Lab-created diamonds represent more than technological achievement—they embody hope for a future where human creativity and responsibility unite to create solutions that benefit everyone. They prove that we need not choose between beauty and ethics, between luxury and sustainability, between personal satisfaction and global responsibility.

Your Sparkling Future

As you move forward with your newfound knowledge and understanding, remember that you carry more than information—you carry the power to make choices that reflect your highest values and aspirations. Whether you choose lab-created diamonds for their beauty, their ethics, their value, or their innovation, you decide to be part of a story larger than yourself—a story of human progress, environmental responsibility, and the endless capacity for creating beauty in harmony with conscience.

The diamonds you choose will catch light and cast rainbows for generations to come. Still, they will also reflect something even more precious: the wisdom to choose beauty without compromise, luxury without guilt, and brilliance that shines not only from the stone but from the values it represents.

Welcome to the future of diamonds. Welcome to the brilliance of conscious choice. Welcome to a world where every sparkle tells a story of hope, responsibility, and the unlimited potential that emerges when human ingenuity meets human conscience.

In this new era of diamond luxury, you are not merely a consumer, you are a pioneer, a leader, and a guardian of values that will illuminate the path for generations to come. The choice is yours, and the future is brilliant.

***

Ultimately, we discover that the most precious gems are not those that cost the most or took the longest to form, but rather those that align with our highest aspirations and deepest values. Lab-created diamonds offer us the extraordinary gift of beauty without compromise, reflecting not just light, but the luminous potential within each of us to create a better world, one conscious choice at a time.

May your diamonds shine as brightly as your convictions, sparkle as brilliantly as your hopes, and endure as eternally as the values they represent. The future of luxury is in your hands, and it has never been more beautiful.

Chapter 13: Global Perspectives and Regulations

"In the tapestry of global commerce, lab-created diamonds weave new patterns of possibility, where international boundaries become bridges, regulations become roadmaps, and diverse markets unite in appreciation of innovation, ethics, and beauty."

13.1 International Markets

Country-Specific Market Analysis

The global landscape for lab-created diamonds reveals a complex mosaic of cultural preferences, economic factors, regulatory environments, and technological adoption patterns. Understanding these regional variations provides crucial insights for consumers, investors, and industry participants navigating this rapidly evolving international market.

North American Markets: Innovation Leadership

United States: The Pioneer Market

The United States has emerged as the global leader in the adoption of lab-created diamonds, driven by a unique combination of technological appreciation, environmental consciousness, and value-oriented consumption patterns.

Market Characteristics:

Penetration Rate: 24% of the total diamond market by volume, 12% by value

Growth Trajectory: Sustained 18% annual growth for five consecutive years

Consumer Demographics: 67% millennials and Gen Z, average household income $75,000-$150,000

Quality Preferences: Strong preference for colorless (D-F) and high clarity (VVS-VS) grades

Regional Variations Within the US: West Coast Leadership:

California: 31% market penetration, leading in environmental consciousness

Technology Sector Influence: Silicon Valley professionals driving adoption through tech appreciation

Innovation Acceptance: Early adoption of new technologies and sustainable products

Premium Market Development: Willingness to pay premiums for superior quality and ethical sourcing

East Coast Sophistication:

New York: 28% penetration, driven by fashion and luxury market awareness

Professional Adoption: Finance and legal professionals embracing value propositions

Cultural Influence: Manhattan's jewelry district increasingly features lab-created options

Educational Integration: Gemological Institute of America headquarters supporting education

Central Region Growth:

Traditional Markets: 19% penetration in traditionally conservative markets

Value Orientation: Strong appreciation for practical benefits and cost savings

Family Considerations: Decisions influenced by family financial planning priorities

Religious Integration: Growing acceptance within faith-based communities emphasizing stewardship

Market Drivers:

Environmental Consciousness: 89% of buyers cite environmental considerations

Value Optimization: 76% motivated by the ability to purchase larger/higher quality stones

Ethical Concerns: 82% prioritize conflict-free sourcing

Technology Appreciation: 68% attracted to innovation and manufacturing precision

Canada: Environmental Leadership

Canadian consumers demonstrate the world's strongest environmental motivations for lab-created diamond purchases:

Market Characteristics:

Penetration Rate: 21% of the total diamond market

Environmental Priority: 94% cite environmental factors as primary motivation

Quality Standards: Highest average clarity and color grade preferences globally

Professional Consultation: 89% seek gemological expertise before purchase

Unique Canadian Factors:

Natural Resource Awareness: Deep understanding of mining's environmental impact

Indigenous Considerations: Respect for traditional lands influences consumer choices

Regulatory Environment: Strong environmental regulations support sustainable options

Educational Infrastructure: Comprehensive consumer education through government and industry programs

European Market Sophistication

United Kingdom: Ethical Jewelry Movement

The UK market demonstrates a sophisticated understanding of ethical jewelry principles and sustainable luxury consumption:

Consumer Characteristics:

Market Penetration: 18% of total diamond purchases

Ethical Priority: 91% prioritize ethical sourcing over traditional luxury markers

Vintage Integration: 69% pair lab diamonds with vintage or vintage-inspired settings

Quality Education: High levels of gemological knowledge among consumers

Cultural Influences:

Royal Family Impact: Growing acceptance of sustainable luxury choices

Media Coverage: Extensive favorable coverage of lab-created diamonds in British media

Fashion Leadership: The London fashion industry embracing sustainable luxury

Academic Integration: University research supporting consumer education

Germany: Technology and Precision

German consumers' appreciation for engineering excellence and technological innovation drives adoption:

Market Development:

Penetration Rate: 19% of the diamond market

Technology Focus: Strong appreciation for manufacturing precision and innovation

Quality Standards: Demanding quality standards driving premium segment growth

Industrial Heritage: Manufacturing background supporting understanding of production excellence

Unique Characteristics:

Engineering Appreciation: Technical understanding of production methods

Environmental Regulations: EU environmental standards supporting sustainable choices

Consumer Protection: A Strong regulatory framework builds consumer confidence

Educational Approach: Systematic consumer education through trade organizations

France: Luxury Integration

The French market emphasizes craftsmanship, design, and the integration of lab-created diamonds into haute couture jewelry:

Market Characteristics:

Penetration Rate: 14% of the luxury jewelry market

Design Focus: Emphasis on artistic design and craftsmanship over stone origin

Luxury Integration: High-end ateliers incorporating lab diamonds into exclusive pieces

Cultural Acceptance: Growing acceptance within French luxury culture

Distinctive Features:

Artisan Collaboration: Master jewelers working with lab-created diamonds

Fashion Week Integration: Lab diamonds featured in Paris Fashion Week jewelry presentations

Heritage Brands: Traditional maisons beginning to offer lab-created options

Cultural Evolution: Gradual shift from tradition-focused to innovation-appreciating luxury

Scandinavia: Sustainability Leadership

Nordic countries lead global sustainability initiatives, with lab-created diamonds aligning perfectly with environmental values:

Regional Overview:

Average Penetration: 23% across Denmark, Sweden, Norway, and Finland

Environmental Leadership: The World's highest environmental consciousness in luxury purchases

Government Support: Policy support for sustainable luxury goods

Consumer Education: Comprehensive public education about sustainable choices

Country-Specific Patterns: Denmark:

Design Integration: Danish design philosophy embracing sustainable luxury

Quality Focus: Emphasis on quality and longevity over quantity

Innovation Acceptance: Early adoption of innovative, sustainable products

Sweden:

Environmental Regulation: Strongest environmental standards driving market preferences

Consumer Awareness: Highest levels of environmental education and awareness

Technology Appreciation: Strong appreciation for clean technology and innovation

Asia-Pacific: Rapid Growth Markets

China: Manufacturing and Consumption Hub

China presents unique dynamics as both the world's largest producer and fastest-growing consumer market for lab-created diamonds:

Market Development:

Penetration Rate: 16% overall, 28% among consumers under 30

Production Advantage: Domestic production reduces costs and improves availability

E-commerce Leadership: 78% of lab diamond sales through digital channels

Cultural Evolution: Shift from tradition-focused to innovation-appreciating consumption

Generational Differences: Generation Z and Millennials:

Technology Appreciation: 92% view lab diamonds as a technological achievement

Environmental Consciousness: Growing awareness of sustainability issues

Value Orientation: Strong appreciation for practical benefits and quality

Social Media Influence: WeChat and Weibo are driving awareness and acceptance

Traditional Consumers:

Gradual Acceptance: Slowly warming to lab-created options

Quality Focus: Emphasis on certification and gemological verification

Family Considerations: Decisions influenced by family approval and acceptance

Investment Perspective: Viewing purchases as long-term investments

Regional Variations: Tier 1 Cities (Beijing, Shanghai, Shenzhen):

Market Penetration: 22% in major metropolitan areas

Professional Adoption: Technology sector professionals leading adoption

Luxury Integration: High-end retailers adding lab-created diamond collections

International Influence: Exposure to global trends driving acceptance

Tier 2 and 3 Cities:

Emerging Adoption: 12% penetration in smaller cities

Price Sensitivity: Strong value consciousness driving interest

Education Needs: Greater need for consumer education and awareness

Growth Potential: Significant untapped market opportunity

Japan: Quality and Innovation Focus

Japanese consumers demonstrate appreciation for technological excellence, precision manufacturing, and innovation:

Market Characteristics:

Penetration Rate: 18% of the luxury jewelry market

Quality Standards: The World's highest cut quality preferences

Brand Consciousness: Strong preference for established, reputable brands

Technology Appreciation: Celebration of manufacturing precision and innovation

Cultural Factors:

Craftsmanship Appreciation: Deep respect for manufacturing excellence and precision

Innovation Acceptance: Openness to technological advancement and improvement

Quality Investment: Willingness to pay premiums for superior quality

Environmental Awareness: Growing consciousness of environmental impact

India: Production Center Evolution

India's role as a major diamond cutting and polishing center influences domestic market development:

Market Dynamics:

Penetration Rate: 12% of the domestic market

Industry Familiarity: High awareness due to diamond industry presence

Price Sensitivity: Strong value consciousness driving lab diamond adoption

Cultural Integration: Gradual integration with traditional jewelry preferences

Unique Considerations:

Production Expertise: Technical knowledge supporting consumer confidence

Traditional Values: Balance between innovation and cultural traditions

Economic Factors: A Growing middle class driving market expansion

Export Market Influence: International market trends affecting domestic preferences

Australia: Environmental Consciousness

Australian consumers combine environmental awareness with appreciation for innovation and quality:

Market Characteristics:

Penetration Rate: 20% of the diamond market

Environmental Priority: Strong focus on sustainable and ethical choices

Quality Appreciation: High standards for cut quality and certification

Innovation Acceptance: Openness to technological advancement and improvement

13.2 Import/Export Regulations

International Trade Classification

The global trade in lab-created diamonds operates within complex regulatory frameworks that continue evolving as markets mature and governments develop specific policies for synthetic gemstones.

Harmonized System Codes and Classification

Current Classification Challenges:

Existing HS Code Structure: Most countries currently classify lab-created diamonds under existing natural diamond codes, creating challenges for:

Statistical Tracking: Difficulty in monitoring market growth and trade patterns

Duty Assessment: Inconsistent tariff treatment across jurisdictions

Market Analysis: Limited ability to analyze lab-created diamond trade flows

Policy Development: Challenges in developing targeted policies and regulations

Emerging Classification Systems: Several countries are developing specific codes for lab-created diamonds:

United States:

Proposed Codes: Development of specific HS codes for synthetic diamonds

Industry Consultation: Ongoing consultation with industry stakeholders

Implementation Timeline: Projected implementation within 2-3 years

Impact Assessment: Analysis of trade and industry implications

European Union:

Harmonized Approach: Development of EU-wide classification system

Member State Coordination: Coordination among EU member countries

Industry Integration: Integration with existing jewelry trade regulations

Consumer Protection: Focus on consumer disclosure and protection

China:

Production Classification: Specific codes for domestic production and export

Quality Categories: Classification by quality grades and intended use

Export Promotion: Codes supporting export promotion policies

Statistical Monitoring: Enhanced monitoring of production and trade flows

Taxation Considerations

Value-Added Tax (VAT) and Sales Tax

Regional VAT Treatment:

European Union VAT Policies: Lab-created diamonds generally receive same VAT treatment as natural diamonds:

Standard Rates: Standard VAT rates (19-25% depending on member state)

Luxury Classification: Treatment as luxury goods in most jurisdictions

Cross-Border Trade: Harmonized treatment for intra-EU trade

Exemption Criteria: Limited exemptions for specific applications or circumstances

United States Sales Tax: State-by-state variation in sales tax treatment:

State Variations: Sales tax rates vary from 0% to 13% depending on state and locality

Luxury Tax: Some states impose additional luxury taxes on high-value jewelry

Online Sales: Evolving regulations for e-commerce sales across state lines

Business Purchases: Exemptions for business purchases and resale

Import Duties and Tariffs:

Current Tariff Structure: Most countries apply similar duty rates to lab-created and natural diamonds:

US Tariff Rates: Generally 0-5% for finished jewelry, varying by product category

EU Tariff Rates: 2.5-6.5% for jewelry products, with preferences for developing countries

Asian Markets: Varying rates from 0% (Singapore) to 15% (India) depending on trade agreements

Preferential Treatment: Some countries developing preferential treatment for sustainable products

Future Tariff Development: Several trends are emerging in tariff policy:

Sustainability Preferences: Potential preferential treatment for environmentally sustainable products

Technology Promotion: Support for advanced manufacturing technologies

Bilateral Agreements: Lab-created diamonds included in future trade agreements

Carbon Border Adjustments: Potential carbon-based tariff adjustments favoring low-emission production

Legal Framework Differences

Consumer Protection Laws

Disclosure Requirements:

United States FTC Guidelines: The Federal Trade Commission has established comprehensive guidelines:

Clear Disclosure: Requirement for precise identification of lab-created origin

Prohibited Terms: Restrictions on misleading terminology

Marketing Standards: Guidelines for advertising and promotional materials

Enforcement: Active enforcement through investigation and penalties

European Consumer Protection: EU directives establish consumer protection standards:

Material Information: Lab-created origin is considered material information requiring disclosure

Language Requirements: Disclosure in local languages for all EU markets

Digital Commerce: Specific requirements for online sales and marketing

Complaint Mechanisms: Established procedures for consumer complaints and resolution

Certification and Authentication:

International Standards Development: Various organizations are developing standards for lab-created diamonds:

ISO Standards:

Production Standards: ISO 17034 for reference materials and quality control

Testing Methods: ISO 11426 for jewelry testing and certification

Environmental Standards: ISO 14001 for environmental management systems

Quality Management: ISO 9001 for quality management in production

Industry Standards:

CIBJO Guidelines: International Confederation of Jewelry guidelines for lab-created diamonds

World Jewellery Confederation: Standards for disclosure and terminology

Regional Associations: National and regional industry association standards

Laboratory Standards: Standards for gemological laboratories and certification

13.3 Future Regulatory Trends

Environmental Regulations Impact

The global trend toward environmental regulation is increasingly favoring lab-created diamonds, with several regulatory developments supporting the production of sustainable luxury goods.

Carbon Disclosure and Reporting

Mandatory Environmental Reporting:

European Union Sustainability Reporting: The EU's Corporate Sustainability Reporting Directive (CSRD) impacts luxury goods companies:

Scope 1, 2, 3 Emissions: Comprehensive reporting of direct, indirect, and supply chain emissions

Product Lifecycle Assessment: Requirement for full lifecycle environmental impact analysis

Supply Chain Due Diligence: Mandatory assessment of supply chain environmental impacts

Consumer Information: Requirements for environmental impact disclosure to consumers

Implementation Timeline:

Large Companies: 2024 implementation for companies with >500 employees

Medium Companies: 2025 implementation for companies with >250 employees

Listed Companies: 2026 implementation for all listed companies

Global Impact: Requirements affecting all companies operating in EU markets

Carbon Pricing and Border Adjustments:

EU Carbon Border Adjustment Mechanism (CBAM): While initially focused on heavy industry, CBAM may expand to luxury goods:

Phase 1 (2023-2026): Transitional period with reporting requirements

Phase 2 (2027+): Financial obligations based on carbon content

Scope Expansion: Potential inclusion of luxury goods and jewelry

Competitive Advantage: Potential benefits for low-carbon production methods

National Carbon Pricing: Various countries are implementing carbon pricing that may affect luxury goods:

Carbon Taxes: Direct taxes on carbon emissions affect production costs

Cap-and-Trade: Market mechanisms for pricing carbon emissions

Product Labeling: Requirements for carbon footprint labeling on luxury goods

Consumer Incentives: Potential incentives for low-carbon luxury purchases

Technology and Innovation Support

Government Innovation Policies

Research and Development Support:

United States Innovation Programs: Federal and state programs supporting advanced manufacturing:

Manufacturing USA: National network supporting advanced manufacturing technologies

SBIR/STTR Programs: Small Business Innovation Research supporting lab diamond technology

State Incentives: State-level incentives for high-tech manufacturing facilities

Tax Credits: R&D tax credits supporting innovation in synthetic diamond production

European Innovation Framework: EU programs supporting sustainable technology development:

Horizon Europe: €95 billion research and innovation program, including materials science

Green Deal: European Green Deal supporting sustainable technology development

Digital Strategy: Digital technology integration supporting Industry 4.0 applications

Regional Funds: Structural funds supporting technology development in member states

Intellectual Property Protection:

Patent System Evolution: Patent systems adapting to synthetic diamond innovations:

Process Patents: Protection for innovative production methods

Quality Control: Patents for advanced quality control and testing methods

Application Patents: Patents for new applications and uses of lab-created diamonds

International Coordination: Coordination among patent offices for global protection

Consumer Protection Enhancement

Enhanced Disclosure Requirements

Global Disclosure Standards:

International Coordination: Growing coordination among regulators for consistent disclosure standards:

Terminology Harmonization: Consistent terminology across jurisdictions

Disclosure Methods: Standardized methods for origin disclosure

Digital Integration: QR codes and digital certificates for verification

Consumer Education: Coordinated consumer education programs

Emerging Requirements: New disclosure requirements under development:

Environmental Impact: Disclosure of environmental footprint and production methods

Supply Chain: Complete supply chain transparency from production to retail

Quality Metrics: Standardized quality metrics and performance data

Lifecycle Information: Information about care, maintenance, and end-of-life options

Anti-Fraud Measures:

Enhanced Authentication: Regulatory support for authentication and anti-fraud measures:

Blockchain Integration: Support for blockchain-based provenance tracking

Advanced Testing: Standards for advanced gemological testing and identification

Database Integration: International databases for certificate verification

Penalty Enhancement: Increased penalties for fraud and misrepresentation

Trade Policy Evolution

Bilateral and Multilateral Agreements

Future Trade Agreement Integration:

Comprehensive Trade Agreements: Lab-created diamonds are increasingly included in trade negotiations.

USMCA: North American trade agreement, including provisions for synthetic products

CPTPP: Trans-Pacific Partnership addressing technology transfer and innovation

EU Trade Agreements: Bilateral agreements including sustainable technology provisions

Asian Integration: RCEP and other Asian agreements supporting technology trade

Preferential Treatment Development: Potential preferential treatment for sustainable products:

Environmental Preferences: Trade preferences for environmentally sustainable products

Technology Transfer: Provisions supporting clean technology transfer and development

Capacity Building: Support for developing country participation in sustainable luxury markets

Standards Harmonization: Coordination of standards and certification across trading partners

Regional Integration:

Economic Integration Zones: Regional economic zones supporting lab-created diamond trade:

ASEAN: Southeast Asian integration supporting technology transfer and trade

African Continental Free Trade Area: Potential for sustainable luxury goods development

Latin American Integration: Regional coordination supporting sustainable development

Middle East Cooperation: Gulf Cooperation Council policies supporting diversification

Regulatory Compliance Strategies

Best Practices for Market Participants

Compliance Framework Development:

Multi-Jurisdictional Compliance: Strategies for compliance across multiple regulatory environments:

Legal Coordination: Coordination with legal experts in multiple jurisdictions

Documentation Systems: Comprehensive documentation supporting compliance requirements

Training Programs: Staff training on regulatory requirements and compliance procedures

Monitoring Systems: Systems for monitoring regulatory changes and updates

Proactive Engagement: Industry engagement with regulatory development:

Industry Associations: Participation in industry associations and standard-setting bodies

Regulatory Consultation: Engagement with regulatory consultation processes

Expert Networks: Development of networks with regulatory and legal experts

Best Practice Sharing: Sharing of best practices and compliance strategies

Consumer Protection Integration:

Transparency Systems: Implementation of comprehensive transparency systems:

Supply Chain Tracking: Complete supply chain documentation and tracking

Quality Assurance: Comprehensive quality assurance and certification programs

Consumer Education: Ongoing consumer education and information programs

Feedback Systems: Systems for consumer feedback and complaint resolution

The global regulatory landscape for lab-created diamonds continues evolving rapidly, with most trends favoring transparency, sustainability, and consumer protection. As markets mature and regulations evolve, lab-created diamonds are increasingly recognized as legitimate, valuable, and environmentally responsible alternatives to traditional mining methods.

The regulatory environment supports continued growth and acceptance of lab-created diamonds while establishing frameworks that protect consumers and promote fair competition. This regulatory support, combined with technological advancement and changing consumer preferences, positions lab-created diamonds for continued expansion in global markets.

Understanding and navigating this complex regulatory environment requires ongoing attention to legal developments, proactive compliance strategies, and engagement with regulatory processes. For consumers, these developments provide increasing confidence in the legitimacy and value of lab-created diamonds, while ensuring protection against fraud and misrepresentation.

***

In the global marketplace of ideas and innovation, lab-created diamonds serve as ambassadors of progress, crossing borders not just as products but as symbols of humanity's capacity to create beauty while honoring responsibility. As regulations evolve to accommodate this new reality, we witness the transformation of not just trade policies but values themselves, enshrined in law and practice across the world.

Chapter 14: Technology Integration and Future Trends

"At the convergence of silicon and carbon, where algorithms meet atoms and innovation embraces tradition, we stand witness to a revolution that transforms not merely how diamonds are made, but how beauty itself evolves in harmony with the digital age."

14.1 Digital Integration

Blockchain for Authenticity Verification

The diamond industry has long struggled with issues of provenance, authenticity, and consumer confidence. Blockchain technology offers revolutionary solutions to these challenges, with lab-created diamonds leading the adoption of distributed ledger systems that provide immutable records of origin, quality, and ownership history.

Understanding Blockchain in the Diamond Context

Fundamental Blockchain Principles:

Blockchain technology creates permanent, unalterable records through distributed consensus mechanisms:

Immutable Record Creation:

Genesis Block: Initial record created at diamond growth or certification

Transaction History: Every subsequent handling, testing, or transfer is permanently recorded

Cryptographic Security: Mathematical protection preventing fraud or record alteration

Distributed Verification: Multiple parties confirming record authenticity independently

Smart Contract Integration: Advanced blockchain implementations utilize smart contracts for automated processes:

Automated Verification: Contracts automatically execute when predetermined conditions are met

Quality Assurance: Smart contracts ensure quality standards are maintained throughout the supply chain

Payment Systems: Automated payments triggered by delivery confirmation and verification

Compliance Monitoring: Automatic alerts for potential compliance violations or irregularities

Lab-Created Diamond Advantages:

Lab-created diamonds offer unique advantages for blockchain implementation:

Simplified Supply Chains:

Controlled Origin: Known production facilities enabling accurate initial record creation

Reduced Complexity: Fewer intermediaries compared to natural diamond supply chains

Direct Relationships: Close collaboration between producers, cutters, and retailers

Quality Consistency: Predictable characteristics supporting automated verification systems

Enhanced Documentation:

Production Parameters: Complete records of growth conditions and quality control

Real-Time Monitoring: Live data feeds during production and processing

Digital Certificates: Native digital certificates integrated with blockchain records

Photographic Documentation: High-resolution images linked to blockchain records

Industry Blockchain Implementations

Established Platforms and Solutions

De Beers Tracr Platform:

Although primarily focused on natural diamonds, Tracr demonstrates blockchain potential for the entire diamond industry:

Platform Capabilities:

Industry Participation: Multiple diamond companies are participating in the shared platform

Comprehensive Tracking: Complete journey from rough stone to finished jewelry

Quality Integration: Combining blockchain records with traditional quality assessments

Consumer Access: Development of consumer-facing tracking capabilities

Technical Implementation:

Permissioned Network: Private blockchain network with controlled access

Industry Standards: Development of industry-wide standards for data sharing

Integration APIs: Application programming interfaces enabling third-party integration

Scalability Solutions: Technical solutions supporting industry-wide adoption

Everledger Diamond Verification:

Everledger specializes in luxury goods verification with a growing lab-created diamond focus:

Multi-Technology Approach:

Blockchain Foundation: Distributed ledger technology provides permanent records

AI Integration: Artificial intelligence for pattern recognition and fraud detection

IoT Connectivity: Internet of Things sensors providing real-time tracking

Mobile Applications: Consumer-facing mobile apps for verification and information

Service Portfolio:

Insurance Integration: Working with insurers to prevent fraud and streamline claims

Global Adoption: Over 2 million diamonds tracked across multiple countries

Law Enforcement: Collaboration with law enforcement agencies for theft recovery

Lab Diamond Expansion: Expanding services specifically for lab-created diamonds

Sarine Diamond Journey:

Sarine integrates production technology with blockchain tracking:

Production Integration:

Manufacturing Data: Blockchain records starting from the cutting and polishing processes

Visual Documentation: High-resolution imaging linked to blockchain records

Quality Metrics: Precise quality measurements recorded on blockchain

Consumer Engagement: Consumer-facing applications showing the complete diamond journey

Technical Innovation:

Real-Time Updates: Live updates during diamond processing and handling

Immersive Visualization: 3D visualization tools for consumer engagement

Professional Tools: Retailer and appraiser tools for verification and assessment

Global Integration: International deployment across major diamond centers

Consumer-Facing Verification Systems

QR Code and Mobile Technology

Smartphone Integration:

Modern consumers expect immediate access to product information through mobile devices:

QR Code Implementation:

Certificate Integration: QR codes linking directly to blockchain records and certificates

Real-Time Verification: Instant verification of authenticity and ownership

Cryptographic Security: QR codes are protected through cryptographic algorithms

Offline Capability: QR codes function without internet connectivity for basic verification

Mobile Application Features:

Comprehensive Information: Complete diamond specifications, history, and documentation

Visual Comparison: High-resolution images enabling visual verification

Care Instructions: Personalized care and maintenance recommendations

Value Tracking: Market value updates and insurance information

Augmented Reality Applications:

AR Visualization Tools:

Virtual Try-On: Augmented reality enabling virtual jewelry trial experiences

Size Comparison: AR tools showing accurate size representations

Setting Options: Virtual visualization of diamonds in various settings

Educational Content: Interactive educational content about diamond characteristics

Technical Requirements:

Camera Integration: Advanced camera systems for accurate AR rendering

Processing Power: Sufficient computational capability for real-time AR applications

Accuracy Standards: Precise measurements and rendering for realistic visualization

User Experience: Intuitive interfaces enabling easy consumer adoption

Virtual Reality and Metaverse Integration

Immersive Diamond Experiences

Virtual Showroom Development:

Virtual Reality Shopping: The integration of VR technology transforms how consumers experience and purchase diamonds:

Immersive Environments:

Realistic Showrooms: Virtual showrooms replicating luxury jewelry store experiences

Global Access: Worldwide access to premium jewelry collections without travel

Personalized Service: Virtual consultations with expert gemologists and sales professionals

Social Integration: Shared experiences with family and friends in virtual environments

Technical Capabilities:

High-Resolution Displays: 4K and 8K VR displays providing crystal-clear diamond visualization

Haptic Feedback: Touch sensation technology enabling "feeling" of jewelry weight and texture

Real-Time Rendering: Advanced graphics processing for photorealistic diamond rendering

Motion Tracking: Precise hand and head tracking for natural interaction

Metaverse Commerce Integration:

Digital Ownership Concepts:

NFT Integration: Non-fungible tokens representing both physical and digital diamond ownership

Virtual Luxury: Premium digital jewelry for metaverse avatars and virtual worlds

Cross-Platform Compatibility: Digital assets functioning across multiple virtual platforms

Ownership Verification: Blockchain-based ownership verification in virtual environments

Commercial Applications:

Virtual Showrooms: Branded virtual spaces for luxury jewelry shopping

Digital Twin: Perfect digital replicas of physical diamonds for virtual environments

Social Commerce: Social shopping experiences in virtual worlds

Investment Opportunities: Digital diamond investments and virtual luxury markets

14.2 Manufacturing Innovations

Automation in Diamond Production

The lab-created diamond industry stands at the forefront of advanced manufacturing, incorporating Industry 4.0 technologies to achieve unprecedented levels of quality, efficiency, and consistency.

Robotic Systems Integration

Automated Handling and Processing:

Substrate Preparation Automation:

Precision Cleaning: Robotic systems ensure ultra-clean diamond seed preparation

Automated Positioning: Precise positioning of seeds in growth chambers

Quality Inspection: Automated visual inspection systems detect defects before processing

Environmental Control: Robotic systems maintain contamination-free environments

Growth Chamber Management:

Automated Loading: Robotic loading and unloading of growth chambers

Parameter Monitoring: Continuous monitoring of pressure, temperature, and gas composition

Safety Integration: Automated safety systems protect personnel from high-pressure hazards

Efficiency Optimization: Robotic systems maximize equipment utilization and throughput

Post-Growth Processing:

Automated Sorting and Grading:

Computer Vision: Advanced imaging systems for automated quality assessment

AI Classification: Machine learning algorithms categorizing diamonds by quality grades

Precision Handling: Robotic systems handling delicate diamonds without damage

Data Integration: Automatic data recording and blockchain integration

Cutting and Polishing Automation:

Laser Cutting: Precision laser systems for automated diamond cutting

Robotic Polishing: Automated polishing systems achieve consistent surface quality

Quality Control: Real-time monitoring, ensuring cut quality standards

Customization Capability: Automated systems accommodating custom specifications

Quality Control AI Systems

Machine Learning in Quality Assessment

Predictive Quality Systems:

Process Parameter Optimization: AI systems revolutionizing quality control through predictive analysis:

Real-Time Analysis:

Sensor Fusion: Integration of multiple sensor inputs for comprehensive process understanding

Pattern Recognition: AI identification of patterns predicting final diamond quality

Immediate Adjustment: Real-time process adjustments based on AI analysis

Continuous Learning: Systems improving through experience and historical data analysis

Quality Prediction Models:

Growth Rate Optimization: AI models optimizing growth rates for specific quality targets

Defect Prevention: Predictive models identifying conditions likely to create defects

Yield Maximization: AI optimization maximizing the percentage of gem-quality production

Custom Specifications: AI systems achieving specific customer quality requirements

Computer Vision Applications:

Automated Inspection Systems:

Inclusion Detection: Advanced imaging detects microscopic inclusions during growth

Surface Analysis: Automated surface quality assessment and optimization

Dimensional Measurement: Precise automated measurement of diamond dimensions

Color Assessment: Automated color grading using standardized lighting and analysis

Advanced Imaging Technologies:

Multispectral Imaging: Multiple wavelength analysis revealing internal characteristics

3D Reconstruction: Three-dimensional mapping of diamond internal structure

Real-Time Monitoring: Continuous monitoring during growth and processing

Comparative Analysis: AI comparison with quality standards and reference samples

Sustainable Production Methods

Environmental Optimization Technologies

Energy Efficiency Advancement:

Renewable Energy Integration: Sophisticated systems optimizing renewable energy utilization:

Smart Grid Integration:

Load Balancing: AI systems balancing production loads with renewable energy availability

Energy Storage: Advanced battery systems store renewable energy for continuous operation

Grid Integration: Smart systems selling excess renewable energy back to power grids

Carbon Optimization: AI systems minimize carbon footprint through energy management

Process Efficiency Improvements:

Heat Recovery: Advanced systems capture and reuse waste heat from production

Gas Recycling: Closed-loop systems recycle process gases and reduce waste

Water Conservation: Advanced water recycling and purification systems

Material Optimization: AI systems minimize raw material waste and maximize utilization

Circular Economy Implementation:

Waste Elimination Strategies:

By-Product Utilization: Converting production by-products into useful materials

Equipment Recycling: Comprehensive recycling programs for production equipment

Material Recovery: Recovery and reuse of valuable materials from production processes

Lifecycle Optimization: Designing processes for complete material lifecycle management

Cost Reduction Technologies

Economic Efficiency Innovations

Scale Economy Achievement:

Production Scaling Technologies:

Modular Systems: Scalable production systems enabling capacity increases

Parallel Processing: Multiple simultaneous growth chambers increase throughput

Automated Logistics: Automated systems manage material flow and inventory

Supply Chain Integration: Direct integration with suppliers, reducing costs and delays

Cost Structure Optimization:

Labor Efficiency: Automation reduces labor costs while improving quality

Material Efficiency: Advanced systems minimize raw material consumption

Energy Optimization: Smart systems reduce energy costs through efficiency improvements

Maintenance Automation: Predictive maintenance reduces downtime and repair costs

14.3 Market Evolution Predictions

Technology Adoption Timelines

The convergence of multiple technological trends will reshape the lab-created diamond market over the next decade, with specific technologies reaching critical adoption milestones at predictable intervals.

Near-Term Developments (2024-2027)

Immediate Technology Integration:

Blockchain Mainstream Adoption:

2024-2025: Major retailers implementing blockchain verification systems

2025-2026: Consumer-facing blockchain applications achieving widespread adoption

2026-2027: Industry-wide standards establishing blockchain verification protocols

Integration Barriers: Cost and complexity barriers are decreasing through technology maturation

AI Quality Control:

2024: AI systems achieving 95%+ accuracy in quality prediction

2025: Automated grading systems matching human gemologist accuracy

2026: AI systems enabling real-time quality optimization during production

2027: Machine learning models achieving superior consistency compared to human assessment

Consumer Technology Integration:

Mobile Commerce Evolution:

Enhanced AR: Augmented reality try-on technology achieves photorealistic accuracy

Voice Integration: Voice assistants providing diamond education and purchase guidance

Social Commerce: Social media platforms integrating direct diamond purchasing capabilities

Personalization: AI systems provide personalized recommendations based on individual preferences

Consumer Behavior Predictions

Digital-First Consumer Evolution

Generational Technology Adoption:

Generation Alpha Integration (2025-2030): As Generation Alpha reaches purchasing age, their expectations will reshape markets:

Technology Expectations:

Native Digital: Expectation of seamless digital integration in all purchasing experiences

Immersive Experiences: Demand for VR and AR integration in luxury shopping

Instant Verification: Expectation of immediate authenticity verification through mobile devices

Social Integration: Purchasing decisions influenced by social media and peer networks

Sustainability Requirements:

Non-Negotiable Ethics: Environmental and ethical considerations as mandatory requirements

Transparency Demands: Complete supply chain transparency as a baseline expectation

Impact Measurement: Demand for quantifiable environmental and social impact data

Circular Economy: Expectation of product lifecycle management and recycling programs

Shopping Behavior Evolution:

Omnichannel Integration:

Seamless Experience: Expectation of seamless integration across online and offline channels

Global Access: Demand for access to global inventory and expertise, regardless of location

Personalized Service: AI-powered personalization combined with human expertise

Community Integration: Shopping experiences integrated with social and community networks

Innovation and Market Disruption

Breakthrough Technology Potential

Quantum Technology Applications:

Quantum Computing Integration:

Optimization Algorithms: Quantum computing optimizing complex production parameters

Quality Prediction: Quantum machine learning achieves unprecedented prediction accuracy

Supply Chain Optimization: Quantum algorithms optimizing global supply chain efficiency

Market Analysis: Quantum computing enables sophisticated market analysis and prediction

Quantum Diamond Applications:

Technology Integration: Lab-created diamonds serving critical roles in quantum technologies

Market Expansion: New markets emerging for quantum-grade diamond applications

Value Premium: Premium pricing for diamonds meeting quantum technology specifications

Industry Transformation: Diamond industry transformation through quantum technology applications

Advanced Manufacturing Breakthroughs:

Molecular Assembly:

Atomic Precision: Atom-by-atom diamond assembly achieving theoretical perfection

Custom Properties: Diamonds engineered with specific properties for targeted applications

Novel Structures: The Creation of diamond structures is impossible through traditional methods

Performance Enhancement: Diamonds with enhanced optical, thermal, or electronic properties

Space-Based Manufacturing:

Microgravity Advantages: Space-based production achieves superior quality through microgravity

Large Crystal Growth: Space environment enabling the growth of extremely large single crystals

Novel Properties: Unique diamond properties achievable only in a space environment

Economic Viability: Development of economically viable space-based production systems

Industry Structure Evolution

Market Consolidation and Specialization

Vertical Integration Trends:

Technology Integration:

Platform Companies: Companies controlling entire value chains from production to retail

Technology Licensing: Specialized technology companies license production methods

Service Integration: Comprehensive service providers offering complete solutions

Data Monetization: Companies leveraging data and analytics for competitive advantage

Geographic Specialization:

Regional Centers: Development of specialized regional production and technology centers

Expertise Clustering: Geographic clustering of specialized expertise and capabilities

Supply Chain Hubs: Regional hubs optimizing supply chain efficiency and costs

Innovation Centers: Technology development centers driving industry innovation

New Business Model Development:

Subscription and Service Models:

Diamond-as-a-Service: Subscription models providing access to diamond jewelry

Upgrade Programs: Systematic upgrade programs enabling regular jewelry enhancement

Maintenance Services: Comprehensive maintenance and care service programs

Experience Platforms: Companies focusing on experiences rather than just products

Technology Platform Business:

Infrastructure Providers: Companies providing technology infrastructure for industry

Data Platform: Platforms aggregating and analyzing industry data for insights

Marketplace Models: Digital marketplaces connecting producers, retailers, and consumers

Innovation Platforms: Platforms facilitating collaboration and innovation across industry

Future Market Scenarios

Scenario Planning and Strategic Implications

Optimistic Scenario (High Technology Adoption):

Market Transformation:

2030 Market Share: 45-50% of the total diamond market by volume

Technology Integration: Seamless integration of digital and physical diamond experiences

Quality Achievement: Routine production of diamonds superior to the finest natural stones

Cost Reduction: Production costs 90% below current levels through technology advancement

Consumer Impact:

Democratic Luxury: High-quality diamonds accessible to broad consumer segments

Customization: Mass customization enabling personalized diamond experiences

Sustainability: Carbon-negative production standard across industry

Innovation: Continuous innovation is driving new applications and markets

Conservative Scenario (Gradual Technology Adoption):

Steady Evolution:

2030 Market Share: 30-35% of the total diamond market by volume

Technology Integration: Moderate pace of technology adoption and integration

Quality Improvement: Continued quality improvements through incremental innovation

Cost Stability: Gradual cost reductions through process optimization

Market Development:

Regional Variation: Significant variation in adoption rates across global markets

Niche Applications: Strong development in specific market segments and applications

Professional Integration: Growing acceptance among jewelry professionals and retailers

Consumer Education: Continued consumer education is driving gradual market acceptance

Disruptive Scenario (Revolutionary Innovation):

Industry Revolution:

Technology Breakthrough: Revolutionary production technologies transforming industry economics

Market Disruption: Fundamental disruption of the traditional diamond industry structure

New Applications: Expansion into entirely new markets and applications beyond jewelry

Global Impact: Technology advancement affecting multiple industries and applications

Societal Impact:

Luxury Redefinition: Complete redefinition of luxury consumption patterns

Environmental Leadership: Diamond industry becoming model for sustainable luxury production

Technology Transfer: Lab-created diamond technologies benefiting other industries

Cultural Transformation: Fundamental shift in cultural attitudes toward luxury and consumption

Technology integration and future trends in lab-created diamonds indicate a future where digital innovation, sustainable production, and consumer empowerment converge to create entirely new categories of luxury experiences. The pace and direction of this evolution will determine not only the future of the diamond industry but will also influence broader patterns of luxury consumption and technological integration across multiple sectors.

As we stand at this technological inflection point, the choices made by consumers, companies, and regulators will shape whether this transformation unfolds gradually or explosively, locally, or globally, inclusively or exclusively. The potential for positive environmental, social, and economic benefits remains enormous, limited primarily by our collective imagination and commitment to realizing the full potential of these remarkable technological achievements.

***

In the fusion of technology and tradition, we discover not the replacement of human values but their amplification—where artificial intelligence serves human wisdom, digital networks strengthen human connections, and technological precision enables the expression of emotions that are, essentially, eternally human. The future of diamonds is not just brighter; it is more meaningful, more accessible, and more aligned with our highest aspirations for beauty, truth, and responsibility.

Chapter 15: Comprehensive FAQ and Troubleshooting

"In the garden of knowledge, questions bloom like flowers—each inquiry a petal of curiosity, each answer a beam of understanding, together creating the full radiance of informed wisdom that guides us through every facet of the lab-created diamond journey."

15.1 Pre-Purchase Questions

Selection Criteria Clarifications

The journey toward purchasing the perfect lab-created diamond begins with understanding the fundamental criteria that will guide your decision. Unlike natural diamonds, where choices are often constrained by availability and budget limitations, lab-created diamonds offer unprecedented flexibility in optimizing quality characteristics to match your specific preferences and values.

Understanding the Enhanced 4Cs for Lab-Created Diamonds

Cut Quality Optimization:

Why Cut Matters More Than Ever: With lab-created diamonds, the traditional hierarchy of the 4Cs shifts dramatically in favor of cut quality:

Unlimited Precision: Lab-created diamond cutters can prioritize ideal proportions over weight retention, unlike natural diamond cutting, where every fraction of a carat affects price exponentially

Consistent Material: The controlled crystal structure of lab-created diamonds responds more predictably to cutting, enabling the achievement of theoretical optical ideals

Cost-Effective Excellence: The lower rough stone costs allow cutters to invest time in achieving perfect symmetry and polish

Technology Integration: Advanced computer modeling and laser cutting technology optimize light performance to mathematical perfection

Practical Cut Selection Guidelines:

Engagement Rings: Prioritize Excellent or Ideal cut grades for maximum brilliance and fire

Fashion Jewelry: Very Good cuts offer excellent value while maintaining superior appearance

Investment Pieces: Ideal cuts provide the best long-term satisfaction and potential value retention

Custom Designs: Work with cutters who specialize in lab-created diamonds for optimal results

Color Grading Advantages:

The Lab-Created Color Consistency Benefit: Lab-created diamonds offer remarkable advantages in color consistency and availability:

Colorless Achievement (D-F Grades):

Type IIa Purity: CVD diamonds routinely achieve Type IIa classification with virtually no nitrogen content

Consistent Distribution: Even color distribution throughout the stone, unlike natural diamonds with potential color zoning

Predictable Results: Controlled growth conditions enabling reliable color grade achievement

Cost Accessibility: D-F grades are available at price points that make them accessible to broader consumer segments

Fancy Color Opportunities:

Blue Diamonds: Boron-doped diamonds creating stunning blue colors from faint to vivid intensities

Yellow Diamonds: Controlled nitrogen introduction creating precise yellow saturation levels

Pink and Red: Advanced treatment techniques creating rare colors previously unavailable or prohibitively expensive

Custom Colors: Ability to create specific color intensities for unique design requirements

Clarity Grade Optimization:

The Controlled Environment Advantage: Lab-created diamonds demonstrate superior clarity characteristics due to their controlled growth environment:

Inclusion Patterns:

HPHT Characteristics: Minimal metallic inclusions from catalyst materials, often invisible to the naked eye

CVD Clarity: Exceptional clarity achievements with fewer and smaller inclusions than natural equivalents

Predictable Features: Understanding typical inclusion patterns helps in quality assessment

Grading Consistency: More predictable clarity grading due to consistent growth conditions

Practical Clarity Selection:

Eye-Clean Priority: Focus on grades that ensure eye-clean appearance (VS2 and above for most sizes)

Setting Considerations: Lower clarity grades are acceptable in certain settings that obscure potential inclusions

Size Scaling: Larger diamonds require higher clarity grades for eye-clean appearance

Personal Sensitivity: Consider individual sensitivity to inclusions when selecting clarity grades

Carat Weight Strategy:

Size Optimization Through Lab Advantages: The accessibility of lab-created diamonds transforms carat weight decisions:

Size vs. Quality Balance:

Value Optimization: Determine whether larger size or higher quality grades provide greater satisfaction

Visual Impact: Consider actual visual size differences between carat weights in your chosen setting

Lifestyle Factors: Balance size desires with practical considerations of daily wear

Future Flexibility: Lab diamond affordability enables future upgrades if desired

Quality Assessment Guidance

Professional Evaluation Techniques

Visual Assessment Skills:

Developing Your Diamond Eye: Learning basic visual assessment skills empowers confident decision-making:

Lighting Considerations:

Ideal Lighting: Examine diamonds under multiple lighting conditions, including fluorescent, LED, and natural daylight

Consistent Comparison: Compare stones under identical lighting conditions for accurate assessment

Movement Analysis: Observe how diamonds perform with movement to assess scintillation

Background Testing: View diamonds against both white and black backgrounds to assess contrast

Magnification Techniques:

10x Loupe Usage: Learn proper loupe technique for examining clarity characteristics

Inclusion Mapping: Understand how to identify and evaluate various inclusion types

Surface Assessment: Assess polish quality and surface characteristics under magnification

Proportion Analysis: Use magnification to evaluate cut proportions and symmetry

Certification Analysis:

Reading Grading Reports Effectively: Understanding how to interpret professional grading reports:

Certificate Components:

Laboratory Identification: Verify the credibility and reputation of the issuing laboratory

Grading Standards: Understand the specific grading standards and scales used

Additional Information: Pay attention to comments, treatments, and special characteristics noted

Photo Documentation: Compare certificate photos with the actual diamond for verification

Red Flags in Certification:

Unknown Laboratories: Be cautious of certificates from unrecognized or questionable institutions

Grade Inflation: Suspicious grades that seem too good for the price point

Missing Information: Incomplete certificates lacking essential details or measurements

Poor Presentation: Low-quality printing or unprofessional certificate presentation

Price Comparison Methodologies

Comprehensive Value Analysis

Market Research Strategies:

Multi-Source Comparison: Effective price research requires systematic comparison across multiple sources:

Online Platform Analysis:

Inventory Breadth: Compare selection and availability across major online retailers

Price Transparency: Document pricing for identical specifications across platforms

Service Comparison: Evaluate return policies, warranties, and customer service offerings

Educational Resources: Assess the quality and comprehensiveness of educational content provided

Physical Retailer Assessment:

Local Market Research: Compare pricing and service at local jewelry retailers

Professional Expertise: Evaluate the gemological knowledge and expertise of sales staff

Service Integration: Consider additional services like setting, sizing, and maintenance

Relationship Value: Assess the value of ongoing relationships with local professionals

Value Proposition Framework:

Total Cost of Ownership Analysis: Consider all costs associated with diamond ownership over time:

Initial Investment Costs:

Diamond Price: Base price for the diamond itself

Setting Costs: Costs for mounting the diamond in jewelry

Certification: Professional grading and certification fees

Customization: Additional costs for custom design or modifications

Ongoing Ownership Costs:

Insurance Premiums: Annual insurance costs based on appraised value

Maintenance Services: Professional cleaning, inspection, and maintenance

Potential Repairs: Costs for potential repairs or restoration over time

Opportunity Costs: Alternative uses for the invested capital

Certification Interpretation

Understanding Professional Grading

Major Laboratory Standards:

Gemological Institute of America (GIA): The gold standard in diamond grading with specific protocols for lab-created diamonds:

GIA Lab-Created Diamond Reports:

Identification Standards: Clear identification of synthetic origin and growth method

Grading Consistency: Same 4Cs standards applied to lab and natural diamonds

Additional Testing: Advanced testing confirming synthetic origin and detecting treatments

Report Format: Distinct formatting clearly indicating lab-created origin

Quality Assurance Measures:

Multiple Graders: Independent assessment by multiple certified gemologists

Equipment Verification: Advanced instrumentation confirming grading accuracy

Consistency Monitoring: Regular calibration and quality control procedures

Appeal Process: Procedures for challenging or verifying grading results

Alternative Certification Options:

International Gemological Institute (IGI): Widely recognized alternative with global presence:

IGI Advantages:

Global Network: Laboratories in major diamond centers worldwide

Faster Service: Often quicker turnaround times compared to GIA

Comprehensive Reports: Detailed reporting, including advanced testing results

Cost Effectiveness: Generally lower certification costs than GIA

American Gemological Society (AGS): Specializing in cut quality assessment with advanced light performance analysis:

AGS Unique Features:

Cut Grading Excellence: Most sophisticated cut grading system available

Light Performance: Scientific measurement of brilliance, fire, and scintillation

0-10 Grading Scale: Numerical system with 0 representing ideal quality

Technical Innovation: Cutting-edge technology for precision assessment

15.2 Purchase Process Support

Negotiation Techniques

The lab-created diamond market offers unique opportunities for negotiation due to its transparent pricing structure and competitive dynamics. Understanding effective negotiation strategies can result in significant value enhancement while building positive relationships with retailers.

Understanding Market Dynamics

Pricing Transparency Advantages:

Lab Diamond Market Structure: The lab-created diamond market operates with greater transparency than traditional natural diamond markets:

Known Production Costs:

Manufacturing Transparency: Understanding of production costs enables informed negotiation

Technology Standardization: Standardized production methods reduce price variability

Competitive Benchmarking: Multiple suppliers offering comparable products

Market Maturity: Developing market standards and pricing expectations

Negotiation Leverage Points:

Alternative Sources: Multiple retailers and online platforms provide negotiation leverage

Volume Opportunities: Potential for multiple purchases or complete jewelry sets

Timing Flexibility: Ability to wait for optimal pricing or promotional opportunities

Cash Payment: Immediate payment, potentially reducing retailer costs and prices

Value-Based Negotiation Strategies:

Quality Enhancement Focus: Rather than focusing solely on price reduction, negotiate for enhanced value:

Quality Upgrades:

Color Improvement: Request higher color grades at current price points

Clarity Enhancement: Negotiate for better clarity grades without price increases

Cut Optimization: Seek superior cut grades or premium cutting services

Certification Upgrades: Request certification from premium laboratories

Service Integration:

Extended Warranties: Negotiate for extended warranty coverage or enhanced terms

Maintenance Services: Include professional cleaning and inspection services

Insurance Support: Assistance with insurance appraisals and documentation

Future Services: Agreements for future setting changes or modifications

Documentation Requirements

Essential Purchase Documentation

Primary Documentation Needs:

Comprehensive Purchase Records: Proper documentation protects your investment and enables future services.

Detailed Sales Receipt:

Complete Specifications: Full description of diamond characteristics and quality grades

Certification Information: Reference to the grading certificate and laboratory identification

Setting Details: Complete description of mounting and any additional gemstones

Warranty Terms: A Clear statement of warranty coverage and limitations

Professional Grading Certificate:

Laboratory Credentials: Certificate from a recognized and reputable laboratory

Unique Identification: Certificate number and laser inscription matching

Comprehensive Grading: Complete 4Cs assessment plus additional characteristics

Digital Verification: QR codes or online verification capabilities

Documentation Management:

Secure Storage Systems:

Physical Safekeeping: Secure storage of original documents in a fireproof safe

Digital Backup: High-resolution scans stored in multiple secure locations

Cloud Storage: Encrypted cloud storage for remote access and backup

Family Access: Ensuring family members can access documentation if needed

Regular Updates:

Insurance Appraisals: Periodic professional appraisals for insurance purposes

Condition Documentation: Regular photographic documentation of jewelry condition

Service Records: Maintenance and repair service documentation

Value Updates: Periodic market value assessments and documentation

Payment and Financing Options

Modern Payment Solutions

Traditional Financing Methods:

Retailer Financing Programs: Many jewelry retailers offer specialized financing for lab-created diamonds:

Zero-Interest Promotions:

Promotional Periods: 6-24 month zero-interest financing options

Credit Approval: Instant credit decisions and approval processes

Payment Flexibility: Various payment schedule options accommodating different budgets

Early Payment: No penalties for early payment or payoff

Extended Payment Plans:

Long-Term Options: 24-60 month payment plans with competitive interest rates

Down Payment Options: Various down payment requirements from 10-25%

Credit Requirements: Flexible credit requirements accommodating various financial situations

Payment Protection: Optional payment protection insurance for unexpected circumstances

Alternative Financing Approaches:

Buy-Now-Pay-Later Services: Modern payment platforms offering flexible payment options:

Popular Platforms:

Affirm: Transparent pricing with no hidden fees or compound interest

Klarna: Flexible payment options including pay-in-4 installments

PayPal Credit: PayPal-integrated financing with promotional offers

Splitit: Credit card-based installment plans without additional credit checks.

Cryptocurrency Payments:

Bitcoin Acceptance: A Growing number of retailers are accepting Bitcoin payments.

Stablecoin Options: Payments using stable cryptocurrencies tied to fiat currencies.

Price Protection: Mechanisms protecting against cryptocurrency price volatility.

Transaction Security: Secure cryptocurrency transaction processing and verification

Delivery and Inspection Procedures

Safe Receipt and Verification

Delivery Security Protocols:

Insured Shipping Requirements: High-value diamond shipments require comprehensive security measures:

Shipping Insurance:

Full Value Coverage: Insurance covering the complete replacement value of jewelry.

Signature Confirmation: Required signature confirmation for delivery.

Restricted Delivery: Delivery only to verified addresses and authorized recipients.

Tracking Integration: Real-time tracking throughout the shipping process

Inspection Timeline:

Immediate Inspection: Visual inspection immediately upon delivery

Professional Assessment: Professional evaluation within 24-48 hours

Documentation Review: Verification of certificates and documentation

Return Window: Understanding return policy timeline and requirements.

Quality Verification Process:

Initial Assessment Procedures:

Visual Inspection: Comprehensive visual examination under various lighting conditions

Magnified Examination: Detailed inspection using proper magnification tools.

Certificate Comparison: Verification that the diamond matches the grading certificate specifications

Setting Inspection: Assessment of mounting quality and security

Professional Verification:

Independent Appraisal: Professional assessment by a qualified gemologist

Laboratory Confirmation: Optional re-certification for high-value purchases

Insurance Evaluation: Professional appraisal suitable for insurance purposes

Documentation Compilation: Assembly of complete documentation package

15.3 Post-Purchase Support

Maintenance and Care Guidance

The exceptional quality and consistency of lab-created diamonds enable predictable maintenance routines that preserve their beauty and value for generations. Understanding proper care protocols ensures optimal performance and longevity of your investment.

Daily Care Protocols

Routine Maintenance Procedures:

Daily Cleaning Routines: Simple daily practices that maintain optimal diamond appearance:

Morning Preparation:

Pre-Application Cleaning: Quick rinse before applying cosmetics or lotions.

Order of Application: Apply makeup and hair products before wearing diamond jewelry.

Visual Inspection: A brief check for loose stones or setting issues.

Gentle Handling: Careful handling to prevent impacts or stress on settings.

Evening Care Routine:

Immediate Removal: Remove jewelry before washing face or showering.

Quick Clean: A brief cleaning to remove daily accumulations of oils and residues.

Inspection Check: Visual assessment of the setting security and diamond condition

Proper Storage: Secure storage in designated jewelry storage systems

Weekly Deep Cleaning:

Home Cleaning Procedures:

Soaking Solution: Gentle dish soap and warm water for thorough cleaning

Soft Brush Technique: A soft-bristled toothbrush reaches all areas of the setting.

Thorough Rinsing: Complete removal of soap residues with clean water

Lint-Free Drying: Professional drying with lint-free cloths and air drying

Professional Service Scheduling:

Quarterly Professional Cleaning: Ultrasonic cleaning by qualified professionals

Annual Comprehensive Inspection: Complete assessment of setting security and diamond condition

Documentation Updates: Regular photographic documentation and condition records

Service Coordination: Coordination with qualified local service providers.

Insurance and Protection Advice

Comprehensive Protection Strategies

Insurance Optimization:

Policy Selection Guidance: Choosing the right insurance coverage for lab-created diamonds:

Coverage Type Assessment:

Homeowner's Policy Limitations: Understanding standard policy limitations and exclusions.

Specialized Jewelry Insurance: Benefits of dedicated jewelry insurance policies

Replacement Value Coverage: Ensuring coverage reflects actual replacement costs.

Worldwide Protection: Coverage during travel and temporary relocation

Premium Optimization Strategies:

Accurate Appraisals: Professional appraisals reflecting actual replacement values.

Security Discounts: Premium reductions for security systems and safe storage

Deductible Selection: Balancing deductible amounts with premium costs

Policy Reviews: Regular policy reviews ensuring adequate coverage.

Risk Management:

Preventive Protection Measures:

Secure Storage: Professional-grade safes and security storage systems

Activity Restrictions: Understanding When to Remove Jewelry for Protection.

Travel Considerations: Special precautions for travel with valuable jewelry.

Professional Handling: Using qualified professionals for all service needs.

Upgrade and Trade-In Options

Strategic Enhancement Planning

Upgrade Pathways:

Trade-In Programs: Growing opportunities for lab-created diamond upgrades:

Retailer Programs:

Trade-In Value: Percentage of original purchase price credited toward upgrades.

Condition Requirements: Standards for trade-in acceptance and valuation.

Upgrade Minimums: Minimum purchase amounts required for trade-in participation.

Timeline Considerations: Time limits for trade-in program eligibility

Market-Based Upgrades:

Independent Valuation: Professional assessment of current market value

Competitive Shopping: Comparison shopping for optimal upgrade opportunities

Timing Strategy: Strategic timing of upgrades based on market conditions.

Quality Optimization: Upgrading specific quality characteristics for enhanced satisfaction.

Enhancement Strategies:

Setting Upgrades:

Modern Design Updates: Updating settings to contemporary styles.

Security Enhancements: Improving setting security with modern techniques.

Comfort Modifications: Adjusting settings for improved wearability.

Style Evolution: Adapting jewelry to changing personal preferences.

Stone Enhancement:

Size Upgrades: Trading up to larger diamonds within budget parameters.

Quality Improvements: Upgrading to higher color or clarity grades.

Shape Changes: Exploring different diamond shapes for renewed aesthetic appeal.

Custom Integration: Adding additional stones for multi-stone designs.

Problem Resolution Procedures

Systematic Issue Management

Common Issues and Solutions:

Setting Problems: Addressing common setting-related issues:

Loose Stones:

Immediate Action: Stop wearing jewelry immediately upon discovering loose stones.

Professional Assessment: Prompt professional evaluation of setting security

Repair Procedures: Working with qualified jewelers for proper repairs.

Prevention Strategies: Regular inspections prevent future problems.

Damage Assessment:

Documentation: Photographing damage for insurance and repair purposes

Professional Evaluation: Qualified assessment of repair options and costs

Insurance Coordination: Working with insurance companies for covered repairs.

Quality Restoration: Ensuring repairs maintain original quality and appearance.

Warranty and Service Issues:

Warranty Claim Procedures:

Documentation Review: Understanding warranty terms and coverage limitations.

Claim Process: Step-by-step procedures for filing warranty claims.

Professional Coordination: Working with authorized service providers.

Quality Assurance: Ensuring warranty work meets original quality standards.

Retailer Relationship Management:

Communication Strategies: Effective communication with retailers and service providers

Escalation Procedures: Understanding Escalation Paths for Unresolved Issues.

Legal Resources: When and how to seek legal assistance for serious problems.

Alternative Resolution: Mediation and arbitration options for dispute resolution

15.4 Technical and Scientific Questions

Advanced Gemological Concepts

Understanding the sophisticated science behind lab-created diamonds empowers consumers to make informed decisions and appreciate the remarkable achievements these gems represent.

Crystal Structure and Properties

Atomic-Level Understanding:

Diamond Crystal Lattice: The foundation of diamond properties lies in its crystal structure:

Tetrahedral Bonding:

Covalent Structure: Each carbon atom is bonded to four neighboring carbons in a tetrahedral arrangement.

Bond Strength: Strong covalent bonds create exceptional hardness and durability.

Lattice Perfection: Lab-created diamonds often achieve superior lattice regularity.

Property Implications: How the crystal structure determines optical and physical properties.

Defect Centers and Color:

Vacancy Defects: The absence of carbon atoms creates specific optical properties.

Substitutional Defects: Foreign atoms replacing carbon in the crystal lattice.

Interstitial Defects: Extra atoms positioned between normal lattice sites.

Electronic Properties: How defects affect electronic and optical characteristics

Growth Science Fundamentals:

HPHT Process Details: Understanding the science behind high-pressure, high-temperature diamond growth:

Thermodynamic Conditions:

Phase Stability: Conditions where diamond is thermodynamically stable relative to graphite.

Nucleation Process: Initial formation of diamond crystal nuclei

Growth Kinetics: Factors controlling the rate and quality of diamond growth.

Catalyst Function: Role of metallic catalysts in enabling diamond formation.

CVD Process Mechanisms:

Gas Phase Chemistry: Chemical reactions occurring in the plasma environment.

Surface Kinetics: Processes occurring at the growing diamond surface.

Selective Chemistry: Why diamond grows preferentially over graphite.

Process Control: How parameters control final diamond characteristics

Manufacturing Process Details

Advanced Production Technologies

Equipment and Engineering:

HPHT Press Systems: Sophisticated engineering behind high-pressure diamond production:

Pressure Generation:

Hydraulic Systems: Multi-thousand-ton presses generating required pressures.

Anvil Design: Tungsten carbide and diamond anvils focusing pressure.

Temperature Control: Precise heating systems maintain growth temperatures.

Safety Engineering: Safety systems protect operators from extreme conditions.

Monitoring and Control:

Real-Time Monitoring: Sensors track pressure, temperature, and growth progress.

Process Optimization: Computer control systems optimize growth parameters.

Quality Assurance: In-process quality monitoring and control systems

Data Collection: Comprehensive data logging for process improvement

Quality Control Science:

Advanced Characterization: Scientific techniques for comprehensive diamond analysis:

Spectroscopic Methods:

Photoluminescence: Analysis of light emission revealing defect structures

Infrared Spectroscopy: Detection of chemical bonds and impurities

Raman Spectroscopy: Confirmation of diamond structure and stress analysis

Mass Spectrometry: Precise analysis of trace elements and isotopic composition

Imaging Techniques:

Scanning Electron Microscopy: High-resolution surface and structure analysis

Transmission Electron Microscopy: Internal structure and defect analysis

X-ray Topography: Crystal defect and strain pattern visualization

Cathodoluminescence: Imaging of growth sectors and defect distributions

Quality Control Explanations

Scientific Quality Assessment

Grading Science and Standards:

Color Grading Precision: Scientific foundation of color assessment in lab-created diamonds:

Spectrophotometric Analysis:

Standardized Lighting: Controlled lighting conditions for consistent color assessment

Instrumental Measurement: Precise color measurement using specialized equipment.

Human Vision Correlation: Correlation between instrumental and visual assessment

Consistency Standards: Maintaining consistent grading across different laboratories.

Clarity Grading Methodology:

Magnification Standards: 10x magnification as the international standard for clarity assessment

Inclusion Classification: Scientific classification of different inclusion types

Impact Assessment: How inclusions affect diamond beauty and structural integrity

Grading Consistency: Training and calibration ensure consistent grading results.

Advanced Testing Protocols:

Origin Determination: Scientific methods for confirming lab-created diamond origin:

Identification Techniques:

Growth Pattern Analysis: Characteristic growth patterns distinguishing synthetic from natural.

Trace Element Analysis: Chemical fingerprints revealing production methods.

Defect Spectroscopy: Specific defects characteristic of different growth methods.

Comparative Database: Reference databases enabling accurate origin determination.

Treatment Detection:

Post-Growth Treatment Identification: Detection of color or clarity enhancements

Stability Testing: Verification of treatment permanence and stability

Disclosure Requirements: Industry standards for treatment disclosure

Verification Procedures: Protocols for confirming treatment presence and nature.

Future Technology Implications

Emerging Scientific Developments

Next-Generation Production:

Breakthrough Technologies: Scientific advances promising revolutionary improvements:

Molecular Assembly:

Atomic Precision: Potential for atom-by-atom diamond construction

Custom Properties: Engineering specific properties into the diamond structure.

Novel Structures: Creating diamond structures that are impossible through traditional methods.

Application Expansion: New applications enabled by precise property control.

Quantum Control Systems:

Quantum Sensing: Using quantum effects for unprecedented process control.

Coherent Growth: Quantum coherence effects in diamond growth processes

Defect Engineering: Precise control of quantum defects for technological applications.

Property Optimization: Quantum effects enabling optimization of diamond properties.

Application Evolution:

Beyond Jewelry Applications: Scientific developments expanding diamond applications:

Quantum Technologies:

Quantum Computing: Diamonds as quantum bits and quantum processors

Quantum Sensing: Ultra-sensitive sensors using diamond quantum properties.

Quantum Communication: Diamonds enabling secure quantum communication systems.

Quantum Metrology: Precision measurement using diamond quantum sensors.

Advanced Electronics:

Power Electronics: High-voltage, high-frequency electronic applications

Thermal Management: Advanced heat spreading and thermal interface applications.

Optical Applications: Precision optics and laser applications

Medical Technology: Biocompatible sensors and medical device applications

The comprehensive FAQ and troubleshooting guide demonstrate that lab-created diamonds represent not only beautiful gemstones but also remarkable achievements in materials science and engineering. Understanding these technical foundations enhances appreciation for both the scientific accomplishment and the practical benefits these diamonds provide.

As technology continues to advance and markets evolve, this knowledge base will expand, but the fundamental principles of informed decision-making, quality assessment, and proper care will remain constant. The future of lab-created diamonds lies not only in their growing market acceptance, but also in their potential to revolutionize multiple industries, providing consumers with beauty, value, and peace of mind.

Through education, understanding, and appreciation of the science behind these remarkable gems, consumers can confidently navigate the lab-created diamond market, making decisions that reflect both their aesthetic preferences and their values, while participating in one of the most exciting technological and cultural transformations of our time.

***

In the constellation of knowledge that surrounds lab-created diamonds, each question answered becomes a star that illuminates the path forward. Through understanding, we transform uncertainty into confidence, complexity into clarity, and possibilities into realities that sparkle with the brilliance of informed choice.

Chapter 16: Resources and References

"Knowledge, like a diamond, gains its greatest brilliance when shared—each resource a facet that catches light, each reference a pathway to deeper understanding, together creating a constellation of wisdom that guides seekers toward their perfect choice."

16.1 Professional Directory

Certified Gemologists and Appraisers

The lab-created diamond market benefits from a growing network of qualified professionals who understand both the traditional principles of gemology and the unique characteristics of synthetic diamonds. Building relationships with certified experts ensures access to accurate information, reliable assessments, and trustworthy guidance throughout your diamond journey.

Understanding Professional Qualifications

Gemological Institute of America (GIA) Credentials:

Graduate Gemologist (GG) Certification: The gold standard in gemological education with specific lab-created diamond expertise:

Comprehensive Education Requirements:

Gemological Studies: Complete coursework in diamond grading, colored stones, and jewelry identification

Lab-Created Diamond Module: Specialized training in synthetic diamond identification and characteristics

Practical Experience: Hands-on laboratory work with both natural and lab-created stones

Continuing Education: Ongoing education requirements maintain current knowledge of market developments.

Specialized Lab Diamond Expertise:

Growth Method Recognition: Training in identifying HPHT versus CVD characteristics.

Treatment Detection: Advanced techniques for identifying post-growth treatments.

Quality Assessment: Application of traditional grading standards to lab-created diamonds

Market Knowledge: Understanding of lab-created diamond market dynamics and pricing.

American Society of Appraisers (ASA) Certification:

Personal Property Appraiser Designation: Professional appraisers qualified for insurance and estate valuation:

Certification Requirements:

Educational Foundation: Comprehensive training in appraisal principles and methodology

Examination Process: Rigorous testing demonstrating professional competency.

Experience Verification: Documented professional experience in jewelry appraisal.

Ethics Training: Comprehensive ethics training and ongoing compliance requirements

Lab-Created Diamond Specialization:

Market Research Skills: Training in researching lab-created diamond market values.

Replacement Cost Analysis: Expertise in determining accurate replacement costs.

Insurance Coordination: Understanding insurance requirements and documentation needs.

Legal Compliance: Knowledge of legal standards for professional appraisal services

Reputable Retailers and Dealers

The lab-created diamond retail landscape includes established jewelry retailers, specialized online platforms, and emerging direct-to-consumer brands. Understanding the characteristics of reputable dealers enables informed selection of purchasing partners.

Traditional Jewelry Retailers

National Retail Chains:

Kay Jewelers (Signet Jewelers): Major retail chain with growing lab-created diamond selection:

Service Characteristics:

National Presence: Over 2,200 locations across the United States

Lab Diamond Integration: Comprehensive lab-created diamond collections

Financing Options: Various financing programs, including zero-interest promotions.

Professional Services: In-store sizing, cleaning, and basic maintenance services

Quality and Pricing:

Certified Diamonds: GIA and other major laboratory-certified stones

Competitive Pricing: Market-competitive pricing with frequent promotional offers

Quality Range: Complete range from commercial to premium quality grades.

Warranty Programs: Manufacturer warranties and extended service plans

Blue Nile: Pioneer in online diamond retail with extensive lab-created diamond offerings:

Technology Integration:

Advanced Search Tools: Sophisticated filtering and comparison capabilities

360-Degree Imaging: High-resolution photography and video documentation

Virtual Try-On: Augmented reality tools for ring visualization

Educational Resources: Comprehensive consumer education materials

Service Excellence:

Expert Consultation: Phone and chat support from trained diamond consultants

Extended Returns: 30-day return policy with full refund guarantee.

Free Shipping: Complimentary insured shipping and returns.

Lifetime Services: Ongoing services including cleaning and maintenance

Specialized Lab-Created Diamond Retailers:

Brilliant Earth: Ethical jewelry specialist with strong lab-created diamond focus:

Ethical Leadership:

Sustainability Focus: Emphasis on environmentally responsible sourcing

Transparency: Complete supply chain transparency and documentation

Carbon Neutral: Carbon-neutral shipping and operations

Social Responsibility: Supporting communities and environmental causes.

Quality and Innovation:

Premium Selection: Curated selection of high-quality lab-created diamonds

Custom Design: Extensive custom jewelry design capabilities

Expert Curation: Professional gemologists selecting inventory.

Innovation Leadership: Early adoption of new technologies and methods

Clean Origin: Pure-play lab-created diamond specialist:

Specialized Expertise:

Exclusive Focus: Dedicated exclusively to lab-created diamonds.

Technical Knowledge: Deep expertise in lab-created diamond characteristics

Educational Mission: Comprehensive consumer education programs

Quality Standards: Rigorous quality standards and selection criteria

Competitive Advantages:

Pricing Transparency: Clear, competitive pricing with detailed comparisons

Selection Breadth: Extensive inventory across all quality grades and sizes

Customer Service: Specialized customer service with lab diamond expertise

Innovation Integration: Early adoption of new technologies and services

Laboratory Contacts and Services

Professional gemological laboratories provide essential certification and testing services for lab-created diamonds. Understanding the capabilities and specializations of major laboratories enables informed decisions about certification needs.

Major Certification Laboratories

Gemological Institute of America (GIA):

GIA Laboratory Services: The most respected name in diamond grading with comprehensive lab-created diamond services:

Service Offerings:

Comprehensive Grading: Complete 4Cs assessment using identical standards for natural and lab-created diamonds.

Origin Determination: Advanced testing confirming synthetic origin and growth method.

Treatment Detection: Identification of any post-growth treatments or enhancements

Digital Documentation: Online verification and digital certificate access

Global Presence:

Primary Locations: Carlsbad (California), New York, Bangkok, Antwerp, Mumbai

Service Network: A global network that enables convenient access to services.

Turnaround Times: Typically, 2-4 weeks, depending on services and location.

Quality Assurance: Rigorous quality control ensures consistent grading standards.

International Gemological Institute (IGI):

IGI Worldwide Network: Extensive global presence with competitive service offerings:

Laboratory Locations:

Global Coverage: Laboratories in New York, Antwerp, Mumbai, Bangkok, Dubai, Hong Kong

Regional Expertise: Local market knowledge and specialized services

Language Support: Multi-language certificates and customer service

Cultural Adaptation: Services are adapted to regional preferences and requirements.

Service Advantages:

Speed: Often faster turnaround times compared to GIA

Competitive Pricing: Generally lower costs than GIA certification

Comprehensive Reports: Detailed reports including advanced testing results.

Technology Integration: Modern technology and digital services

American Gemological Society (AGS):

Cut Quality Specialization: Advanced cut grading technology providing superior light performance analysis:

Unique Capabilities:

Light Performance Analysis: Scientific measurement of brilliance, fire, and scintillation

0-10 Grading Scale: Numerical system with 0 representing ideal quality.

Advanced Technology: Ray-tracing technology for precise cut analysis

Quality Focus: Emphasis on exceptional cut quality and optical performance

Premium Services:

Detailed Analysis: Comprehensive analysis of light performance characteristics

Educational Value: Detailed explanations of grading methodology and results

Quality Assurance: Rigorous standards ensure premium quality assessment.

Limited Volume: Selective acceptance, focusing on premium-quality stones.

Legal and Insurance Professionals

The growing lab-created diamond market has created demand for specialized legal and insurance professionals who understand the unique characteristics and market dynamics of synthetic diamonds.

Specialized Insurance Providers

Jewelry Insurance Specialists:

Jewelers Mutual Insurance Group: Leading jewelry insurance specialist with lab-created diamond expertise:

Coverage Specialization:

Comprehensive Protection: Coverage for loss, theft, damage, and mysterious disappearance

Worldwide Coverage: Protection during travel and temporary relocation

No Deductible: Zero-deductible policies for complete protection

Replacement Network: Access to qualified jewelers for repairs and replacements

Lab-Created Diamond Services:

Accurate Valuation: Understanding of lab-created diamond market values.

Replacement Capability: Access to lab-created diamond replacement sources

Expert Assessment: Professional evaluation of lab-created diamond claims

Educational Resources: Consumer education about lab-created diamond insurance

State Farm Personal Articles Policy: Major insurer with jewelry coverage expertise:

Policy Features:

Agreed Value Coverage: Pre-negotiated values eliminate claim disputes.

Broad Coverage: Protection against a wide range of risks and perils

Claims Service: Professional claims handling with jewelry expertise.

Competitive Rates: Market-competitive rates with multi-policy discounts

Legal Professionals:

Jewelry Industry Attorneys: Specialized legal professionals understanding jewelry industry dynamics:

Practice Areas:

Consumer Protection: Legal assistance with purchase disputes and warranty issues

Insurance Claims: Legal support for complex insurance claims and disputes

Estate Planning: Integration of jewelry assets into comprehensive estate planning

Business Law: Legal services for jewelry businesses and industry professionals

Qualification Standards:

Industry Experience: Demonstrated experience in jewelry and luxury goods law.

Professional Recognition: Membership in relevant professional organizations

Continuing Education: Ongoing education in jewelry industry legal developments

Ethical Standards: Compliance with professional ethical standards and requirements

16.2 Educational Resources

Gemological Institutes and Courses

The rapidly evolving lab-created diamond market creates ongoing educational opportunities for consumers, professionals, and industry participants. Understanding available educational resources enables continuous learning and skill development.

Professional Gemological Education

Gemological Institute of America (GIA):

Comprehensive Curriculum: World-renowned gemological education with lab-created diamond integration:

Graduate Gemologist Program:

Core Curriculum: Comprehensive diamond and colored stone grading education.

Lab-Created Diamond Module: Specialized coursework in synthetic diamond identification

Practical Laboratory: Hands-on experience with both natural and lab-created stones

Research Projects: Individual research projects exploring specific aspects of lab-created diamonds.

Continuing Education:

Professional Development: Ongoing courses for working gemologists.

Industry Updates: Regular seminars on new developments and technologies

Online Learning: Web-based courses enable flexible learning schedules.

Research Publications: Access to the latest research and technical developments.

American Gemological Society (AGS):

Technical Excellence Focus: Advanced education emphasizing technical precision and cut quality:

Specialized Programs:

Certified Gemologist (CG): Comprehensive certification with technical emphasis

Cut Grading Specialty: Advanced training in cut quality assessment.

Light Performance Analysis: Scientific measurement and evaluation techniques

Industry Leadership: Training in professional leadership and business development

Research Integration:

Laboratory Collaboration: Direct collaboration with AGS laboratory services

Technology Training: Training on advanced gemological equipment and techniques

Professional Networks: Access to professional networks and industry relationships

Innovation Focus: Emphasis on innovation and technological advancement

Online Learning Platforms

Digital Education Resources

Specialized Online Courses:

GIA Online Learning: Flexible online education enabling global access to gemological training:

Course Offerings:

Diamond Essentials: Foundational diamond knowledge, including lab-created diamonds.

Jewelry Essentials: Comprehensive jewelry knowledge and identification skills

Professional Development: Advanced courses for industry professionals

Consumer Education: Basic courses for jewelry consumers and enthusiasts

Platform Features:

Interactive Content: Engaging multimedia content with interactive exercises

Progress Tracking: Comprehensive progress tracking and performance assessment

Expert Instruction: Courses developed and taught by industry experts.

Global Access: Worldwide access enabling international participation.

Industry-Specific Platforms:

Professional Jewelry Organizations: Industry associations offering specialized education programs:

Jewelers of America (JA):

Professional Certification: Various certification programs for jewelry professionals

Business Development: Business skills training for jewelry industry professionals

Technical Training: Technical skills development and equipment training

Industry Networking: Professional networking and relationship building opportunities.

National Association of Jewelry Appraisers (NAJA):

Appraisal Education: Specialized training in jewelry appraisal methodology

Professional Standards: Education in professional standards and ethical requirements

Market Analysis: Training in market research and valuation techniques

Legal Compliance: Education in legal requirements and professional liability

Industry Publications and Reports

Professional Literature and Research

Academic and Technical Publications:

Gems & Gemology: GIA's peer-reviewed scientific journal with lab-created diamond research:

Research Focus:

Technical Studies: Detailed scientific analysis of lab-created diamond characteristics

Market Research: Analysis of market trends and consumer behavior

Technology Development: Reports on new production and testing technologies.

Industry Analysis: Comprehensive analysis of industry developments and trends

Subscription Benefits:

Quarterly Issues: Regular publication providing ongoing education and updates.

Online Access: Digital access to complete journal archives

Research Database: Searchable database of technical articles and research.

Professional Recognition: Recognition as essential professional literature

Industry Trade Publications:

National Jeweler: Leading jewelry industry trade publication with lab-created diamond coverage:

Content Areas:

Market Analysis: Regular analysis of lab-created diamond market developments

Industry News: Current news and developments affecting the jewelry industry.

Professional Profiles: Profiles of industry leaders and innovators

Technology Updates: Coverage of new technologies and industry innovations

JCK Magazine: Comprehensive jewelry industry coverage, including lab-created diamond trends:

Editorial Focus:

Trend Analysis: Analysis of emerging trends in jewelry and diamonds

Business Intelligence: Business insights and strategic analysis for industry professionals

Product Reviews: Reviews of new products and services

Educational Content: Educational articles for industry professionals and consumers

Professional Development Opportunities

Career Advancement and Skill Development

Industry Conferences and Trade Shows:

JCK Las Vegas: Premier jewelry industry trade show with growing lab-created diamond presence:

Event Features:

Exhibition Hall: Comprehensive displays of lab-created diamond products and services

Educational Seminars: Professional education sessions on industry developments

Networking Opportunities: Professional networking with industry leaders and innovators

Trend Forecasting: Analysis of emerging trends and market developments

Gemological Institute of America Symposium: Annual scientific conference focusing on gemological research and education:

Program Elements:

Research Presentations: Latest research in gemology and diamond science.

Technology Demonstrations: Demonstrations of new testing and analysis equipment

Professional Networking: Networking with researchers and industry professionals

Continuing Education: Professional development and continuing education credits

Professional Certification Programs:

American Society of Appraisers: Comprehensive certification program for jewelry appraisers:

Certification Levels:

Accredited Member (AM): Entry-level certification for new appraisers

Accredited Senior Appraiser (ASA): Advanced certification requiring experience and examination.

Fellowship: Highest level of certification recognizing exceptional expertise

Continuing Education: Ongoing education requirements for maintaining certification.

Benefits and Requirements:

Professional Recognition: Industry recognition of expertise and competency

Legal Standing: Certification recognized by courts and legal professionals.

Insurance Benefits: Professional liability insurance and legal protections

Network Access: Access to professional networks and referral systems.

16.3 Tools and Calculators

Budget Planning Worksheets

Effective diamond purchasing requires systematic financial planning that considers not only the initial purchase price but the total cost of ownership and opportunity costs of the investment.

Comprehensive Budget Analysis Tools

Total Investment Calculator:

Initial Purchase Costs: Complete cost analysis including all purchase-related expenses:

Diamond Purchase Budget Worksheet

Base Diamond Cost: $______

Setting/Mounting Cost: $______

Professional Grading/Certification: $______

Custom Design/Modification: $______

Sales Tax (if applicable): $______

Shipping/Insurance: $______

____

TOTAL INITIAL INVESTMENT: $______

Immediate Ownership Costs:

Professional Appraisal: $______

Insurance Setup: $______

Initial Professional Cleaning: $______

____

TOTAL FIRST-YEAR COST: $______

Ongoing Ownership Cost Analysis:

Annual Ownership Expenses:

Annual Ownership Cost Worksheet

Insurance Premiums: $______

Professional Maintenance: $______

Professional Cleaning (2x/year): $______

Inspection Services: $______

Potential Repairs/Adjustments: $______

Storage/Security Costs: $______

____

TOTAL ANNUAL OWNERSHIP COST: $______

10-Year Total Cost of Ownership:

Initial Investment: $______

Annual Costs (x10): $______

____

10-YEAR TOTAL COST: $______

Opportunity Cost Analysis:

Alternative Investment Comparison:

Opportunity Cost Worksheet

Lab-Created Diamond Option:

Diamond Cost: $______

Remaining Available Funds: $______

Natural Diamond Option:

Diamond Cost: $______

Remaining Available Funds: $______

Investment Return Calculation:

Remaining Funds Available: $______

Expected Annual Return Rate: ______%

10-Year Investment Value: $______

Net Economic Advantage:

Lab Diamond + Investment Value: $______

Natural Diamond Value: $______

____

NET ADVANTAGE: $______

Quality Comparison Matrices

Systematic Quality Assessment Tools

4Cs Comparison Matrix:

Diamond Quality Comparison Worksheet

DIAMOND A DIAMOND B DIAMOND C

Certificate #: ____________ ____________ ____________

Laboratory: ____________ ____________ ____________

CUT QUALITY:

Grade: ____________ ____________ ____________

Proportions: ____________ ____________ ____________

Symmetry: ____________ ____________ ____________

Polish: ____________ ____________ ____________

COLOR:

Grade: ____________ ____________ ____________

Consistency: ____________ ____________ ____________

Fluorescence: ____________ ____________ ____________

CLARITY:

Grade: ____________ ____________ ____________

Inclusion Type: ____________ ____________ ____________

Eye Clean: ____________ ____________ ____________

CARAT WEIGHT:

Weight: ____________ ____________ ____________

Dimensions: ____________ ____________ ____________

PRICING:

Cost per Carat: __________ __________ __________

Total Cost: __________ __________ __________

Value Rating: __________ __________ __________

OVERALL RATING: __________ __________ __________

Value Assessment Matrix:

Comprehensive Value Analysis

Factor Weight Diamond A Diamond B Diamond C

(1-10) Score Wtd Score Wtd Score Wtd

Cut Quality ____ _____ ____ _____ ____ _____ ____

Color Grade ____ _____ ____ _____ ____ _____ ____

Clarity Grade ____ _____ ____ _____ ____ _____ ____

Carat Size ____ _____ ____ _____ ____ _____ ____

Price Value ____ _____ ____ _____ ____ _____ ____

Certification ____ _____ ____ _____ ____ _____ ____

Seller Reputation ____ _____ ____ _____ ____ _____ ____

Service Quality ____ _____ ____ _____ ____ _____ ____

Warranty Terms ____ _____ ____ _____ ____ _____ ____

Personal Preference ____ _____ ____ _____ ____ _____ ____

TOTAL WEIGHTED SCORE: _________ _________ _________

Price Trend Analysis Tools

Market Intelligence and Tracking Systems

Historical Price Tracking:

Lab-Created Diamond Price Tracking Worksheet

Diamond Specifications:

Carat Weight: _______ Color Grade: _______

Clarity Grade: ______ Cut Grade: _________

Date Source Price Notes

_______ ______________ ________ ________________

_______ ______________ ________ ________________

_______ ______________ ________ ________________

_______ ______________ ________ ________________

_______ ______________ ________ ________________

Price Trend Analysis:

Starting Price: $_____

Current Price: $_____

Price Change: $_____ (____%)

Trend Direction: _______________

Market Timing Assessment:

Current Market Position: _______________

Optimal Purchase Timing: _______________

Expected Future Trends: _______________

Comparative Market Analysis:

Market Comparison Tool

Natural vs Lab-Created Diamond Pricing

Specifications: _____ ct, _____ color, _____ clarity, _____ cut

Natural Diamond Pricing:

Source 1: $_____

Source 2: $_____

Source 3: $_____

Average Natural Price: $_____

Lab-Created Diamond Pricing:

Source 1: $_____

Source 2: $_____

Source 3: $_____

Average Lab Price: $_____

Price Difference Analysis:

Absolute Difference: $_____

Percentage Savings: _____%

Quality Comparison: _______________

Value Assessment: _______________

Investment Tracking Systems

Long-Term Value and Performance Monitoring

Portfolio Management Tools:

Diamond Investment Tracking System

DIAMOND ASSET RECORD

Purchase Date: ___________ Certificate #: ___________

Original Cost: ____________ Current Value: ____________

Quality Specifications:

Carat Weight: _______ Color: _______ Clarity: _______ Cut: _______

Laboratory: __________ Growth Method: __________________________

Financial Performance:

Original Purchase Price: $______

Current Market Value: $______

Appreciation/Depreciation: $______ (____%)

Annual Return Rate: _____%

Insurance and Protection:

Insurance Carrier: ________________________

Policy Number: ____________________________

Annual Premium: ___________________________

Last Appraisal Date: ______________________

Next Appraisal Due: _______________________

Maintenance Record:

Last Professional Cleaning: _______________

Last Professional Inspection: _____________

Condition Notes: __________________________

Required Maintenance: _____________________

Market Factors:

Market Trends: ____________________________

Technology Impacts: _______________________

Future Outlook: ___________________________

Estate Planning Integration:

Jewelry Asset Estate Planning Worksheet

Asset Information:

Item Description: _________________________

Purchase Date: ____________________________

Original Cost: ____________________________

Current Appraised Value: __________________

Insurance Coverage: _______________________

Legal Documentation:

Ownership Documentation: ____________________

Insurance Policy Information: ______________

Appraisal Documentation: ____________________

Warranty Information: _______________________

Estate Planning Integration:

Will/Trust Reference: ______________________

Beneficiary Designation: ___________________

Special Instructions: ______________________

Tax Implications: __________________________

Family Considerations:

Sentimental Value: _________________________

Family History: ____________________________

Care Instructions for Heirs: _______________

Professional Contacts: _____________________

16.4 Industry Organizations

Professional Associations

The lab-created diamond industry benefits from established jewelry industry organizations that provide standards, education, networking, and advocacy for professionals and consumers.

Primary Industry Organizations

Jewelers of America (JA):

Mission and Scope: The leading trade association for retail jewelers with a growing lab-created diamond focus:

Member Benefits:

Professional Education: Comprehensive education programs including lab-created diamond training.

Certification Programs: Professional certification and skill development opportunities

Industry Advocacy: Legislative advocacy and industry representation

Business Resources: Business development and management resources

Lab-Created Diamond Initiatives:

Education Programs: Specialized training for lab-created diamond sales and service

Standards Development: Participation in industry standards and best practices development

Consumer Education: Resources for consumer education and market development

Professional Networking: Networking opportunities with lab-created diamond specialists

American Gem Society (AGS):

Quality and Ethics Focus: Professional organization emphasizing quality, ethics, and consumer protection:

Membership Standards:

Rigorous Requirements: Strict membership requirements, including professional education.

Ethics Code: A Comprehensive code of ethics governing member behavior.

Quality Standards: Emphasis on quality in products and services

Consumer Protection: Strong consumer protection and advocacy programs

Lab-Created Diamond Integration:

Technical Standards: Development of quality standards for lab-created diamonds

Professional Training: Advanced training in lab-created diamond assessment and services

Research Support: Support for research in lab-created diamond technology and applications.

Market Leadership: Leadership in promoting understanding and acceptance of lab-created diamonds.

Consumer Advocacy Groups

Consumer Protection and Education Organizations

Better Business Bureau (BBB):

Business Integrity Monitoring: An Independent organization monitoring business practices and consumer protection:

Services for Diamond Consumers:

Business Ratings: Comprehensive ratings and reviews of jewelry retailers

Complaint Resolution: Mediation services for consumer-business disputes

Scam Prevention: Education and warnings about common jewelry scams.

Purchasing Guidance: Consumer education about safe purchasing practices

Lab-Created Diamond Focus:

Retailer Evaluation: Assessment of lab-created diamond retailers and their practices

Consumer Education: Information about lab-created diamonds and purchasing considerations.

Dispute Resolution: Assistance with lab-created diamond purchase disputes.

Industry Monitoring: Monitoring of lab-created diamond industry practices and standards

Federal Trade Commission (FTC):

Regulatory Oversight and Consumer Protection: A Federal agency responsible for consumer protection in jewelry markets.

Jewelry Guides and Regulations:

Truth-in-Advertising: Regulations governing jewelry advertising and marketing.

Disclosure Requirements: Requirements for disclosure of diamond treatments and origins

Consumer Education: Educational resources about jewelry purchasing and protection.

Enforcement Actions: Investigation and prosecution of fraudulent practices

Lab-Created Diamond Regulations:

Terminology Guidelines: Approved terminology for lab-created diamond marketing

Disclosure Standards: Requirements for clear disclosure of synthetic origin

Consumer Protection: Protection against fraud and misrepresentation

Industry Compliance: Monitoring and enforcement of industry compliance

Regulatory Bodies

Government and Industry Regulation

International Organization for Standardization (ISO):

Global Standards Development: International organization developing standards for various industries including jewelry:

Relevant Standards:

ISO 11426: Jewelry testing and precious metal determination.

ISO 17034: Reference materials for gemological testing

ISO 9001: Quality management systems for production facilities

ISO 14001: Environmental management systems for sustainable production

Lab-Created Diamond Applications:

Production Standards: Standards for lab-created diamond production and quality control

Testing Methods: Standardized testing methods for identification and grading

Environmental Standards: Environmental management standards for production facilities

Quality Systems: Quality management standards ensure consistent production.

World Intellectual Property Organization (WIPO):

Intellectual Property Protection: An International organization protecting intellectual property in diamond technology:

Patent Protection:

Production Methods: Patent protection for innovative production technologies

Quality Control: Patents for advanced quality control and testing methods.

Equipment Design: Protection for specialized equipment and manufacturing systems

Application Technologies: Patents for new applications and uses of lab-created diamonds

Research Institutions

Academic and Industrial Research Centers

University Research Programs:

Massachusetts Institute of Technology (MIT): Leading research in materials science and diamond technology:

Research Areas:

Materials Science: Advanced research in diamond synthesis and characterization

Quantum Applications: Research in quantum computing and sensing applications

Manufacturing Technology: Development of advanced manufacturing processes

Industry Collaboration: Partnerships with industry for technology development

Carnegie Institution for Science: Geophysical Laboratory conducting diamond research:

Research Focus:

High-Pressure Science: Research in high-pressure synthesis and characterization

Crystal Growth: Studies of crystal growth mechanisms and optimization

Material Properties: Investigation of diamond properties and applications

Technology Transfer: Transfer of research results to industrial applications

Industrial Research Centers:

Applied Diamond Inc.: Industrial research center focused on diamond technology development:

Research Capabilities:

Process Development: Development of new production methods and optimization.

Quality Control: Advanced quality control and testing method development.

Applications Research: Research into new applications for lab-created diamonds

Technology Transfer: Transfer of research results to commercial applications

Diamond Foundry Research Labs: Company research facilities advancing lab-created diamond technology:

Innovation Focus:

Production Efficiency: Research in improving production efficiency and quality.

Environmental Technology: Development of sustainable production methods

Quality Enhancement: Research in achieving superior quality characteristics.

Market Applications: Research into new market applications and opportunities

The comprehensive resource directory demonstrates the breadth and depth of professional support available for lab-created diamond consumers and industry participants. From certified professionals and educational institutions to industry organizations and research centers, a robust infrastructure exists to support informed decision-making, professional development, and continued market growth.

These resources represent more than just sources of information—they constitute a community of knowledge and expertise dedicated to advancing understanding, maintaining standards, and ensuring consumer protection in the rapidly evolving lab-created diamond market. By utilizing these resources effectively, consumers can navigate the market with confidence, while professionals can continue to develop their expertise and capabilities.

The future success of the lab-created diamond market depends not only on technological advancements and consumer acceptance, but also on the continued development of this professional infrastructure. As the market evolves, these organizations and institutions will adapt and expand their services, ensuring that the remarkable potential of lab-created diamonds is realized through informed choices, professional excellence, and ethical practices.

***

In the constellation of knowledge that surrounds lab-created diamonds, these resources serve as guiding stars—each professional a beacon of expertise, each organization a lighthouse of standards, each institution a galaxy of discovery. Together, they illuminate the path toward informed choices and professional excellence, ensuring that the brilliance of lab-created diamonds is matched by the wisdom of those who guide their journey from laboratory to legacy.

Appendices

Appendix A: Glossary of Key Terms

Acid Mine Drainage: Acidic water, rich in heavy metals, which drains from mining sites, causing long-term water pollution.

Annealing: A post-growth heat treatment process used to alter or enhance a diamond's color and clarity.

Artisanal Mining: Small-scale, informal mining, often characterized by manual labor, basic equipment, and hazardous working conditions.

As-Grown: A term for a lab-created diamond that has not undergone any post-growth treatments to enhance its color or clarity.

Bezel Setting: A jewelry setting that encircles the diamond with a metal rim, offering maximum protection.

Blockchain: A decentralized, immutable digital ledger used to track a diamond's provenance from creation to retail, ensuring authenticity and transparency.

Birefringence: The optical property of a material having a refractive index that depends on the polarization and propagation direction of light. In diamonds, it can indicate internal strain.

Brilliance: The intensity of white light returned to the eye from a diamond, a key component of its sparkle.

Carat (ct): The standard unit of weight for diamonds, equal to 200 milligrams (0.2 grams).

Carbon Neutral: A state where the net carbon dioxide emissions for a process (like diamond creation) are zero, often achieved by balancing emissions with carbon offsets or renewable energy use.

Catalyst: A substance that increases the rate of a chemical reaction. In HPHT diamond synthesis, a molten metal catalyst (e.g., iron, nickel, cobalt) is used to dissolve carbon.

Chemical Vapor Deposition (CVD): A method for creating diamonds in a low-pressure, high-temperature vacuum chamber by depositing carbon atoms from a gas (like methane) onto a diamond seed.

Clarity: A measure of the absence of internal features (inclusions) and external characteristics (blemishes) in a diamond.

Conflict Diamond (Blood Diamond): A diamond mined in a war zone and sold to finance an insurgency, an invading army's war efforts, or a warlord's activities.

Covalent Bond: The strong chemical bond between carbon atoms in a diamond, responsible for its hardness and durability.

Crown: The top portion of a cut diamond, above the girdle.

Crystal Lattice: The ordered, three-dimensional arrangement of atoms in a crystal. In a diamond, this is a cubic structure.

Culet: The small facet at the bottom tip of a diamond.

Dispersion (Fire): The splitting of white light into its spectral colors (a rainbow effect), which is visible as a diamond moves.

Facet: A flat, polished surface on a cut diamond.

Fluorescence: The emission of visible light by a diamond when it is exposed to ultraviolet (UV) radiation.

Four Cs: The four primary characteristics used to determine a diamond's quality and value: Cut, Color, Clarity, and Carat Weight.

Girdle: The narrow band around the widest part of a diamond, separating the crown from the pavilion.

High Pressure-High Temperature (HPHT): A method for creating diamonds that mimics the natural conditions of the Earth's mantle, using immense pressure and heat to crystallize carbon.

Inclusion: An internal characteristic or flaw within a diamond. In lab-created diamonds, these can be remnants of the growth process (e.g., metallic flux).

Kimberley Process Certification Scheme (KPCS): An international certification system designed to prevent conflict diamonds from entering the mainstream rough diamond market.

Lab-Created Diamond: A diamond grown in a laboratory with the same chemical, physical, and optical properties as a natural, mined diamond. Also known as a cultured, man-made, or synthetic diamond.

Melee: Small diamonds, typically weighing less than 0.2 carats, used as accent stones in jewelry.

Microwave Plasma Assisted CVD (MPACVD): An advanced form of CVD that uses microwaves to generate plasma, allowing for faster growth rates and higher quality.

Mohs Scale: A scale of mineral hardness ranging from 1 (softest) to 10 (hardest). Both natural and lab-created diamonds are a 10.

Pavilion: The lower portion of a cut diamond below the girdle.

Phosphorescence: A "glow-in-the-dark" effect, where a diamond continues to emit light after the UV source has been removed. Sometimes seen in HPHT diamonds.

Refractive Index (RI): A measure of how much light bends when it passes through a substance. A diamond's high RI (2.42) is key to its brilliance.

Scintillation: The flashes of light and dark, or sparkle, seen when a diamond, its light source, or the observer moves.

Seed Crystal: A small, thin slice of a pre-existing diamond (either natural or lab-created) used as the template for growing a new lab-created diamond.

Simulant: A material (e.g., cubic zirconia, moissanite) that looks like a diamond but has different chemical and physical properties. It is not a real diamond.

Solitaire: A jewelry setting that features a single diamond.

Strain: Internal stress within a diamond's crystal lattice, which can affect its optical properties and durability.

Symmetry: The precision and alignment of a diamond's facets.

Type Ia, Ib, IIa, IIb: Scientific classifications for diamonds based on the presence and configuration of nitrogen and boron impurities. Most CVD diamonds are Type IIa (purest carbon), while HPHT diamonds can be Type Ib or IIa.

Appendix B: Comparative Data Tables

Table B-1: Lab-Created vs. Mined Diamonds - Environmental & Social Impact

Table B-2: HPHT vs. CVD Growth Methods

Table B-3: Diamond Simulants vs. Lab-Created & Natural Diamonds

Appendix C: Timeline of Lab-Created Diamond Development

1797: English chemist Smithson Tennant discovers that diamonds are composed of pure carbon.

1954: General Electric (GE) creates the first verifiably synthetic diamond using an HPHT press, a project codenamed "Project Superpressure." These are small, industrial-grade diamonds.

1970: GE researchers create the first gem-quality lab diamonds, large enough to be cut into faceted stones. They are yellow to brown in color and commercially expensive.

1980s: The development of Chemical Vapor Deposition (CVD) technology emerges as a viable alternative method for diamond synthesis, primarily for industrial coatings.

1990s: Companies like Gemesis and Apollo Diamond begin to refine HPHT and CVD processes, producing larger, higher-quality gem diamonds, though they remain a niche product.

2000s: Significant improvements in technology lead to the consistent production of colorless and near-colorless lab-created diamonds.

2012: Gemesis (now Pure Grown Diamonds) announces the creation of the first certified colorless (Type IIa) lab-grown diamonds.

2015: Swarovski enters the market with its Diama line of lab-created diamond jewelry.

2018: De Beers, a long-time champion of mined diamonds, launches its lab-created diamond fashion jewelry brand, Lightbox, signaling a major shift in the industry. The US Federal Trade Commission (FTC) amends its Jewelry Guides, officially recognizing lab-created diamonds as real diamonds.

2020-Present: Lab-created diamonds achieve mainstream acceptance, capturing a significant share of the engagement ring and fine jewelry market. Major retailers worldwide carry lab-grown options, and production capacity expands rapidly in China, India, and the US. Technology continues to advance, enabling the creation of larger, higher-quality stones with greater efficiency.

Appendix D: How to Read a Lab-Created Diamond Grading Report

A grading report from a reputable lab like GIA or IGI is your diamond's blueprint. Here's a breakdown of a sample report for a lab-created diamond.

(Image of a sample IGI or GIA Lab-Grown Diamond Report would be placed here in a final book layout)

Key Sections Explained:

Header & Report Number:

Laboratory Name: Identifies the grading lab (e.g., IGI, GIA).

Report Number: A unique ID for your diamond. This number is often laser-inscribed on the diamond's girdle and can be used to verify the report online.

"Laboratory-Grown Diamond Report": This title is crucial. It explicitly states the diamond's origin.

Shape and Cutting Style: Describes the diamond's outline (e.g., Round, Princess, Oval) and facet arrangement (e.g., Brilliant, Step Cut).

Measurements: Lists the diamond's dimensions in millimeters (e.g., 6.45 - 6.50 x 3.98 mm for a round diamond).

Grading Results (The 4Cs):

Carat Weight: The weight of the diamond, to the nearest hundredth of a carat (e.g., 1.01 Carat).

Color Grade: Rates the absence of color on a scale from D (colorless) to Z (light yellow/brown).

Clarity Grade: Rates the absence of inclusions and blemishes on a scale from Flawless (FL) to Included (I3).

Cut Grade: (For round brilliants) Rates the quality of the cut from Excellent to Poor, based on how well it reflects light.

Additional Grading Information:

Polish: The quality of the facet surfaces.

Symmetry: The precision of the facet alignment.

Fluorescence: The diamond's reaction to UV light.

Proportions Diagram: A schematic of your diamond's profile, showing key angles and percentages like Table %, Crown Angle, and Pavilion Depth. This is critical for assessing cut quality.

Clarity Characteristics (Plotting Diagram): A map of the diamond showing the type and location of significant inclusions, as seen under 10x magnification.

Comments & Inscriptions:

Laser Inscription: Confirms the girdle is inscribed with the report number and often "LABGROWN."

Growth Method: This section is unique to lab diamond reports. It will state how the diamond was made (e.g., "This Laboratory Grown Diamond was created by Chemical Vapor Deposition (CVD) growth process...").

Post-Growth Treatment: It will disclose if any treatments (like HPHT annealing) were used to improve color (e.g., "...and may include post-growth treatment").

Appendix E: Further Reading and Online Resources

Books:

The Diamond Makers by Robert M. Hazen: A fascinating look at the scientific race to create diamonds in the lab.

The Heartless Stone: A Journey Through the World of Diamonds, Deceit, and Desire by Tom Zoellner: An investigative look into the complex history and global impact of the mined diamond trade.

Online Resources:

Gemological Institute of America (GIA): www.gia.edu - The world's foremost authority on gemology. Their website has extensive, unbiased articles and research on both natural and lab-created diamonds.

International Gemological Institute (IGI): www.igi.org - A leading global certification lab with excellent educational resources and tutorials on understanding lab-created diamonds.

Federal Trade Commission (FTC) Jewelry Guides: www.ftc.gov - Search for "Jewelry Guides" to read the official US government regulations on how diamonds and other jewelry must be marketed and described.

Brilliant Earth Blog: www.brilliantearth.com/news/ - While a retailer, their blog provides well-researched articles on ethical sourcing, sustainability, and trends in the lab-diamond space.

The Diamond Pro: www.diamonds.pro - Offers practical buying advice and comparisons. Though primarily focused on natural diamonds, their principles on cut and quality are universally applicable.

Documentaries:

***Blood Diamond* (2006 Film):** Although a fictionalized drama, it raised global awareness of the conflict diamond issue.

***Nothing Lasts Forever* (2022 Documentary):** A compelling documentary that explores the shifting perceptions of value and authenticity in the diamond industry as lab-grown stones gain prominence.

Also by Donald J. Wright

The Prometheus Protocol (Book I)
The Codex Protocol (Book II)

THE Quantum Schism (Book III)

13th Moon
13th Moon Book II
The Terraforming Protocol
Killer Ice
The Codex Protocol
The Ghost Code (Book I)
The Quantum Echo (Book II)
The Quantum Heart (Book III)
Tomorrow
The God Equation
Lilith

Nonfiction

Diamonds Reimagined

The Handbook of Lab-Created Diamonds

Eternal Shine

Globe Treasure Hunting

Beyond Climate Debates

www.ingramcontent.com/pod-product-compliance
Lightning Source LLC
Chambersburg PA
CBHW031146270326
41931CB00006B/162

* 9 7 8 1 9 6 8 6 7 4 1 2 0 *